THE THIRD STATISTICAL ACCOUNT
OF SCOTLAND

THE COUNTY OF
SHETLAND

THE THIRD STATISTICAL ACCOUNT
OF SCOTLAND

THE COUNTY OF
SHETLAND

EDITED BY

JAMES R. COULL

SCOTTISH ACADEMIC PRESS
EDINBURGH
1985

Published by
Scottish Academic Press Ltd,
33 Montgomery Street
Edinburgh EH7 5JX

SBN 7073 0433 4

Printed in Great Britain by
Clark Constable
Edinburgh, London, Melbourne

CONTENTS

ILLUSTRATIONS

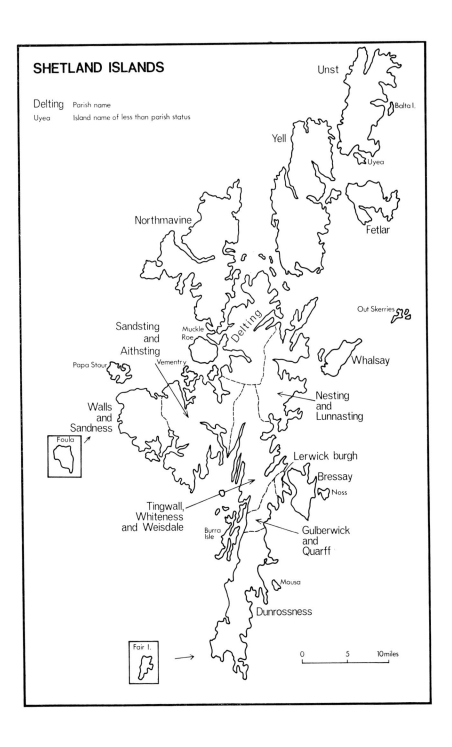

SHETLAND ISLANDS

Delting   Parish name
Uyea   Island name of less than parish status

Unst

Balta I.

Yell

Uyea

Northmavine

Fetlar

Out Skerries

Sandsting
and
Aithsting

Muckle
Roe

Delting

Vementry

Whalsay

Papa Stour

Walls
and
Sandness

Nesting
and
Lunnasting

Foula

Lerwick burgh

Bressay

Noss

Tingwall,
Whiteness
and Weisdale

Burra
Isle

Gulberwick
and
Quarff

Mousa

Dunrossness

Fair I.

0   5   10 miles

FOREWORD

I have great pleasure on behalf of the Scottish Council for Community and Voluntary Organisations in welcoming the Shetland volume of *The Third Statistical Account of Scotland*. When the scheme was conceived after the war, and the parish accounts written in the early 1950s, the picture was different from what obtains today, and Dr Coull has been wise to note in his Introduction many of the important developments of recent years. The original individual parish accounts also have been revised to take note of relevant changes and in one or two instances, where the originals have disappeared, a fresh account has been given. In all cases, appropriate dates have been inserted, and we believe that this volume maintains the tradition set in the eighteenth century by Sir John Sinclair, of reflecting local opinion, local history, and local ways.

The Scottish Council for Community and Voluntary Organisations is greatly indebted to various people and organisations for help in the production of the Shetland volume. The Shetland Islands Council have given a most generous grant, and the Carnegie Trust for the Universities of Scotland, always anxious to encourage Scottish publications, have also helped. The University of Aberdeen has been behind the project, and thanks are particularly due to Professors Maxwell Gaskin and E. H. Mellor. Above all we must thank Dr Coull for what we have found a fascinating and important volume.

ALEXANDER LAW
Vice-President
Scottish Council for Community
and Voluntary Organisations

PREFACE

It has given me great personal pleasure to edit *The Third Statistical Account* of the Shetland Islands. I have now been visiting these islands for over quarter of a century, and have come greatly to like their people. My hope is that this description will be acceptable in Shetland, and that in editing these writings of Shetland people I have not significantly influenced what they wish to say about their own islands.

For a variety of reasons *The Third Statistical Account of Scotland* has had a protracted passage since it was launched in 1946; and its completion for Shetland and several other counties has been considerably delayed. With the changes there have been in the islands in the interim—especially the advent of the oil industry in the 1970s—there have been inevitable problems in producing parish descriptions in parallel with those written earlier for other parts of the country. It was felt that for descriptions finalised in the 1980s for a series in which the first volume was published in 1951, the best procedure was to review developments since World War II. This has necessitated some adjustment in the organisation of the descriptions. Another problem is that the basic unit of the civil parish, although still in existence, has meant less since the reorganisation of local government of 1974. In this respect, however, it appeared clear that it was best to maintain the framework of parish units, which are still meaningful statistical divisions, and this also maintains a parallel organisation with volumes in the series already published.

From the start of my involvement with *The Third Statistical Account*, I have been impressed by the interest and enthusiasm of those who have contributed descriptions. The extent and quality of what they have written speaks for itself. While in editing it has been necessary to bring the different descriptions into a broad general framework, the main principle I have sought to apply has been to allow the writers as far as possible to say what they wish in their own way. It is they who best know their own people and their own parishes, and I feel it is appropriate to respect the emphasis and balance they themselves have given in their descriptions. On occasion opinions have been expressed on controversial issues, and it seems to me that this is a freedom which should be allowed.

For the most part, those who have contributed to this work are acknowledged at the heads of the appropriate descriptions, but there are others who do not appear in that context. My work in making contact with authors was greatly facilitated by Mr John Burgess and his staff in the Research and Development Department of Shetland Islands Council;

in particular my thanks are due to John Holme; they are also due to Mr Michael Peterson, and to Mr Thomas Watt of Shetland Museum, for the trouble they took to obtain the photographic illustrations: I am indebted to Mrs Margaret Souter and Mrs Grace Mather for preparing the typescript. Prof. R. E. H. Mellor of the Geography Department and Prof. M. Gaskin of the Political Economy Department, both of the University of Aberdeen, played essential parts in initiating the work. I should also wish to thank Prof. R. Miller, who has edited the Orkney volume, for his co-operation in the work. Miss Mairi MacArthur and Mr Alistair Bruce of the Scottish Council for Community and Voluntary Organisations have also been most helpful in clarifying issues of editorial policy.

September 1983   JAMES R. COULL, M.A., PH.D.

INTRODUCTION

by James R. Coull, M.A., Ph.D.

The Shetland Islands, Britain's northmost outpost, have become known world-wide in recent years with their role in the oil industry, and in particular with the development of the oil-fields of the East Shetland Basin in the North Sea, which has been a technological frontier in a difficult and demanding environment. The islands have also figured prominently in recent years in the context of the European Economic Community, with the controversies over the fisheries of the Shetland area—their main traditional resource. While these developments have inevitably influenced life on the islands, Shetland still remains a distinctive community and has been not unsuccessful in harmonising its strong traditional base with modern demands.

The period after World War II witnessed a 20-year period of decline in the islands, as the rise in living standards lagged behind, and there was a scarcity of employment and consequent emigration. From the mid 1960s however an encouraging recovery began, mainly through developments in fishing and knitwear, and aided by the Highlands and Islands Development Board. On top of this Shetland in the 1970s sustained the massive impact of one of the most important and vital of modern industries with the development of oil.

PHYSICAL BASIS

The Shetland archipelago is deeply penetrated by the sea and now has a total of 16 inhabited islands; the total area is 552 sq. miles, and only at one place is it possible to get as much as three miles away from the sea. Geologically the islands consist mainly of an assemblage of Precambrian rocks of the Dalradian group, but with some areas based on Old Red Sandstone. The relief is best described as hilly or undulating, and only at Ronas Hill in the North Mainland and at the Sneug on the island of Foula does it exceed 1,000 feet. Many of the hills and not a little of the low ground is covered with blanket peat, and rock outcrops for the most part are fairly infrequent, despite a history of glacial erosion. On the other hand, in many places drainage has been sufficiently modified to give many small lochs. The more exposed parts of the coast have almost everywhere been eroded to give prominent cliffs, and the highest of these—the Kame on the island of Foula—is over 1,200 feet high. On more sheltered parts of the coast there can occur bay and shingle bars, and sometimes tombolos linking islands to the mainland.

The climate of the islands is certainly less severe than its popular image would suggest. In winter Shetland is not significantly colder than the great part of Britain; and although summers are certainly cooler than in other parts of the country there is some compensation in the long daylight. While average wind strengths are on the high side, recorded rainfall shows that the islands are less wet than almost anywhere on the west coast of Britain. The islands may be somewhat poor in most types of wild life, but the great number and variety of sea-birds, especially in summer, is a really outstanding feature.

THE CROFT BASE

As in other crofting counties, the population of Shetland over the modern period has continued to be mainly rural despite the growth of towns; and a large proportion of the people continue to be croft-based. Farms as opposed to crofts, in Shetland are very few. Although the croft has continued to be the home base of many, there have been far-reaching changes. From being the part-time holding characteristic of Shetland, the croft has become either the spare-time holding for the majority, or the full-time holding for the few. The basic problem with the crofts is that the big majority of them are simply too small to be economic units. They represent the historical legacy of holdings worked largely by hand methods which produced the main part of the food supply for a people whose main source of cash income was from fishing. The Crofters Commission has since 1955 given good grants for the improvement of crofts, and this has resulted not only in considerable apportionment and reclamation of 'scattald' (common rough grazing), but also in fencing, drainage, and other improvements. In some cases, as for example at Quendale in the South Mainland and on the island of Fetlar, this has helped the creation of economic farming units.

However, the trend has continued throughout the 20th century that more and more land has been put down to sheep, and there has been a big increase in the amount of croft land in permanent grass, while the cultivated area has declined to a fraction of its former extent. At one time virtually every crofter kept cattle, and the milk cow was a basic necessity. The extra work involved in keeping cattle, together with poor returns in recent times, has meant that they have been abandoned on the big majority of crofts; and most crofters are now spare-time rather than part-time small farmers. For the crofters who are able to make a living from the land, this is done generally by acquiring several crofts and often by reclaiming hill land as well. While they do keep more cattle, they now concentrate mainly on beef stock.

Despite modern trends, crofting still gives a welcome measure of flexibility in rural Shetland. There are crofters categorised as 'spare-time' who work their land well, and who put in on the croft almost the number of hours of their full-time paid employment. It is also possible for some to keep the croft 'ticking over' when other employment is available, and to work it to capacity at other times.

New encouragement to crofters and farmers is now being given by the Shetland Islands Council's Agricultural Development Plan, which will give further aids to develop a viable modern agriculture, and which will include incentives towards more cropping and more cattle husbandry.

FISHING

Until the earlier part of the present century, the great part of the active man-power in the islands was involved in fishing, and looked to it as the main source of cash income to supplement the subsistence yield of the crofts.

In the 18th and most of the 19th century, the main activity was the 'haaf' fishery for cod and ling, operated with open 'sixerns' with long lines. In the 1880s Shetland was involved in a herring boom, and the main fishery became that for herring, operated with decked sail-boats using drift-nets. In the 20th century the sail-boats started to give way to steam drifters and motor-boats, while activity in fisheries became more concentrated in the islands of Burra and Whalsay.

In the second half of this century, change in the fisheries has accelerated. In the period after World War II a new fleet of dual purpose diesel-powered boats was built up which was involved in the drift-net fishery for herring in summer, and ground-seining for white fish in the remainder of the year. More recently boats have tended to become more specialised. This can mean ground-seining or trawling for white fish all year; but the strongest-going men have generally invested in bigger boats built of steel rather than wood which specialise in pelagic fishing with the purse-net for mackerel or herring, as available under modern conservation regulations. However, activity has also become more diversified, with the fishery for scallops and crabs added to the traditional small-boat fishery for lobsters; and now Norway pout and sand-eels are both caught for reduction to meal and oil.

In fish processing, the traditional dry salting of cod and ling and the curing of herring in barrels have both gone completely. Fish filleting and freezing was successfully established in the 1960s, considerably helped by market outlets in the U.S.A. There is some difficulty in maintaining adequate supplies to the fish plants in face of the attraction of bigger markets at Peterhead and Aberdeen. During the oil boom it was also difficult for the plants to maintain their labour and some of them closed, but with the islands now over the peak of the boom this is now less of a problem. A big number of products has now been developed in accordance with market demand. These include both catering and consumer packs, and the range includes various fillets and cutlets along with high value preparations like paté and crab meat.

With the persistent tendency now to overfishing within E.E.C. waters, there has been increasing concern for the future of the industry in the islands. In the 20th century Shetland boats have caught only a small proportion of the fish taken in Shetland waters, the rest going to vessels from other parts of Britain and other countries. There is now strong feeling that the islands' fishermen should be guaranteed a better share of the fish from grounds around the archipelago. While the E.E.C. fisheries policy does make some concessions to the Shetland men, there are real fears that there are inadequate restraints on the operation of non-Shetland boats. There is a widespread recognition that fishing will have to be the major component of the economy once oil is exhausted.

OTHER SEAFARING OCCUPATIONS

Shetlanders have for many years been involved in other seafaring occupations, including the Royal Navy, the Merchant Marine and whaling. Outside actual wartime the numbers in the Royal Navy have been small, but service in the Merchant Marine took big numbers in the late 19th and earlier 20th centuries. While Shetlanders still 'go sailing' new opportunities at home and the decline of British shipping have reduced the numbers to a handful. Shetlanders also went in their hundreds in the 19th century on British ships whaling in the Arctic. When that fishery had declined to extinction, in the 20th century Shetland men went on the ships of Salvesens of Leith when they went whaling in the Antarctic. This proved a convenient arrangement, as they could be away during the southern summer, and also be at home for work on the croft in the northern summer. However declining yields at the Antarctic whaling caused the end of British participation in it in the early 1960s.

KNITWEAR

Shetland knitwear, now a modernised version of a traditional craft, has been an important supplementary source of income to many households throughout the modern period, and is the main occupation for some. The traditional hand-knit patterns are now often executed in a wider variety of colours, and the work of hand-knitters is now supplemented by knitting machine. Knitwear played an important part in the economic recovery of the islands in the 1960s; and although the products have never enjoyed until recently the protection of an effective trade mark, they have been widely marketed in America and Europe. As a fashion industry it does suffer from market fluctuations and competition, but does make a distinctive Shetland product very widely known.

THE OIL BOOM

As is internationally known, oil and oil-related developments have dominated the Shetland scene since 1970. As well as causing inevitable upheaval in the life of the islands generally, this has involved the setting up of oil-servicing bases at Lerwick and Sandwick; but the really massive investment has been in the oil terminal at Sullom with its facilities for oil storage, tanker berthing, pilotage and pollution control. This has also involved the building of big temporary work camps at Firth and Toft, and the re-activation of the wartime airstrip at Scatsta. Activity at Sumburgh Airport was also intense, with greatly increased frequency of service and charter flights to and from mainland destinations, as well as large-scale helicopter operations to service oil rigs and platforms. More recently, however, the new Chinook helicopters have been able to service the oil-fields direct from Aberdeen Airport, and there has been an incentive for this as big investment in improvements at Sumburgh have resulted in considerably higher landing charges. (The total investment at Sumburgh was £34 million.)

As far as possible, outside labour has been brought into Shetland for oil-related developments. The objectives have been to give the minimum of disturbance to local employment and local life, and to maintain a healthy balance when the big construction phase of the oil industry is past. None the less, the oil era has brought the best employment situation the isles have ever known, although it has of course brought a host of problems in its train. Not the least of these is the management of finance by local government on a new scale, especially in the light of the decision by the local authority to borrow to build the harbour facilities and to lease out the site of the terminal for operation. However the construction phase of the oil industry is now over, and it appears that Shetland's future here lies in being a gathering and shipment point for oil. There appears little likelihood of the establishment of petro-chemical industries. Even in the absence of these, it is clear that oil-related employment will be of major importance for Shetland at least till the end of this century.

LOCAL GOVERNMENT

A very important event in the life of the islands was the setting up of the all-purpose local authority, the Shetland Islands Council (S.I.C.) in 1974 under the act for the reorganisation of local government in Scotland. This is one of the island authorities which has avoided the two-tier (regional and district) structure of modern local government, although Shetland does have also the basic level of community councils as do other local authorities. The inception of the S.I.C., especially in the circumstances of the oil boom, has done much to regenerate interest in the life of the islands and to orientate the administration. Previous to this the successful moving of a private parliamentary bill by the former Zetland

County Council to plan for and control oil development had provided a basis to shape the changes of the oil era.

The S.I.C. has also in recent years been playing an increasingly important and direct role in the economy of the islands, giving support for existing industry and encouraging new ventures.

HOUSING AND AMENITIES

A far-reaching series of improvements in living conditions and amenities have been made since World War II. Through a series of local schemes, mains water has now been extended to almost every house, and mains electricity has been supplied everywhere except the smallest inhabited islands. Tarred roads have been extended to virtually every settlement, and (especially in the oil era) several of the main roads have been widened and their alignments improved.

In housing, although various internal improvements and extensions have been made throughout the islands in the post-war period, there had been limited additions to the basic housing stock (other than in Lerwick) until the 1970s. Previous to this the main developments had been the expansion of Lerwick with council housing and some private building. Outside Lerwick a few groups of council houses were built at central points, with some private housing—the latter most evident in the prosperous fishing islands of Whalsay and Burra. In the special case of the island of Unst, the building of Services housing added to the stock.

During the oil boom there has been the building of modern housing of varied types in a very wide range of locations—certainly not confined just to the main areas immediately affected by oil-related activity. As well as private building, council and Scottish Special Housing building has included accommodation for oil workers and for the elderly, including the much valued sheltered housing.

The organisation of education has also considerably changed in the modern period. This has also included the thinning out of the rural schools, with the selection of a number of central points to which children are transported, and at which more complete facilities (including meals) are provided. Most recently some very fine new school buildings have been constructed; they are provided with an admirable range of facilities. A rural community like Shetland has had problems in developing a system of comprehensive education as is now required. There is still the one full secondary school in Lerwick, now named the Anderson High School; there are also seven junior high schools in the islands as well as 36 primaries.

With the aid of the resources of the Charitable Trust, set up with oil revenues, Shetland now enjoys a particularly high standard of social provision. For the elderly repairs to houses have been financed, while there has been an increased provision of sheltered housing for those who require it. Other provision includes for example the free supply of vehicles to invalids.

Leisure provision has also been extended. There has been the building of new community halls, and the improvement and extension of existing ones; help has been given to various organisations and groups to improve their facilities; and at present the building of a big new indoor leisure complex at Clickimin, Lerwick, is under way.

TRANSPORT

A degree of isolation and related transport problems have always been part of island life. The modern Shetland transport system now includes air services as well as roads and ferries, and there remains the steamer link with Aberdeen. However there is an enduring problem in providing and financing adequate services to a relatively small and scattered population.

The main link to the islands has continued to be the steamer service from Aberdeen, which allows Shetland to be reached by an overnight sailing. This is now operated by P. and O. Ferries. Until the 1970s there were two return trips per week, but thereafter a bigger 'roll-on roll-off' vessel was acquired which could handle the increased cargo of the oil era in a more efficient way, and it now makes three return trips per week. In the earlier post-war period, Shetland also had a steamer connection with Leith via Aberdeen and Kirkwall: there were two services a week in summer and one in winter, but with declining profitability this service was finally discontinued in the 1960s. There is still, however, a conventional cargo service to Grangemouth operated by the Shetland Line, and a 'Ro-Ro' cargo service to Leith operated by P. and O. Ferries.

There have been air services to and from Shetland throughout the post-war period, although before the oil era this was limited to one or two flights a day. They were at first operated by B.E.A. and subsequently by British Airways. The main contact has been with Aberdeen, and with the big increase in oil-related traffic there have been up to six services a day, while terminal facilities at Sumburgh Airport have been greatly extended and improved. In addition there was a boom in other services (mainly charter), and these include direct contacts with the mainland from the airports at Scatsta, Tingwall and Balta Sound.

Within the islands communications have in most respects considerably improved. The most significant development has been the replacement of the *Earl of Zetland* steamer, which provided the link between Lerwick and the north isles, with a system of drive-on drive-off vehicular ferries which have speeded up contacts by connecting up the road system via the shortest sea crossings. For the islands of Muckle Roe, Trondra and Burra even better has been the building of bridges across the narrow sounds to give direct road connection. On the other hand,

Skerries and Fair Isle are still dependent on services by vessels of small fishing boat size; and Foula and Papa Stour on smaller motor-boats.

Internal air services have also made a contribution to the transport system, and are especially valuable for urgent purposes—especially medical emergencies. All the inhabited islands except Bressay and Yell now have airstrips approved for charter use, although not sanctioned for full air services.

In one respect public transport services have deteriorated—that of buses, the inevitable consequence of a high rate of car ownership. Reduced bus services still extend from Lerwick to nearly all parts of the mainland, and through the northern isles of Yell and Unst. Only the most populous parts now have a daily service.

The service of delivery vans for shopping in rural areas has also considerably declined. While this is a minor inconvenience for most, for households with no car this is a problem, and bears especially hard on the elderly.

POPULATION

The population trend in Shetland over the modern period has much in common with the remainder of Scotland's Highlands and Islands. There was a sustained increase till the mid-19th century, followed by a century of decline, but which has now been reversed.

Throughout the 19th century more and more people were leaving Shetland, because of the restricted opportunities available at home, and the better opportunities available elsewhere, in Britain and abroad. However the 19th century was still the time of big families, and population continued to increase until 1861 when the total was 31,670 compared with the first Census figure of 22,379 in 1801. Subsequently numbers fell with accelerated emigration, which was linked in part to clearances of crofters and by appropriation of their scattald grazings; and with the trend towards smaller families from the end of last century, the population continued to fall for a full century to 1961 when the total was 17,814. Economic recovery in the 1960s led to a turn of the tide, and the oil boom has been associated with rapid growth with the result that the 1981 figure was 27,271, although this was considerably boosted by the big number of construction workers who were temporary residents. A more realistic figure is c. 23,000, the estimate of permanent residents produced by Shetland Health Board.

There have also been important changes in the distribution and composition of population. In distribution, the main trend is the concentration at central points, especially in Lerwick itself, which now has almost one-third of the total population. Other central points, including Scalloway, Hamnavoe, Brae, Firth/Mossbank, Sandwick and Balta Sound have continued to grow, and indeed this gathering of population into local centres is seen in some degree throughout the islands. The counterpart to this has been the thinning out of population elsewhere as croft and cottar houses have continued to be abandoned. The run-down of rural population is most seen in the remoter areas, including especially the small islands. While numbers of small islands have become deserted since the middle of last century, none have actually been abandoned in the last 50 years, although the population in some is now around one-tenth of their 19th century peak. The survival of the communities in the remaining small islands is now delicately poised, but they all so far retain the basic essential facilities of shop, post-office and school, along with the personnel of schoolteacher-missionary and nurse.

The composition of the population has also inevitably changed. Prominent here is the different age structure from former times which is usual in developed countries, with a greater proportion of elderly and fewer young people now. For most of the present century nearly all parts of the islands have had more females than males, as young men have been more prone to emigrate. However the 1981 Census figures show that the considerable immigration of males during the oil boom has changed the sex balance in favour of males in the great majority of parishes. This new immigration has included a big number of returning Shetlanders, but also considerable numbers without previous island connections. The population now thus shows the marks of the enhanced mobility that is characteristic of modern society.

SHETLAND NOW

Life in Shetland has greatly changed in the modern period, as it has throughout the western world. There is now a much higher standard of security and amenity than before, although there are considerable problems. In the age of mass consumption, however, Shetland people still generally know their neighbours, and indeed know many of the other Shetlanders. On the other hand the co-operation and teamwork which formerly was strong in crofting and in other work is now less in evidence.

In the 1950s and early 1960s restricted employment opportunities and continued emigration were a steady drain on the life of the islands; and included in those lost were many of the most able young people, who obtained qualifications in higher education and could not find employment in Shetland commensurate with their ability. However the persistent move to the cities which dominated the western world for well over a century has now eased, and in Shetland the development of oil along with the re-organisation of local government has done much to re-invigorate the community. Shetland can claim to have coped well with the stresses of oil development, and now faces the challenge of planning for the future once the oil has gone.

September 1983

THE ISLAND AND PARISH OF BRESSAY

by Stella Sutherland

PHYSICAL BASIS

The island of Bressay lies to the east of the Shetland mainland and in effect encloses the stretch of water known as Bressay Sound or Lerwick Harbour, which has enabled Lerwick to grow up as Shetland's main port. In a document of 1490, Bressay appears as Brusøy, suggesting a derivation from the man's name Brusi. It has also been surmised that the Breideyjarsund in Shetland in which King Harald lay in 1263 is Bressay Sound, which would give an original Breidey, i.e., 'broad island'. The island is about seven miles long by three miles at its widest. It contains some interesting caves and rock formations, notably the Orkneyman's Cave at the point of the Bard Head, and the Giant's Leg near the lighthouse. To Bressay's east side, across a narrow sound (200 yards at its narrowest) lies the bird sanctuary island of Noss. The area of Bressay is 7,419 acres and that of Noss 774 acres. The whole area is composed of Upper Old Red Sandstone. In general, Bressay is low-lying, the only notable hills being the Ward (742 feet O.D.) and Anderhill (460 feet O.D.); and in Noss, the Noup (592 feet O.D.). A curious feature of Anderhill is that, no matter from which direction it is looked at, it has the same whale-backed outline. There are several lochs of good size in Bressay containing some trout. The Loch of Brough provides the island's water supply and is also the venue for races of a local model yacht club.

HISTORY

From at least 1490 up to the late 17th century, a Norwegian nobleman named Sigurd Jonsson and his descendants owned considerable estates in Shetland, including Noss and part of Bressay. In 1660, Noss and the Bressay interests passed into the hands of John Neven the Younger from Unst and subsequently to the Hendersons, the progenitors of the Mouats of Garth. The Hendersons were themselves an ancient family of Norwegian origin. The Bolts of Cruister were the only other notable landlords (Magnus Bult was 'Foude' of Bressay in 1612). Their lands were acquired by the Mouats in the early 19th century and their 'Haa' (i.e., the hall) at Cruister is now a ruin, only an outbuilding remaining in good condition. Arthur Anderson, a co-founder of the P. & O. Company and donor of the Anderson Educational Institute (now the Anderson High School) in Lerwick, began his working life as a beach boy in Thomas Bolt's fishcuring business, later becoming his clerk and rising from that position. The present laird of Bressay is Mr John Hamilton Scott of Garth, in succession to his late uncle, Mr Norman Ogilvie Mouat Cameron of Garth, whose father, William Cameron, was a Bishop of Cape Town. Mr Scott farms Maryfield (1,118 acres) and is active in agricultural matters in Shetland generally.

The Gardie Papers are an important collection and have had a preliminary survey by the National Register of Archives (Scotland), the survey number being 0450.

Bressay Lighthouse was first lit in 1858, and is now on the list for conversion to automatic operation. At present there are three lightkeepers, as well as a local assistant, and two occasional helpers.

At one time Bressay supplied peats to Lerwick, and also provided the whole of Shetland with 'slates' (i.e., thin flagstone slabs), which are still to be seen on the roofs of some of Lerwick's older buildings.

In 1774, 400 foreign 'busses', mostly Dutch, visited Bressay Sound, and up to the early 1900s the Dutch were still fishing in large numbers around these shores, giving rise to the local saying that 'Amsterdam was biggit oot o'da back o'Bressa'. During the herring fishing boom in the early years of this century, several fishcuring stations were established on Bressay's western foreshores, notably Milligan's at Ham; Low's or Moar's at Leraness; Buchan's, Duthie's, Watt's and R. Gordon's at Cruister; and E. Gordon's and White & Willows' at Heogan. There were earlier and other fishcuring stations, including one on the Holm of the Mail in the 1880s. During the Peninsular War, Bressay was harassed by the press gang seeking men for the Navy. Also as elsewhere, clearances took place of small crofters to create sheep walks, notably at Wadbister, Culliesbrough, Noss, Noss Sound, Hoversta, Maryfield and Aith. 1871 was known locally as 'da year 'at Walker made da uproar', Walker being factor to the then laird, Miss Mouat. Gunnista would have suffered the same fate, but for the fact that no tenant could be found offering a higher rent than the combined rents of the sitting crofters. Walker built the present Maryfield House and named it for his wife; the site was formerly a croft aptly named Troubletoon. The Walkers too had their sorrows—a baby son is buried in the churchyard at the Mail.

Kirk Session Records are available from 1764-1806. Old parochial registers have survived from 1737, but there are several blank years. There are also earlier presbytery records.

There were three early churches. At Kirkabister there was St John's of which little is left now but the tradition, and the name Da Kirk Gait, and that all but forgotten; St Mary's at Culliesbrough, a fragment of the walls of which remains; and St Ola or Olaf at Gunnista, which was the parish church prior to 1722. From presbytery records of that year it is clear that the minister resided at Culliesbrough and used the 'chappell there in case of sickness, weakness or infirmity whereby he was unable to travel to the foresaid parish church at Gunelsta [sic] being a mile and a half distant'. The minister of 1722, Mr John Duncan (not to be confused with an assistant of the same name who served Bressay about 80 years later) was in dispute with the then laird, William Henderson of Gardie. Henderson had begun building a new church at the west side of the island and wished to take the timbers of the Gunnista church and those of the Culliesbrough chapel for the use of the new building. Duncan brought the matter before the presbytery and obtained a decision against the laird. It would appear, however, that Henderson got his way, for in 1722 church and manse were removed to the west side. The Gunnista church was demolished and on its site a tomb was erected for the Henderson family. (The tomb itself is now falling into disrepair.)

In 1775 the first west-side church received a new roof and was lengthened, but in 1812 it was condemned and a new church built about 1814, presumably on the same site since no other remains exist, nor is there tradition of any other site on the west side of the island. The 1814 church accommodated 370 'and no free sittings'!

A new manse had been built in 1786 and repaired in the 1790s 'at very great expence'. It would seem that this was situated on the croft still known as the Old Manse (incidentally the birthplace of the present writer). About 1819 this manse was replaced by another building, which in its turn gave way to the present manse, built about 1951. The 1819 building, renovated and re-named Mizpah House, is still occupied.

Gardie House itself was built about 1700. About 1900 the façade as it presently appears was created. It is one of the most attractive small mansion houses in Shetland.

In the Culliesbrough churchyard are several interesting tombstones, including one uncovered about 1965, commemorating Marjorie Gifford (of the Giffords of Busta) wife of Hugh Leigh, minister of Bressay. She died, the mother of twins, the year after her wedding in 1670. Leigh married again, to Elizabeth Williamson, daughter of a shipmaster in Bressay, and was suspended in 1702 for beating his wife, but 'reponed' in 1704. Marjorie Gifford's tombstone does not appear in the Inventory of Ancient and Historical Monuments for the very good reason that it formerly lay hidden, having been grown over with grass. Four others are included, one being that of a Dutch captain, Claes Jansen Bruyn of Durgerdam, and another commemorating Agnes Gifford 'ane virtuous and discreet gentlewoman, spouse to Andrew Robertson', almost certainly the same 'Nanse Giffert' whose name appears in the Register of Testaments, Commissariat Records of Orkney and Shetland, with the date 7 August 1630. Her actual date of death was 20 October 1628, but it must have taken some time for her affairs to be wound up.

The Bressay Stone was found near here. The Norwegian historian Brøgger (1929) dates it between the 6th and 8th centuries A.D.; but the 19th century architect, Sir Henry Dryden gives the date as the 9th or early 10th century; it is now in the Scottish National Museum of Antiquities. Other interesting remains, including at least four brochs, are listed under Nos. 1085-1109 in the official Inventory of Ancient and Historic Monuments. William Umphray, who became minister of Bressay in 1581, bequeathed in 1637 a capital sum of £100 Scots and the rent of four merks of land for maintenance of a reader and other pious purposes. This land, a park of about 60 acres, is still known as the Mortified Land (mortification here signifying a bequest to some charitable institution), and is still rented out by the Church. Two communion cups, which are still in regular use, bear William Umphray's name and the date 1628.

At Aithsness and Bard Head, Bressay's two extremes, heavy guns were sited during World War I, and remain in remarkably good condition for their age. In World War II, heavy artillery batteries were placed on Cruister Hill and Setter Hill, and light batteries at Leraness and Maryfield. These guns were removed after the war and only the foundations and magazines remain.

POPULATION

Bressay's population stands now at just over 300. From 1841 to 1891 it remained between 800 and 900. From 1911 there was a steady decline of about 100 each decade to 269 in 1961, since when there has been a slight increase. Most of the population is concentrated on the west side, with the three council housing estates together containing about 40 per cent of the total. Only 11 people reside on the east side of Bressay, while Gunnista and Beosetter to the north contain respectively four and seven people.

HOUSING

Since the 1914 war, many older buildings have fallen into disrepair or disappeared completely. Bressay was slower than some districts to begin house improvements, since so many people emigrated abroad or went to work and settled in Lerwick, Leith or elsewhere. This left an ageing population whom poverty or disinclination prevented from improving their houses. Since the 1939-45 war, government grants and loans have encouraged building and renovation. In the past 20 years, 15 houses (including new croft houses) have been built and 28 others improved or enlarged, following the coming of electricity and piped water in the 1950s. Also in the 1950s, the Council built 12 houses at Voeside, and more recently two further housing estates at Glebe Park and Fullaburn have been developed. Six sheltered houses in one block exist within the Glebe Park complex. The occupants are independent in their homes, but there is a warden on call. A community room in the sheltered housing provides a venue for occasional Women's Guild meetings, slide shows, and coffee mornings for charitable purposes; these events create interest and outside contacts for those of the occupants who wish to attend.

PUBLIC AND SOCIAL SERVICES

A car ferry service began in the autumn of 1975 and has proved a great benefit, linking Bressay with the Shetland Mainland by a shorter crossing than formerly. Many more local people now work in shops, offices and elsewhere in and around Lerwick. Children attending the Anderson High School can now live at home the year round, where formerly, during the winter months, they had to be accommodated in Lerwick during the school week. About 75 per cent of Bressay householders have become car owners since the car ferry came, while only about 25 per cent possessed cars before. Roads have been improved, though they are still narrow and rough in places. Electricity and piped water (from the 1950s) have brought comfort and convenience. There has been an efficient nursing service since about 1914, the present nurse being a local woman. A doctor visited the island once a week up to the 1970s, but again, the coming of the car ferry, which runs every hour from either side and more often in event of emergency, made this less necessary. There is a weekly refuse collection. Home helps are provided for those who need them, and meals-on-wheels for the elderly. There is a thriving playgroup for pre-school children. A library van comes over once a month and is greatly appreciated. Few houses are without the telephone. The TV station on the Ward serves the whole of Shetland, and when there is a power cut, Bressay can be sure of prompt attention. Once a farmhouse, Maryfield House has been developed as a hotel and public house.

There has been a public hall since the 1890s, almost entirely provided by local subscription. Even the poorest gave something, the women knitting shawls and other woollen goods for sale as their contribution. Because the Church gave a grant towards the cost, for many years the building was run as a church hall and its use was severely restricted. Almost nothing of a secular nature was permitted and it was only in the 1930s that some relaxation of the position began. The hall was used as a Church of Scotland canteen for servicemen during the Second World War and has been twice renovated since then. It provides accommodation for the playgroup, a community group and other activities, such as sales of work, whist drives, concerts, dances, the annual local Up-Helly-Aa festival held in February, sales organised by visitors, and occasional services of religious bodies.

A Women's Guild (Church of Scotland) and a branch of the S.W.R.I. exist, although the latter is in abeyance at present.

EDUCATION

Fifty years before the Education Act of 1872, two schools existed in Bressay, the parochial one on the east side (now a roofless but still imposing ruin) and the Assembly one on the west (now Hoversta farm-house). There is also the tradition of a dame school at Kirkabister. The east side school had as one of its masters John Ross, who is commemorated in one of the stained glass windows in the church, placed there by his son David, who became a leading figure in technical education in Scotland. (In 1895 David Ross also presented the font which is in the parish church at Lerwick.)

The present school dates from about 1880. Its first headmaster was George Linklater, a local man, brought up at Gunnista and at the Old Manse croft already mentioned. The school has been enlarged and extended more than once. At present there are 21 pupils, and two teachers. There is a commodious schoolhouse and also separate accommodation for an assistant; these are rented out as the teachers do not require them.

CHURCH

There is a Church of Scotland membership of about 80. An evening service is held each Sunday by the resident missionary reader, who is also assistant in the joint parish of Lerwick and Bressay. Communion is dispensed twice a year, usually in May and November, by the minister in charge of the parish. The church is a substantial building and appears to be that built in 1814. During a renovation in 1957 traces of an outside stair were found on the outside of the east gable. There is a gallery which is rarely used now. The pulpit, on the south side, is flanked by two handsome stained glass windows. That depicting St Peter is to the memory of John Ross already mentioned, who was the schoolmaster of this parish, during the period 1843-1878. The other shows St Paul and commemorates Sir Robert George Cruickshank Hamilton, (1836-1895), who was born at the manse (now Mizpah House), son of Zachary Macaulay Hamilton and of his first wife. Z. M. Hamilton was minister of Bressay from 1833 to 1876, and was a cousin of Lord Macaulay. Sir Robert was appointed Under-Secretary for Ireland in 1882, and became Governor of Tasmania in 1886; he also held other important political offices. His son, also Sir Robert, was a judge and at one time Liberal M.P. for Orkney and Shetland. Two memorial tablets, one at either side of these main windows, bear the names of two former lairds, William Mouat of Garth, who died in 1836, and his half-sister Mrs Cameron Mouat who succeeded him, and who died in 1871 at the age of 91. (It was her grandson William Cameron who was a Bishop of Cape Town, and after him the family name was Cameron of Garth.) A brass plate near the vestry door states that the electric lighting of the church was presented by James Yorston, Melbourne, Australia, in memory of his parents Mr and Mrs Robert Yorston, Hoversta. There is an electric organ, gifted by Mrs William Laurenson, formerly of Heogan, in memory of her husband and of her parents. Two local ladies (the present writer is one) play the organ on alternate Sundays. On the outside wall on either side of the west door are memorials to the local dead of the World Wars 1914-18 and 1939-45. The bell of Bressay Church, unused since the Second World War, is still in place. It was cast in Hamburg in 1723 'for the use of this kirk'. In 1957 the church was renovated and redecorated, mainly by voluntary labour and subscription.

The Pentecostal Church in Shetland maintains its minister in a recently-built manse in Bressay: he commutes to services in Lerwick. The head of the Mormon Church in Shetland also lives in Bressay.

AGRICULTURE AND INDUSTRY

There are three farms, Maryfield (1,118 acres), Setter (872 acres), and Hoversta (135 acres). These are mostly given over to sheep rearing, but with some beef cattle. There has been no dairy farm since the 1960s, and milk is brought in. Silage is made at Maryfield and Hoversta but elsewhere grass is cured by the traditional haymaking method. About 40 acres of oats and barley are grown annually for feeding stock and about 15 acres of rape annually for 'finishing' sheep. Cultivation of potatoes and turnips is small-scale and is mostly only sufficient for the household and some animal feed. Cabbage plant cultivation, once a useful part of the croft income, has all but disappeared. There are about 60 crofters, some of whom tenant more than one croft and several of whom own their crofts. Of these holdings about half are actively worked. Since 1945, the farms and cultivated crofts have had tractors and tractor implements; crofters who have insufficient machinery employ one of the farmers in his spare time.

Approximate agricultural figures for 1982
Stock: 3,000 breeding sheep
            70 (beef) breeding cows
            2 bulls
Product: 2,600 lambs
            70 calves

Together with wool and subsidies this gives a figure for gross agricultural income over £100,000 for 1982.

There is no commercial fishing from Bressay now, but the fish meal and oil plant at Heogan remains, as it has been since 1888, the main local employer of labour. New factory premises have been built during the past year and are in process of occupation. About 20 people are employed at Heogan, including canteen and office staffs. At one time there was a second fishmeal factory, at Aith, but it ceased to operate about 1930.

Approximate output of Heogan Factory for 1982
From 35,196 tons of fish landed:
7,419 tons meal   (approximate value £250/ton)
  553 tons oil   (,,   ,,   £200/ton)

EMPLOYMENT

Apart from the ferry crew and those engaged in the refuse collection, there is little other local employment: there are a school cook; a part-time postmistress; two or three assistants at one of the local shops (the other is family-run); casual workers at the public house; a local assistant light-keeper and two occasional helpers; two or three home helps; and one resident teacher. Roads are maintained from Lerwick by the Islands Council. Maryfield Farm employs two men, including the farmer, full-time. The 60 crofters may be said to be part-time, since either they have other employment or are pensioners. A few people have knitting machines but handknitting and finishing are now at a minimal level.

NOSS

The island of Noss (774 acres) is now run as part of Maryfield Farm. Noss is interesting in its own right and not just as a bird sanctuary and nature reserve, for which it is best known. Between 1841 and 1871 its population averaged over 20, but after 1871 ('da year 'at Walker made da uproar') numbers diminished to three and were never again to rise above seven. The island has not been continuously inhabited since 1939, although Laurence Sutherland (husband of the present writer), then joint tenant of the island, spent 25 summers from 1945 till 1969 in Noss, looking after his sheep and acting as warden and boatman. About 1969, some of the flagstones surrounding the dwelling house collapsed, and he discovered an underground passage about 2 foot 6 inches wide, with stone-built sides, largely obscured by sand and rubble. For safety's sake the hole was filled in and the flagstones replaced. On the ness in front of the house there is the site of an ancient chapel with a graveyard, which is being eroded by the sea on the east side, bones being sometimes exposed. Dr James Copland who published the *Dictionary of Medicine* in 1832, was a son of the farmer of Noss, also named James Copland, of whose butter and milk Patrick Neill declared on a visit in 1806, that it was the best he had seen in Shetland. Butter was regularly carried to Lerwick for sale. The rent was £40. 5s. and the tenant was 'allowed to fish on his own behoof'. James Copland, who originally came from Orkney, built a house and pier in Lerwick for his own use. The house is now Nos. 2-6, Commercial Street; the pier is now known as Gellie's Pier.

The Marquis of Londonderry leased Noss from 1871-1900 and reared Shetland ponies there for use in his Durham coal mines. The steading at the back of the dwelling house has only two others like it in Shetland, one at Swinister (Delting) and one at Kirkabister (Yell). It is a well-built square with corners heightened for effect or to prevent stock escaping. Inside are (or were: they are disintegrating) lean-to shelters for stock, roofed with heavy Bressay slate; there are also roofless horse-boxes in the centre of the square; there are two entrances, opposite each other, east and west. The last dwelling houses (other than the present one) were at Setter, on the south-west coast, but these are now in ruins.

The Nature Conservancy maintains a warden in Noss during the summer months and a boatman is also in residence then. Visitors must shout to attract attention and a flag is displayed when weather conditions are unsuitable for crossing.

The Holm of Noss, sometimes called the Cradle Holm from the cradle that was used to put sheep on the Holm for grazing, is no longer used for this purpose. By tradition, the original cradle was fastened by a Foula man who successfully climbed the steep Holm. Instead of returning the easy way, by the cradle now in place, he elected to climb back down, and in so doing lost his life. The cradle was dismantled many years ago and the Holm is occupied only by seabirds. About 1969, a fall of rock from the Noss side blocked the channel, so that small boats cannot as hitherto use it as a passage.

There are traditions of shipwrecks on Noss and on the nearby Bressay shore, mariners sometimes mistaking the Bressay–Noss channel for that between Bressay and Lerwick. One tale has it that a quantity of gold was found at Burgie Geo on the Bressay side, just below the ruined broch.

WAY OF LIFE

This has changed a great deal, particularly in the last 20 years. The coming of electricity and piped water transformed habits based on the necessity of doing things by hand. Fewer peats are cut, and carrying water is a thing of the past. Comparatively full employment and higher incomes have raised the standard of living; though still modest, it is well above the poverty level. The older generations deplore the passing of informal visits among neighbours; the need to lock doors nowadays when going out; and the decline in behavioural standards. Churchgoing has diminished, the weekly congregation numbering rarely above 20, and at Communion services 40 to 50. But Bressay is still very much a caring community, sympathetic, neighbourly and helpful. The incomers who have made their homes here have integrated well, being accepted themselves, and with few exceptions, making some worthwhile contribution to the community. The new housing estates, being mainly occupied by local people re-housed from older accommodation, and in some cases married to incomers, do not separate themselves from the mainstream of local life and indeed may be said to enrich it.

In general the community is law-abiding, although habits and ideas are more relaxed than those of a generation ago. Vandalism and petty crime are minimal, the occasional domestic squabble or drunk driver being the most usual reason for police visits. There is no resident police-man. Bressay is a good place in which to live and work. There is a feeling of stability, permanence, and continuity and there is a wish to remain. The old ways are being modified but not abandoned entirely.

March 1983

THE PARISH OF DELTING

Original description by A. N. Sutherland, B.Sc.(Agri.), 1953
Extensively revised by Laureen M. Johnson, M.A., 1983

PHYSICAL BASIS

The parish of Delting covers an area 12 miles long by from one to five miles broad, and lies towards the north end of the Shetland Mainland. To the south and south-east it has land boundaries, but the remainder is all bounded by the sea apart from the narrow isthmus of the Mavis Grind which links it to the parish of Northmavine to the north-west. The land is hilly or undulating, and the main trend of the hills, several of which reach over 750 feet O.D., is north to south. The coast is considerably indented, and the inlets of Dales Voe, Colla Firth and Olna Firth are in effect small-scale, steep-sided fiords. Between Delting and Northmavine parish lies the inlet of Sullom Voe, now internationally known for its oil terminal; and to the north-east of Delting lies Yell Sound with its strong tidal currents. There are a number of off-shore islands, several of which were formerly inhabited; but the only inhabited 'island' remaining is Muckle Roe, which is in fact connected by a bridge.

HISTORY OF THE COMMUNITY

There have of course been far-reaching changes since the earlier Statistical Accounts were written. The history of the parish since the middle of last century has been a strange mixture of progress and retrogression, accompanied by steady depopulation for a century until the mid-1960s.

We see the people gradually turning their backs on the sea, both as a means of livelihood and transport. When the *Old and New Statistical Accounts* were written the 'sixern' fishing was in full swing. The boat from which it got its name (the sixern) was a six-oared open boat of 18 to 20 feet keel, in which a very hazardous line fishing was prosecuted, often miles out to sea. When these craft were caught in a gale the toll of life could be heavy, and the sixern gradually gave way to larger decked boats. With the diminution of cod on the Shetland banks, these bigger boats went further afield and soon were discovering new fishing banks at Faroe and Iceland. Delting was well situated for this fishing and Voe, at the inner end of Olna Firth, became one of the main centres of departure and arrival of the Faroe smacks. This important fishing went on into the present century, with fishing trips not only to the Faroe and Iceland banks, but also to the cod banks off Rockall.

Fishing has always been hazardous, and Delting had its own worst disaster here in 1900 when a sudden fierce gale in the month of December caught seven boats at the haddock fishing. Four of the boats were lost with a total of 22 men, mostly from the townships of Firth and Toft; and they left 15 widows and 51 fatherless children.

Delting men also took part in the summer herring fishing from the end of last century, but as a rule they did not operate from local stations. The only part of Delting where herring curing took place was at Mossbank where curing on a small scale was carried on for a time. Other parts of the parish were too far from the open sea and the fishing grounds, and Delting boats often operated from the isle of Papa Stour on the west side of Shetland. Gradually, with the substitution of engines for sail, the Shetland herring fishing was centralised at Lerwick, and Delting boats faded from the picture.

One other kind of fishing, however, flourished for a number of years with headquarters in Delting. Fifty years ago whales were plentiful around these islands and in the early years of this century a Norwegian company set up a whaling station on the north side of Olna Firth, where a plentiful supply of water could be obtained from a nearby loch. The whales were captured by whale chasers off the west coast of Shetland and towed to the station where the oil was extracted. This fishing was suspended during World War I when the whaling station was partly utilised by the Navy. It was resumed after the war and operated until 1929, when it was finally closed down and dismantled. By that time the whales, once so plentiful, had been so reduced by overfishing, that the enterprise had become uneconomic. A number of local men were employed in various capacities, especially during the latter years of the station's operations. Today little trace of this once busy centre remains.

During the first half of this century the crofter-fisherman, the typical Shetlander of a bygone generation, has gradually disappeared. Fishing now is a full-time occupation, and while two or three districts in Shetland have become definite fishing centres, the men of Delting have almost all forsaken the fishing. Even so, at certain times of the year when haddock and whiting are plentiful in St. Magnus Bay, Voe because of its geographical position becomes quite a busy little fishing centre. But it is seine net boats and trawlers from Burra Isle, Scalloway and other parts of Shetland which are landing their catches there, to be transported by lorry to Scalloway or Lerwick.

During the decline and specialisation of Shetland fishing the Delting men gradually disappeared from the ranks of Shetland fishermen. But the land could only provide at best a partial living, and once again the men turned to the sea. More and more men became seamen and sought their livelihood all over the globe. Some of these men eventually settled down in Leith, Shields or other shipping ports, but the majority maintained their homes in their native isles. Often they were away on long voyages for two or three years and then came home for two or three months before again embarking on long voyages. Many men from Delting, as from elsewhere in Shetland, worked their way by perseverance and study from before the mast to positions as officers and captains. During both world wars a number of Delting seamen of both the Merchant Navy and Royal Navy paid the supreme sacrifice.

With the decline in fishing considerable increase in agriculture might have been expected. That such has not been the case, except in the case of sheep, is shown from the following table:

Year	Arable acreage	No. of cattle	No. of sheep
1870	941	1,473	9,454
1890	1,022	1,551	12,110
1910	919	1,056	18,186
1930	642	668	16,995
1950	474	333	25,570

Throughout the 19th century the landlords, who were also the fish buyers and merchants, were all-powerful. Unfortunately they often used this power to enrich themselves and keep their tenants in poverty and often in debt. In order to provide homes for as many as possible for the fishing they subdivided the crofts. Each croft became so small that the utmost had to be made of its potentialities to produce food, mainly in the form of potatoes and oats. But even while the poorer crofts were being subdivided, the slide to depopulation was started by evictions from the better holdings. As long ago as the 1780s Gideon Gifford of Busta turned out the crofters on the south and west side of Olna Firth in order to make room for sheep. This first attempt at sheep farming proved unsuccessful as the flock became infected with sheep scab (the practice of sheep dipping to prevent scab was not known at that time, at least in Shetland). The crofters were allowed to return and occupy their holdings, but in 1852 they were again turned out, this time for good. Some of the best districts in the parish were cleared in this way, and many unfortunate families were forced to emigrate. It is significant that the population of Delting reached a maximum of 2,144 in 1851. From that time depopulation set in. By 1901 the population had fallen to 1,389, rather fewer than it had been in 1801. The population in 1951 had dropped to 864, a decrease of 59 per cent in a century. But although depopulation started with the clearances, it certainly did not stop when the landlords were at last deprived by law of their powers of summary eviction.

DEVELOPMENTS SINCE WORLD WAR II

There have been many changes in the parish of Delting during the last 30 years. The most notable of these changes have of course occurred since the coming of the oil industry, but it must not be assumed that nothing else of any importance has happened in Delting in 30 years, nor that oil was the only factor in turning the tide of depopulation which had ebbed for more than a century.

The period falls roughly into three phases:

1. the 1950s and early 1960s
2. the mid 1960s and early 1970s
3. the 'oil boom' period, from the mid 1970s up to the end of 1982.

Delting has not for many years now been involved in fishing, the former main commercial activity. There are a few individual fishermen, and small fishing boats often land catches at the Voe pier, but there are no fishing boats of any size based in Delting. Even during the lobster boom in the 1960s only a handful of men were full-time lobster fishermen, although not a few owned suitable boats and would set some creels in their spare time. A similar situation exists now with scallop fishing. Recent developments in fishing, therefore, affected this parish hardly at all.

THE 1950s AND EARLY 1960s

The economy of Delting in the 1950s was sustained partly by crofting and partly by light industries, especially the hosiery and tweed trade. The average man was very likely to have both a croft and other work, as few could make enough of a livelihood from their holdings to exist solely off the land.

Agriculture in Delting, as in the rest of Shetland, received a great boost in the late 1950s when government grants began, through the Crofters Commission, to enable the crofter to fence and reclaim apportionments of the 'scattald' or common grazing land. From 1959 onwards there was a great deal of apportionment, until by the early 1970s almost all the readily accessible hill land was fenced and held by one crofter or another. An added incentive to re-seeding and land improvement was a high subsidy on lime.

Reclamation of scattald had two major results for the enterprising crofter: it gave him a larger, more viable agricultural unit to work, and it made him less dependent on his neighbours. It is always difficult, when the scattald sheep have to be dipped, clipped, etc. to fix upon a day and a time which suits all the crofters involved, when most of them have other employment. If a man has even *some* of his sheep on his own apportionment, he can work with them when he pleases, and when the weather is suitable.

By the 1960s, agricultural machinery, especially tractors, began to become more common. In the early 1950s, only a few crofters had a tractor, and much cultivation was still done by hand.

However as crofting was, and still remains, only a part-time occupation in most cases, agricultural advances in themselves could not sustain the population. There had to be other employment.

In the early 1950s the main sources of employment were machine-knitting and weaving tweed, the two being carried out side by side in Mossbank and in Voe; at the latter place the long-established firm of T. M. Adie & Sons employed 62 people in 1955. The firm also had a shop, a bakery and a farm, but it is noteworthy that 32 of these employees were employed in the manufacture of tweed.

At this time 90 per cent of the finished tweed was exported to the United States, but the trade soon went into decline when the U.S.A. brought in a quota system to limit the import of woollen fabrics. It never recovered. Today Adie's still produce tweed, but only three workers are employed in its manufacture.

Knitwear, too, was subject to the vagaries of the market, and the demand of the early 1950s was not maintained.

The London owners of the Mossbank tweed and hosiery business went bankrupt. Tweed production had ceased by 1955, but a little hosiery manufacture was carried on until 1960, when the company went into liquidation.

A number of Delting men had been accustomed to go every winter season to the Antarctic whaling. During the 1950s this too began to decline, was very much reduced by 1959, and ceased altogether in 1962 to 1963.

Some welcome employment was brought by the coming of the North of Scotland Hydro-Electric Board, and by public works such as the County Council water schemes. Electricity reached Voe and part of Brae in 1957, went from Brae to Muckle Roe in 1959, and was connected to Mossbank in 1960. The Brae water scheme was completed in 1955 and extended to Muckle Roe in 1958. Work was very labour-intensive at this time, before the days of heavy machinery. Bigland and Mowat, a well-known local firm, which after World War II had had six employees, employed about 30 men on the Brae water scheme. It employed a similar number in the building of a six house council housing scheme in Brae which was completed in 1957. There was always a certain amount of work on the roads, and all side roads in Delting were now being tarred, e.g., the road to Toft was tarred in 1957.

But these employment opportunities were short-lived. At the end of the 1950s and in the early 1960s work was scarce locally. 1961 was described by the *Shetland Times* as 'a black year for unemployment'. And the 1961 census revealed that the population of Delting had fallen yet again, from 863 in 1951 to a new low point of 701, a decrease of 18·7 per cent.

Electricity and water schemes arrived too late to save some of the smaller communities, which were already empty apart from one or two houses, usually the homes of elderly people unwilling to leave. This was the case in Toft, which at the end of the war had had between 20 and 30 inhabitants. The last person from Swinister, north Delting, left in 1964. Grobsness, in the south-west corner of the parish, was empty of all its original inhabitants by 1961.

In Firth, near Mossbank, all the croft houses on the east side of the Voe had old rhyming names, e.g.: 'Peerie Löt, Muckle Löt, Pund O'Löt and Holla, Whilbiegarth, Tiptigarth, Newhouse and Upper Scolla'. The rhyme continued to include another 9 croft names. Depopulation had been going on for a long time in Firth. By the 1960s, only two old ladies lived on the east side of the voe. There were only two houses and the Firth and Mossbank school on the other side.

And almost unnoticed, a small group of crofts on the outlying Calback Ness, on the shores of Sullom Voe, fell empty. The last inhabitant moved out in 1958, leaving Calback to the sheep.

The main communities, Brae, Voe and Mossbank, were losing people too, especially young people who had to move away to find work. In 1958, the County Council had to advertise to find tenants for two empty council houses in Mossbank. By 1963 the Brae primary school roll had fallen to 17, whereas in 1955 there had been 26 primary pupils from Brae. The Firth (and Mossbank) primary school roll was down to 25 in 1963 from 35 in 1956. Olna Firth Primary School in Voe, a new two-teacher building opened in 1960, was maintaining its roll in 1963 at about 30, but was obviously about to decline drastically from 1965 onwards, and was reduced to one-teacher status in 1966. Collafirth Side School, near Voe, had closed in 1955 with only two pupils, who were sent to Voe.

MID 1960s—EARLY 1970s

The problems of depopulation were common throughout rural Shetland, and 1965 saw the advent of the application of the principle of 'holding points', a scheme whereby the Zetland County Council selected certain places in Shetland as key centres for the rural population. These were to be encouraged to grow and develop industries to absorb people who were not actively involved in agriculture. The remaining rural areas would be allowed to become still more thinly populated, but it was hoped that larger, more efficient agricultural units would develop as a result. The Brae–Voe area was nominated as a 'holding point' for the north mainland. From now on, any new housing, industries or amenities would be directed towards this area, although in practice most developments took place in Brae.

In the mid 1960s, there began a phase of remarkable industrial development, side by side with the agricultural developments which had already begun. Grant assistance became available for all kinds of projects from various sources, including, from 1965 onwards, the Highlands and Islands Development Board. Local firms and individuals did not hesitate to take up the assistance offered.

Several local ventures started up about this time, some of which were to be very successful. Notable among these was the knitwear firm of Thuleknit, started in a croft house in Muckle Roe in 1965 by Peter and Chrissie Johnson. In 1968 they moved into a small factory at Brae, which they extended in 1972 to install modern machinery for washing and pressing knitwear. At their peak of production they employed 38 people on their premises, and approximately 300 knitters in their own homes. Their hosiery van, delivering yarn and collecting jumpers, ran as far as Scousburgh in the south mainland of Shetland, as well as to the West Side and to the island of Yell.

The hosiery trade had been revived in Mossbank in 1962 by Mr Peter Robertson, the local shop-keeper, who found a market in France. By 1966 he was producing 1,000 garments a week, and was employing 15 people full-time, although not all of these lived in Mossbank. He also had 70 part-time knitters and finishers. When he sold the business in 1971 it was still going well.

Fish processing was making good headway in Shetland, and in 1969 a processing factory was opened in Weathersta, Brae, by Williamson's of Scalloway. This employed about 40 people at its peak in 1972. Sullom Voe Fish Processing Ltd., a firm set up by two local men aided and advised by a big crab processing firm from England, opened a factory at Graven in 1968 for processing crabs and later scallops—the first scallops ever to be processed in Shetland.

Also at Graven, the Brae firm of Manson Bros. set up a concrete block factory in 1967. This firm was also involved in quarrying and haulage. It rebuilt the old council quarrying plant at Sullom quarry in 1971-72, and at the height of its operations ran a fleet of 10 trucks and employed 32 men in all.

The building trade began to flourish as grants for house renovations and house-building became better and more widely available, and as the new industries required premises and their workers accommodation. Bigland and Mowat, who in 1965 had only three or four employees, by 1969 were building eight council houses at Skelladale in Brae, employing 16 men to do so. By the early 1970s there was a real building boom and Bigland and Mowat found they were turning down as much work as they undertook. Smaller building concerns, too, had plenty of work to do, as did local garages, hauliers, etc.

The unemployment figures for Delting in the early 1970s were very low, e.g., the figures in the month of May were 6 in 1972, 1 in 1973, 2 in 1974.

The 1971 census showed that the population of Delting was now 674, a decrease of 27 from 1961. However, there had been a special census in 1966, when the population had stood at 654; thus in the five years from 1966, there was actually an increase of 20 people, the first known increase in 120 years.

In 1961, there were 222 households in the parish, including 22 council houses. Only 75 (33·8 per cent) had hot and cold water, bath and w.c., although many more had one or more of these amenities. In 1971 there were 210 occupied households, of which 130 (61·90 per cent) had all four amenities. As only 30 of these households were council houses, this reflects the amount of private house improvement that had been completed, and was still continuing.

The 'holding point' principle meant centralisation of facilities, including schools. In 1968, Muckle Roe Primary School closed, and its 10 pupils transferred with their teacher to Brae Primary. Sullom School in nearby Northmavine was also closed at this time, and its six pupils sent to Brae. This meant a Brae Primary School roll of 41, whereas the previous year it had stood at 20. The roll rose steadily to 67 in 1975, reflecting the increase in housing and population in the area. A further 10 council houses had been completed in Brae in 1972.

Urafirth Junior Secondary School in Northmavine closed in 1969 and sent its pupils to Brae, bringing the Brae roll to 41 (from 29 the previous year). Brae was now the only junior secondary school in the north mainland of Shetland, with pupils from Northmavine, Delting and Lunnasting. In 1970 Shetland's junior secondary schools became junior high schools, offering two years of fully comprehensive secondary education. Pupils wishing to sit a full range of O-grades would now transfer to Lerwick at the beginning of their third year rather than immediately after primary school. This was a welcome development in the eyes of many people, as it had often been felt that 11 or 12 was too early an age at which to send a child into lodgings or hostel in Lerwick, and not infrequently home-sickness led to a bright child relinquishing the chance of O-grades or highers.

The County Education Committee pressed for the closure of Firth primary school, an antiquated building. There was strong local opposition, but in 1972, when the roll had fallen to 15 and would obviously fall still further, the school did close. Ten pupils and their teachers transferred to Voe. By now the Voe school roll was increasing, from 14 in 1970 to 23 in 1972. In the period 1972 to 1975 the number of primary pupils from Mossbank fell to seven. Evidently Mossbank was still losing its young people, even with the increased prosperity in the parish.

There were other developments during this period. In 1968 the U.S. Coastguard commissioned a small Loran station at the seaward end of the old wartime aerodrome at Scatsta. There were 15 military personnel, some of whom brought their families and lived in the surrounding districts. They were a source of great interest in those days when incomers were relatively uncommon! The station is still in operation, and there have been a few marriages of American servicemen and Shetland girls.

Public spending increased, and added both to employment and amenities. A council refuse collection service began to operate throughout the parish. The mobile library had begun operations in 1964. Voe got its water scheme in 1969, and that of Mossbank followed.

Two Lerwick banks began to send out vans to the country districts. This was a boon, especially to small businesses.

Old or disabled people in the parish could now benefit from a home help scheme, run and financed by the Council's Social Work Department; and a 'meals on wheels' service began.

With electricity well-established in the parish, the 1960s saw a great increase in electrical household amenities such as washing-machines. Perhaps the item which made the most impact was the 'deep freeze' unit. Soon almost every household was to have one. In Delting, nearly everyone who was not a crofter was bound to have a relation, neighbour or friend who was. Everyone had access to a stock of meat for the winter, and 'filling the freezer' after sheep slaughter time in autumn became very much part of the yearly routine.

Television had arrived in Shetland in 1964, and although it was restricted to BBC 1 in black and white, for a time it did have the expected effect of decline on small local gatherings such as whist drives and socials.

Football became very popular, and a new football pitch was built in Brae; a children's playground was later added beside it.

During the 1960s and early 1970s, social life for the young centred around the dances which were held almost every Friday and Saturday night in one district or another. By the mid 1960s, car ownership had increased greatly, and spread to the under-20's, so that most young people now arrived at dances in groups in each other's cars. In the 1950s, motor cycles had been more common, and groups of young people would hire transport.

The main social events of the year were the Regatta dances which were held during the summer, commencing with the Brae Regatta at the beginning of July, and followed by regattas in other parishes. These dances were well patronised by people of all ages, but young people would drive many miles to attend. They were usually so crowded that dancing was very restricted, but they were certainly good places to meet people!

THE OIL BOOM PERIOD:—MID 1970S—END 1982

Delting in the early 1970s was a busy and thriving place, when there came rumours of a new and disturbingly massive development, the coming of the oil industry.

Oil from the North Sea was to be piped ashore in Shetland and it was soon being said that an oil terminal was to be built in the Delting area. Some said this terminal was to be at Sullom Voe, the site of the wartime R.A.F. base. But no, others argued, surely Yell Sound was no place for tankers. Swarbacks Minn, on the south-west side of the parish, was much more suitable. Jetties would be built along the shores of Muckle Roe, and the island of Linga was to be flattened.

The people of Delting waited to hear the fate of their parish with mixed feelings. Obviously great changes were imminent. It was rumoured that an oil refinery might also be built. What sort of place would Delting become in the years ahead?

PLANS

In 1973 the Zetland County Council's plans for Delting were laid before the public. The Council had commissioned a report on the parish by the firm of Livesey and Henderson, consulting engineers, and the recommendations of this report were published in a series of pamphlets, copies of which were soon in every home in Delting.

Sullom Voe, and Calback Ness in particular, had indeed been selected as the oil terminal site. There was to be no oil refinery, at least for the time being, although the report allowed for the possibility of this at some future date, as well as for some other eventualities such as a gas liquefaction plant. It was made clear that oil development would fall into two stages, those of construction and actual operation. These stages would overlap, but the construction period would require a large number of temporary workers, who would mostly be incomers to be housed in a construction camp. Operations staff, also mostly incomers, would be permanently employed and would bring their families with them. This would mean a great increase in housing in the parish.

The report suggested that, depending on the amount of oil development which eventually took place, 1,000 new houses might be needed in the parish, 550 of these in the first five years of development. The suggestion was that these should be distributed among Voe, Brae, Mossbank and Toft, and areas of each district were mapped out as suitable for housing and provision of amenities. The number of occupied houses in Delting in 1971 was actually 210.

OIL DEVELOPMENTS

Development began soon afterwards. Pipe-lines from the Brent and Ninian oil-fields were brought ashore at the head of Firths Voe and continued overland to Calback Ness. A construction camp was built on the top of Firth Hill. It was originally intended to house 600 men, then extended to hold 1,200. Construction of the terminal itself began in February 1975. Little Orka Voe, at the back of Calback Ness, was gradually filled in with peat, deep layers of which were removed during preparation of the site. The first oil came ashore in 1976.

The terminal covers 800 acres and is designed for a throughput of 1·41 million barrels of oil per day. (The first billion barrels had been shipped out by the end of 1978.) It was soon obvious that many more construction workers would be needed, and work began in January 1977 on a second, even larger construction camp in Toft, which eventually housed 2,500. Still this could not cope with the numbers, and two accommodation ships, the *Rangatira* and the *Stena Baltica*, were moored near to the construction site. At the peak of construction in 1980 there were over 6,000 employees on site.

At nearby Sellaness a harbour was constructed for tug-boats and pilot boats, and headquarters were built for the Ports and Harbour Department, Pollution Control, etc.

The old wartime aerodrome at Scatsta was partly re-surfaced and opened in 1978 as Scatsta Airport, where plane loads of workers flew in and out daily. Previously they had to make long coach trips to and from Sumburgh. In 1980, Scatsta had 6,278 fixed wing aircraft movements and 128 helicopter movements.

Parallel to the activity on and around the terminal site, much had to be done in the rest of the parish. Roads, in some places almost literally collapsing under the weight of heavy construction traffic, were renewed, widened and straightened, as was the road to Lerwick. House building was going ahead at a steady rate. Many of the houses, especially those built in Firth and Mossbank, though eventually planned for permanent staff and families, had to be used immediately by groups of workers. Also, some construction staff were entitled to bring their families with them, and houses were usually occupied as soon as they were ready.

The Shetland Islands Council had a scheme of 100 council houses ready in Brae in 1976-77. The scheme was built to a new design, the houses being rather squat and short in appearance, and distributed around the site in little groups. It became known throughout the parish as 'Toytown'! The name persists, despite the late decision by its tenants to re-name it 'Moorfield'.

One hundred council houses were completed in Firth by 1977-78, a further 51 in Mossbank by 1977, and 18 in Voe by 1977. In practice, no housing developments took place in Toft as Livesey and Henderson had suggested. Firth was developed instead, the new houses being built below the construction camp, facing the line of old empty crofts on the other side of Firths Voe.

In addition to the council schemes, a number of private housing schemes were built for, or purchased by, British Petroleum and associated companies. Notable among these were two schemes, including 80 houses in all at Firth. B.P. also bought up a number of vacant local houses as and when they came on the market, and several more were rented by oil or construction companies for their staff.

There was also, of course, an increase in house building by private individuals. By 1982, a total of 746 houses were on the valuation roll in

Delting, compared with 210 in the 1971 census. At an average of three persons per household (the average in both the 1971 and the 1961 census), this gives an estimated population in 1982 of over 2,200, and does not include people living in caravans or in the camps.

A big new primary school was built in Brae in anticipation of the population explosion. It opened in 1976, when the school roll had already started to rise. During the following years the roll rose dramatically with the influx of workers: August 1976, 83 pupils; August 1977, 114 pupils; August 1978, 174 pupils; August 1979, 249 pupils.

These years were very difficult for both staff and pupils, as more and more children at all stages of education and from all parts of the country arrived almost from week to week. The situation was eased when in January 1980 the new Mossbank Primary School was opened and 114 Mossbank pupils could now attend their own school. Fourteen Mossbank pupils had been attending Olna Firth Primary School in Voe, and they too were recalled to Mossbank.

In August 1982 the rolls of the primary schools in Brae and Voe had steadied at 169 and 46 respectively, although they still fluctuate a little. The roll of Mossbank Primary School fluctuates more at present. It was 115 in August 1982, and expected to increase in 1983, having been as high as 145 in the 1981-1982 session. However, the school has still not reached the capacity it was built for.

EFFECTS ON LOCAL INDUSTRIES

The oil boom provided for the first time a chance for local people to earn really high wages. Although sometimes this involved long tedious working hours, or a seven-day week (or both) the offer of big money was very tempting. Very often far more could be earned in unskilled work at the camps or the terminal site than in many a highly-qualified post. A local man with an honours degree in electronic engineering left his London post, which was the designing of radar circuits, to 'fit light bulbs in Firth' for double the wages.

In face of the oil industry, what became of the local firms which had been so vital to the parish in previous years? Their fate depended to a large extent on how well they could serve the needs of the boom period. Wages of course had to rise, where this was possible, to compete at all with those on offer in the oil industry or oil-related construction.

Excavating firms did well, expanding greatly both in staff and equipment. Quarrying, haulage and block-making promised to be profitable, and the successful firm of Manson Brothers, together with most of its employees, was taken over by a large firm from the south in 1974.

Although large building projects were contracted to big mainland firms, local builders were busier than ever, sub-contracting and building private houses. Bigland and Mowat, who had been building houses by the timber-frame method since 1972, built a factory at Weathersta in 1975 to produce timber-framed 'kit' houses, anticipating the housing demand which soon materialised. They also built 24 private houses in Brae and nine in Voe which they sold to oil or construction companies. They were very busy from 1975 to 1980, employing up to 30 men.

Fish processing and knitwear could not compete with oil industry wages, and went into decline. The fish factories at Weathersta and Graven closed, leasing their cold stores to firms supplying food to the construction camps. Thuleknit knitwear carried on on a reduced scale right up to 1981.

An added difficulty for the knitwear industry was that most of its former home knitters were women who, for the first time, now had the chance to go out and work in the camps or the site canteens, and found this much more attractive than working at home on a knitting machine in isolation. Women of all ages took jobs at Sullom Voe; some were quite elderly and had not worked outside the home since before they were married. It was an experience which most of them enjoyed very much, but they did not forsake their knitting. Anyone who could knit had ample opportunity to sell knitwear among the construction workers, who were willing customers.

Other sections of the community also profited. People who had formerly kept tourists in summer found, especially in the early days of the oil boom, that they could keep oil workers all the year round and be paid very handsomely. A similar situation existed where anyone owned an empty house or a caravan which could be rented out.

Taxi drivers and car hirers had more trade than they could cope with.

A public house was opened in Brae in 1974, another in Voe in 1977, and a third in Mossbank in 1978 (significantly, in the premises formerly used as a knitwear factory). These were all run by local people. There was also a bar in the Sullom Voe Hotel in Graven, and all four establishments were well patronised during the boom.

The construction workers

The construction workers who arrived first stood the best chance of getting to know the local people, particularly if they did not have to live in a camp but in a community. It was generally felt by the locals that the Irish workers mixed best with the Delting folk. One particular group of Irishmen were among the first to come and the last to leave. They stayed for eight years in all, attending local functions and making many friends, and were reluctant to go.

Many construction workers saw little of Delting or the rest of Shetland; they saw only the work site and the camp, during their five-week stints of work, with perhaps an occasional outing to a local public house or Lerwick dance hall, or a fishing expedition on a summer evening.

Local people worried about trouble in bars and at dances. Open dances ceased for a time in the parish, and dances became 'ticket only' affairs. In fact, although there were always incidents from time to time, there was little trouble, considering the number of construction workers and the amount of money circulating and the drink consumed. There were huge sports halls and entertainment centres in the camps themselves, where top artistes from the south often appeared, and no encouragement was given to workers to leave the camps at all outside working hours. If they wished to do so, they had to make their own arrangements. Anyone causing trouble immediately lost his accommodation, which meant, in practice, his job as well.

There was a police presence in Delting from 1977 onwards, when two policemen occupied houses in Brae. Brae Police Station was opened in 1979, and a sergeant and two constables are based there. Three constables are based at Firth. Security duty at the terminal is carried out for B.P. by the firm of Securicor. Local police feel, as does the parish, that crimes and offences increased and decreased with the numbers of construction workers, but that even during the worst period there was not much really serious crime.

ILL-EFFECTS OF THE OIL BOOM

The oil boom, however, has not been without its ill-effects. The increased amount of money and material possessions did not always bring happiness. Work for women, shift work, the seven-day week, and the high-spending habits of unattached workmates, could all cause a certain amount of strain in family life. Most families thus affected adjusted well; some did not. Several marriages broke up during this period. This caused general regret in the local community, where marital separation and divorce had never been common, although they were not unknown.

Delting has not for many years been a 'dry 'area, but drink was now more widely available, and people had far more money to spend. It is not surprising that some people feel that alcohol abuse is much worse than it used to be. Certainly drinking has caused a lot of heartbreak in some families. Other people point out that drink was never hard to obtain in Delting, and that drink was a problem for some long before the oil boom.

House building costs soared during the boom period. It became difficult to find anyone to do repairs and minor building work.

The parish roads, although wider and straighter, were much faster than before and carried a vastly increased volume of often heavy traffic. Scores of hill sheep were killed on the roads. People living near main roads began to fear for the safety of their children. There were two fatal car accidents in the parish within two weeks in 1978, and there have been other fatalities.

THE END OF THE BOOM

The Queen came to inaugurate the oil terminal on 9th May 1981, and now at the end of 1982, the boom is definitely over. Construction has at last finished. The terminal is producing 1·1 million barrels per day. Toft Camp lies empty and forlorn, its fate still undecided. Firth Camp, too, is empty. It is to be maintained in some as yet unspecified form. The *Stena Baltica* left long since; the *Rangatira* followed her, and is at present in the Falkland Islands.

There is no more digging, no more bulldozing, no more beds to make, comparatively few canteens. Hardly any new houses are being built. Building firms, greatly reduced in size, are mostly engaged in repairs and maintenance, or agricultural building. The parish is settling down to live with the fully operational oil terminal.

THE AFTERMATH OF THE OIL BOOM

The end of the construction boom brings the expected results. Unemployment figures are up (44 in October 1982, 66 in January 1983) but, says the Lerwick Job Centre, these include a number of people temporarily resident in the parish, who may move on. People worry about the young who still have to find work, and those who have become used to high wages which have now finished. And surely never again will there be so much work for women.

But, so far, Delting appears not to be so badly affected as many people feared. A good proportion of Delting people never were involved with oil construction in the first place. Also, many local people now have permanent posts at the oil terminal, as of course do the great majority of incomers.

Living with permanent oil developments is also having varying effects upon the parish.

At the back of many people's minds there is now an underlying fear of oil pollution. These fears were realised at the New Year in 1979, when a sizeable spill of bunker oil from the tanker *Esso Bernicia* polluted Sullom Voe, off-shore islands, and both sides of Yell Sound. Since this early disaster, the oil industry has made great efforts to improve its pollution control. It is the fervent hope of everyone in Delting that a major oil spill will never occur. Its effects, particularly when distributed by the fast-flowing currents in Yell Sound, would be devastating.

With the influx of so many new-comers from south, the loss of the old sense of community was widely feared among local folk, and this has inevitably happened in varying degrees. It must be said however that among the incomers there are many people willing to give of their time and talents to serve the community, and some who are more interested in their surroundings than many locals are. Some have integrated very well. But although there has been little friction, there are several factors which hamper integration, not the least of these being the Shetland dialect. Some city people find it difficult to settle in Delting. Oil operations staff are often transferred from Shetland within three to five years, just after they have become established in the community. The biggest drawback has been the sheer size and speed of the influx of population. People mix well where there is a shared project or point of interest, e.g., clubs, playgroups, or the 'Up-Helly-Aa' festivals in Mossbank and Brae. But there remains, at least among the adults, a certain amount of recognised distinction between 'locals' and 'incomers', albeit with goodwill on both sides. The children, of course, mix happily as a rule.

Local children surrounded by mainland accents are tending to lose the dialect, ironically, at a time when, after more than a century of repression, the dialect is at last receiving encouragement in Shetland schools.

There is a small troublesome element among the teenagers, but this is not entirely a new thing, and seems almost inevitable in a period of such social change, with people from all parts of the country being brought together.

There is an obvious element of class distinction among some of the incomers, a new and unwelcome feature in Delting.

However, the parish enjoys many new facilities as a direct result of the influx of population, e.g., new schools, better roads, sewage disposal schemes, and T.V. booster stations. There are buses to Lerwick every day the shops are open, and an increase in leisure activities and entertainment.

LIFE IN DELTING, 1982

MOSSBANK AND FIRTH

The community of Mossbank and Firth is the part of Delting which has changed most drastically. There were 292 houses on the 1982 Valuation Roll in Mossbank and Firth; 255 of these belong to housing schemes completed from 1977 onwards. When Mossbank Primary School opened, only seven of its 131 pupils were natives of Mossbank, and fewer than 10 per cent of its present pupils were born in Shetland.

This area does have the facilities of Firth Camp nearby for sports, etc. and there is a public house but otherwise it is comparatively poorly provided for. There is just one shop, a post office and a petrol station. Moves are being made to set up a community co-operative shop in Firth.

The Shetland Islands Council intends to turn the old primary school at Firth into a community centre, but this has not even begun as yet.

It is very commendable that Mossbank has just been able to open a new public hall, on a par with anything in Shetland. It cost £150,000 and although most of this was paid by grant assistance, a good sum of money was raised locally. The hall is certain to be in constant use, as several clubs and organisations have formed in the district. Notable among these is the drama group, which has an active junior section.

Graven and Scatsta

The oil terminal is, in many ways, a world of its own. It is far enough from the main road as to be amazingly unobtrusive. Far more of it is visible from Northmavine parish on the other side of Sullom Voe.

The new terminal road has bypassed the quiet village of Graven (nine houses) which remains much as it was, still surrounded by ruins of wartime buildings. The Sullom Voe Hotel, in Graven, a 14-bed establishment which was once an R.A.F. officers' mess, has recently applied to build a large extension.

The harbour at Sella Ness is neat and trim. The activities of tankers, tugboats and pilot boats in the voe are of interest to local people. Nearby Scatsta Airport, landscaped and cleanly laid out, is a pleasure to behold, especially when one remembers how rutted and desolate the old airstrip had become. In January 1981, 41 people were employed here. Scatsta's future, now that the construction period has ended, is somewhat in doubt, but everyone would be sorry to see it close.

The whole Scatsta and Graven area is dominated by the huge terminal flarestack which burns night and day. Its light can be seen for many miles as a glow in the night sky.

Brae

Brae has grown and changed a great deal. On the 1982 valuation roll there were 244 houses in Brae (not including Weathersta). 166 of these houses belong to housing schemes, council and private, built since 1976. A good number of private houses have also been built recently. There seems to be a good balance of local people and incomers. Quite a few people have moved to Brae from other parts of Shetland. In November 1982, 49 per cent of pupils in Brae primary School were Shetland-born.

Brae has a post office and two shops, including a small newly opened supermarket with an adjoining cafe. It has two garages, a building supplies shop, a hairdresser's and a bank which opens three days a week. And in part of the old Thuleknit premises, a young Brae couple have started up a knitwear business again.

Adjoining the public house is the Brae Hotel, opened in 1979, which has 25 bedrooms plus 20 rooms in annexe accommodation and four suites of rooms. Across the voe, Busta House, in previous centuries the home of the Giffords, lairds of the district, and latterly the home of Sir Basil Neven-Spence, Lord Lieutenant of Shetland, has been tastefully converted into an 11-bedroom hotel.

Beside the Brae Police Station is the fire station, also opened in 1979. It has 14 retained (i.e., part-time) firemen and two water tenders. Close by is the health centre, where the two local doctors have their surgeries. Formerly, the Delting doctor's surgery was at Voe. The health centre, which opened in 1981, also houses a dentist, a physiotherapist and a health visitor, and is the headquarters for the north mainland district nurses and the local social worker.

As in Mossbank, the increased population has led to a great increase in clubs and organised activities. The primary school has an excellent hall which is frequently in use. Brae always had a sailing club, and there proved to be keen sailors at Sullom Voe, who for a time had a club of their own. Now the two are amalgamated and have built a clubhouse. This has become a popular social centre, where local musicians often provide entertainment.

Brae suffers from the lack of an adequate hall, as the present one is much too small. Plans are ready for the building of a new hall, but work has been held up because of delay in government assistance. It is hoped to start work in 1983.

The new Brae Primary School was ready before it was needed, but the new junior high school was not ready until October 1981, by which time the roll had risen to 166, from 66 in 1975. The secondary department struggled on with ever-increasing numbers in an assortment of old buildings and huts, the pupils having to either walk or go by bus nearly half a mile each way for physical education and canteen dinners at the primary department. The new secondary school, however, was worth waiting for. It is roomy, attractive, and provided with the latest and best of modern equipment. Staff and pupils are justly proud of it.

In November 1982, the proportion of Shetland-born children in the secondary department was 36 per cent. Teachers report that the children have integrated very well.

In August 1982, Brae Junior High School began to provide a full range of four-year O-grade courses. Local parents were greatly in favour of this. Any pupils wishing to take examinations at higher grade will transfer to Lerwick after their O-grades.

It was regretted by many in the growing communities of Delting that a swimming-pool had not been included in the new Brae school. A North Mainland Swimming Pool Association has been formed with the aim of providing a pool in the near future.

MUCKLE ROE

The island of Muckle Roe is the least changed of Delting's communities. It has held its population at about the same level, as the following statistics show:

1951	1961	1971	1982
110	103	94	100

There are several new houses, but very few incomers. There are 12 children of primary school age, similar to the numbers 30 years ago. Muckle Roe remains a close-knit, croft based community, and seems to

Plate 1. CLIFF SCENERY, Sandness

Marine erosion has regularly eroded the parts of the coast open to the sea into impressive cliffs.

(J. D. Ratter. Courtesy Shetland Museum and Library)

Plate 2

SANDSPIT OR TOMBOLO, Dunrossness

This sandspit links St. Ninian's Isle to the Shetland Mainland. Such features have been constructed by wave action in certain places in sheltered water. In the foreground are the ruins of the Medieval Church dedicated to St. Ninian.

(Courtesy Shetland Museum and Library)

exist quite happily while using Brae for shopping, entertainment, etc. The small Muckle Roe hall is not much used at present as it needs improving.

VOE

Voe is widely regarded as one of the most picturesque villages in Shetland. It had a total of 108 houses (excluding Dale and Gonfirth) on the valuation roll in 1982. It has not been extended as was first envisaged at the start of the oil boom, as only 44 houses in council and private schemes have been occupied since 1977. In addition, ten small council houses are now about to be occupied. There has also been some individual private building, although it is often difficult to obtain planning permission to build a house in Voe. The most attractive part of the village is a conservation area, and no building is allowed between the Tagon road and the foreshore.

Voe grew up round the firm of T. M. Adie & Sons, which has been in business since 1830. The firm still carries on, although both tweed and knitwear now operate on a very small scale, e.g., in 1981 there were ten employees, including shop workers. The Voe post office is at Adie's shop. The bakery, now known as Johnson & Wood, was taken over by the bakers themselves in 1964. It is a very busy place, full of modern equipment, supplying bread throughout Shetland, and always experimenting with new products, e.g., their pizzas are currently much in demand.

Voe House, an Adie family home for many years, was sold in 1966 to an English couple who ran it very successfully as a small first-class hotel with a reputation for good food. It passed into the hands of B.P. when the oil boom began, and now houses the oil terminal manager.

There is another general merchant's shop in Voe, at Tagon. Nearby is the public house, and the only remaining dairy farm in the parish, where John Jamieson has a herd of 13 cattle, with eight milking cows producing about 20 gallons of milk per day. This does not even supply the whole of Voe, but it is still a real asset to the community.

A children's play area has recently been built behind the school. The Voe Hall is sizeable, and was extended in 1975 to provide extra kitchen and clubroom space. There are not so many clubs or activities in Voe as in Brae or Mossbank, but there is a thriving playgroup, adult and junior badminton, a group of cubs and a branch of the S.W.R.I.

Voe has retained much of its old sense of community, and recent years have seen the revival of two traditional features of life in Voe. The concert party was revived in 1978, after a lapse of almost twenty years, putting on shows of dialect songs and sketches upon contemporary local themes. And in 1980, a movement began to revive the Voe Agricultural Show, last held in the 1930s. It was a big undertaking and many people were sceptical of its success. However, a success it certainly was, both in 1981 and 1982, and the Voe Show now seems established as one of the highlights of the summer. Much credit is due to the show committee, who are drawn from all over the north mainland of Shetland.

There are new houses all through the parish outwith the main communities: in Gonfirth, Dale, Voxter, Weathersta and along the shores of Olna Firth. There are even new houses in Toft, the inhabitants all being incomers. In Grobsness, an incoming family renovated a house in 1979 and have become very much part of the community in Gonfirth and Voe.

Voe, Brae and Mossbank each have, included in their new housing schemes, a small group of sheltered houses for the elderly.

CROFTING

Generally speaking, native Delting people have become much less involved with the land than was previously the case. This change began before the oil boom days, with the coming of steady full employment. Full employment means less time for croft work. The tendency has therefore been less and less towards time-consuming cultivation and cattle rearing and more towards sheep husbandry. Full employment also means that it becomes possible to live well without a croft at all. Crofts which fell empty, instead of being taken up by young people looking for land, were usually bought up by the larger-scale crofters and farmers. As they often lived quite a distance away, sheep-rearing was again the most practical purpose for the croft.

In 1950, 25,570 sheep had been kept in Delting, most of these being Shetland sheep. By 1958, with continuing depopulation, and before much agricultural development took place, the figure was 19,369. In 1973, it had risen again, to 26,903. Even sheep numbers, however, fell back a little during the oil boom. In 1980, they numbered 24,578. Crofters, of course, are rather fewer, and the trend is now to keep much larger sheep breeds, although there are still Shetland sheep on the scattald (hill grazing). Usually Cheviot-Shetland cross ewes are kept on inbye ground, and there has been a big trend to the use of Suffolk rams.

In 30 years, the number of cattle in the parish has not dropped very far, but the number of crofters who keep cattle has decreased markedly. In 1950, when many crofts still possessed a cow or two, there were 333 cattle in Delting. In 1982, the Cattle Compensation Society had 215 Delting animals on its books, all owned by only 12 people. There are probably no more than 250 cattle, and 15 owners, in the whole parish. The oil boom has probably had an impact on cattle numbers too, as immediately before the boom in 1973, they stood at 360.

Hay, straw and turnips as animal fodder have largely given way to silage, which is more quickly harvested and less affected by weather. There has been a tremendous increase in imported animal feed stuffs, which people can now better afford. The average crofter still grows potatoes and a few vegetables for home consumption, and may keep a few hens. Pigs are very rare.

Grant assistance, hill land reclamation and the availability of additional empty crofts have, since the early 1960s, enabled the interested crofter to expand and develop his holdings. Perhaps the end of the oil boom will mean more people wanting to return to the land, or to make better use of the land they have. Certainly there will be more assistance than ever available through the Shetland Ten-Year Plan for Agriculture, which uses oil reserve fund money. Already in Voe, two crofters have undertaken the very latest scheme in scattald reclamation, bulldozing the rough hill land flat for re-seeding.

PEAT CUTTING

In the first spate of house-building in the 1960s the first houses without chimneys appeared in Delting. Oil-fired central heating was at first the fashion, followed (when oil prices soared) by various kinds of electric heating. Whole schemes of houses have been built without chimneys, although now it is noticeable that this pattern is changing. Many people however, chose to continue with the traditional fuel, peat, cut and worked by hand. Despite the not inconsiderable work involved, peat-burning is much cheaper than any other form of heating, as all it costs is a family's own time and perhaps the hire of a lorry to bring the peats home. The very latest thing, in fact, featured in several of the newest houses, is a peat-fired cooker which can successfully cook, provide hot water and heat the whole house as well—a most economical arrangement.

RELIGION

The Church of Scotland parish minister lives in the Brae manse. His work is much more demanding than it used to be, as in the 1950s he had a missionary assistant at Firth. Now, he not only has the whole parish of Delting in his charge, but (since 1977) also the neighbouring parish of Nesting and Lunnasting. The present minister, the Rev. Mr Sim, is a young man who can cope with this, but it is a widespread area with six different churches. At present, there are weekly church services in Brae, Voe and Mossbank, and a fortnightly one in Muckle Roe.

Church attendance among the local people is, in general, poorer than it was thirty years ago. However, the number of Church of Scotland members is currently showing an increase, although not a great number of young people are joining. Sunday Schools flourish in Brae, Voe and Mossbank, and there is a branch of the Women's Guild for Brae and Muckle Roe. A Scripture Union branch has recently been set up in Brae Junior High School.

With the influx of people from the south, several other religious denominations have gained ground lately. There is no form of religious discrimination in Delting. There is a Methodist service in the Brae Church of Scotland once a month, and a Baptist meeting every Sunday in Brae Junior High School. A small group of Roman Catholics meet fortnightly in Voe Hall. A new Gospel Hall was recently built in Brae for a flourishing branch of the Plymouth Brethern, who also have an active Sunday School.

Sunday observance has noticeably decreased in the last 30 years. It is perhaps debatable, however, whether this practice was really religious in nature or more a matter of tradition and habit.

SOCIAL LIFE

Delting people still visit each other, though not as much as they used to when little other entertainment was available. Family ties are still important. One happy result of increased prosperity is that several local people have been able to visit family members as far away as Australia and New Zealand.

At home, most people have colour television, and video recorders are rapidly gaining ground. As in the rest of Shetland, country and western music is very popular among the 'native' Delting folk. The guitar has replaced the fiddle as the most commonly played instrument, but a good fiddler is highly prized—and very frequently invited out! Scottish, Irish and Shetland dance music is still very popular, and quite a few incomers share the local enthusiasm for a good dance tune. This interest is not confined to the older generation, e.g., at the moment there is a waiting list of Voe children wishing to learn to play the fiddle.

A local wedding is still likely to be one of the biggest social events of the year. As many people are invited as the hall can comfortably hold, e.g., 350 to 400 in the Voe Hall. Pride is taken in offering plenty of food and drink, and dancing continues until 2 to 3 a.m. Thirty years ago, it was common practice for a wedding to last until 5 to 6 a.m. and to be followed by a second night of dancing. Second nights are still held occasionally. However long it lasts, a good lively wedding is a most enjoyable occasion.

Christmas and New Year are both important social events, when a good deal of house-to-house visiting goes on. Nowadays, New Year seems to be more heartily celebrated. Many people agree, however, that both are quieter occasions than used to be the case, with fewer people on the move. This is attributed to various causes, such as the number of other minor celebrations throughout the year, the advent of the breathalyser, and, in recent years, the pattern of shift work at Sullom Voe.

Young people were quick to follow the national fashion for discos, a trend which baffles their parents. One local father, returning from a brief look at a disco in Brae, described it as 'just like a night of thunder and lightning'! Discos have tended to replace the weekend dances of the

1960s and the early 1970s, but many young people enjoy the old-fashioned kind of dance too.

The most popular dance bands have to be booked months in advance. There are no dance bands currently based in Delting, but the Muckle Roe Band, popular for many years in the parish, will still play on special occasions such as the old folks' Christmas party, when people will nod their heads and remark that there are few that can beat them yet.

Although not many Delting men earn a living from the sea, many have small boats and enjoy fishing, usually for piltocks (saithe), mackerel and inshore white fish. Many incomers share this interest. The modern boat is as likely to be of fibre-glass as of wood, and will probably have a powerful engine. This is almost essential nowadays, not (as the older men sometimes assert) because people are lazier, but because fish are often very scarce now in the voes themselves and must be sought in deeper water. This is largely attributed to the ever more intensive fishing methods employed by modern fishing boats. Complaints are also made about the appetites of the black seal population, which has increased ever since the black seal became protected in 1971. However, it is still possible to spend a pleasant and productive night at the fishing, and one's neighbours are still glad of some really fresh fish.

When there is a glut, people still salt and dry fish for winter. In olden days, this was a lifeline; now, 'it makes a change'.

CONCLUSION

Life in Delting has been many things lately, but it has certainly not been dull. A great deal has been written and said about the parish over the past seven or eight years. The place has been studied by surveyors, engineers, conservationists, sociologists, newspaper and television reporters, all ranks and kinds of officialdom, and curious visitors from all parts of the globe who wished to see 'the effects of oil development'. The parish has been on show to the whole world. It will be quite glad to settle down now. It has, perhaps, survived better than it thought it might, and faces the future with cheerfulness, and a normal mixture of hopes and fears.

February 1983

THE PARISH OF DUNROSSNESS

Original description by Robert W. Tait, F.E.I.S., 1952
New version by James W. Irvine, M.A., 1983

PHYSICAL BASIS

The parish of Dunrossness is essentially the peninsula at the south end of the Shetland Mainland, and its name derives from the Old Norse 'dyn rost' which refers to the strong tide race off its southern end. It is 16 miles long and from 2 to 5 miles in breadth. Included in the parish are the off-shore islands of Mousa, Colsay and St Ninian's Isle, although the latter is in fact connected to the mainland by a sandspit which is passable at all stages of the tide. None of these islands have been inhabited for many years. Also included in Dunrossness is Fair Isle, midway between Orkney and Shetland, which is separately described.

Prominent in the parish is a hilly main spine, which runs southwards from the north margin of the parish for 10 miles to end in the Ward of Scousburgh. The bedrock of this ridge consists of Dalradian gneiss, and its hill tops range from 500 to over 900 feet O.D. The great part of the ridge is covered by blanket peat, and only occasionally are rock outcrops to be seen. This main spine is flanked, especially on the east and south, by considerable areas of low ground, mainly on Old Red Sandstone bedrock: these areas constitute some of the best farming and crofting land in Shetland. The hill mass of Fitful Head in the south-west is also a Dalradian gneiss, and is separated from the main hill ridge by the depression in which lies the Lochs of Spiggie and Brow.

As in much of Shetland, the coast is scenically impressive and consists mainly of cliffs, which tend to be higher and steeper where they front the open sea; in the case of Fitful Head, they reach a height of over 900 feet. On the coast are a number of prominent headlands, especially in the Sandwick and Cunningsburgh areas to the east, and at the extreme south end where Sumburgh Head has an important lighthouse.

The bays generally have shingle or sand beaches. As well as the half-mile long sandspit linking St Ninian's Isle to the mainland, a broad sandbar of comparable length closes off the north end of the Loch of Spiggie. Quendale Bay in the south is a mile wide, and landward from it is a considerable sand spread. Historically this encroached on arable land over a period of centuries, and covered a former church at Quendale, but it is now fairly well covered by vegetation and is stable.

HISTORY

Dunrossness is a veritable treasure-house for archaeologists. A wealth of sites in the area have provided—and have doubtless still to provide—a great store of knowledge about the life, the skills, the economy and the beliefs of the settlers of the prehistoric period and later. But pride of place in this respect must surely go to an event which occurred in 1977. In that year workers from a firm of contractors were engaged on work at Sumburgh Airport when they chanced to excavate some human bones. Closer examination showed the site to be a multiple burial of disarticulated human bones in a rough cist. Altogether the bones represented at least 18 individuals, and radio-carbon tests revealed that they dated from about 3200 B.C. It was an unprecedented discovery for Shetland, and was the first definite evidence of such early occupation of the islands.

JARLSHOF

Jarlshof, near Sumburgh Head, is probably the most famous archaeological site in Shetland, and is certainly one of the most remarkable archaeological sites ever excavated in Britain. For here the excavations show clearly that the site was in continuous occupation from the Stone Age, and through the Bronze and Iron Ages, to the Viking period and medieval times; and later there was here the building referred to by Walter Scott in his novel *The Pirate*. The Department of the Environment now controls and maintains the site, and a guide is in attendance.

MOUSA BROCH

On the island of Mousa stands the Broch of Mousa, which is reputed to be the most perfect extant example of this type of fortification. The walls of the broch still rise to over 43 feet in height, and at the base they are 15 feet thick. The diameter of the broch at its base is 50 feet, narrowing to about 40 feet at the top. This broch was probably occupied for centuries. There is record of a Norwegian eloping couple living there for a time about A.D. 900, and there is further historical record of young Erland Ongi carrying off Margaret, Countess of Athlone, in 1153 and, with the countess, ensconcing himself in the broch, where he was later besieged by an avenging Harald, Earl of Orkney.

Two other broch sites have been excavated at Levenwick and Clumlie, but there are many others in the area. For instance, opposite the Broch of Mousa, on the mainland, stands the Broch of Burraland, much broken down and dilapidated, but situated in a position of great natural strength. Without giving an exhaustive list, others can be found at Gord, Mail, Aithsetter in Cunningsburgh, Clumlie, Dalsetter, Clevigarth, Brough Head, Lunabister and the Loch of Brow.

At the Ness of Burgi, Scatness, are the remains of a fortified place.

This site, it is thought, exemplifies a stage in the development of the brochs, as there is a degree of sophistication in its structure which seems to bear a strong resemblance to features of broch design.

ST NINIAN'S ISLE

This isle is joined to the mainland at Bigton by a sandy 'ayre', or beach but was probably once really an island, because a seventeenth century cartographer shows a ship at anchor in the area now covered by the sand. Excavation which has been done on the island shows occupation going back to at least the Bronze Age. But the most important discovery so far made on the island was during excavations on the site of what was assumed to be a Celtic church. There, below the earth floor, under a thin slab on which was lightly scratched a cross, a great silver treasure was found which included brooches, seven bowls (including one hanging bowl), two implements for giving the sacrament in a way still practised in the Greek Orthodox Church, and other objects of unknown use.

POPULATION, HOUSING AND EMPLOYMENT

In 1861 the population of Dunrossness reached a peak of 4,447. At that time crofting and fishing provided a hard-won and precarious living for the people, and the large families of the time lived in primitive conditions in little thatched-roof cottages.

But over the years the population gradually declined until by 1931 the total had dropped to 2,596, and it continued to drop for the next forty years. In the early 1970s oil came to Shetland and the trend was reversed. This can be best illustrated by tabulating the population figures for the period:

	Dunrossness	Fair Isle
1861	4,447	380
1931	2,596	108
1951	2,397	73
1961	2,030	64
1971	1,968	65
1974*	2,289	79
1976*	2,506	76
1978*	2,856	79
1979*	2,972	76
1980*	3,157	72
1981	2,896	59
1982*	2,746	72

* Years marked with an asterisk are estimates. The others are census totals.

From the figures it can be seen that the modern peak was probably reached in 1980, when the total was 60 per cent up on 1971. Since that date the decrease has been in the region of 13 per cent.

In the recent past, employment opportunities in this parish have changed almost beyond recognition, and while this has affected all aspects of life, the community has adapted with substantial success.

Formerly crofting and fishing were the main occupations here as elsewhere in Shetland. Dunrossness has some of the best land in the islands and has always been one of the most productive areas, although it still has a considerable number of townships with their houses in groups, and some land in run-rig. There has been considerable hill reclamation and the Quendale crofters from the 1950s were pioneers in this respect. In fishing, as well as the older open-boat line fishing for white fish, the parish had in the 19th century some of the main herring stations in Shetland; but in the 20th century activity in this fishery became very much centred on Lerwick. During the 20th century employment opportunities have also widened somewhat with work in various service occupations.

When the oil industry came to Shetland in the early 1970s it had a tremendous effect on Shetland as a whole, but on some areas more than others. Dunrossness was one area where the effects were dramatic. The islands' main airport is situated at Sumburgh, and it very quickly became an important staging-post for the crews of rigs and platforms in the East Shetland Basin. Fixed-wing aircraft brought the crews to Sumburgh where they transferred to helicopters for the last lap of their journey. Many millions of pounds were spent at Sumburgh Airport on improving runways, building a large new terminal complex, and modernising landing aids. The result was that the airport quickly became by far the largest source of employment in the Dunrossness area. In 1972, 70,000 passengers passed through the airport; and in 1978, the top year, the total was 685,000—nine times the 1972 total, and that increase achieved in only six years. In 1980, 748 people were shown as employed in and around the airport.

To cope with the dramatic rise in population many new houses were built by a number of agencies, including Shetland Islands Council, the Civil Aviation Authority, Bristows' Helicopters, British Airways, the Scottish Special Housing Association and Hjaltland Housing Association. In addition numerous private houses were completed. At the same time provision was made for the increased social and recreational needs.

But the dramatic upsurge came to an abrupt halt, and for this there were two main reasons. Firstly, the very large sums spent on improving the airport resulted in very high landing charges having to be imposed in order to recoup the expenditure. Secondly, the development of long-range, twin-engined helicopters, carrying much increased passenger loads, made it possible to effect crew changes for the platforms and rigs direct from Aberdeen.

At the end of 1982 the population of Dunrossness was accommodated in about 1,000 houses, an average of 2·74 people per house. Of these houses, 29 per cent were rented, while the remainder were either croft houses or owner-occupied houses. Within these figures there were marked differences in different areas, e.g., in the Sumburgh area 51 per cent of the houses were rented, in Sandwick 31 per cent, in Cunningsburgh 24 per cent, and in Levenwick, Ireland and Maywick virtually none. Again, at the end of 1982, approximately 60 houses were unoccupied in the Dunrossness area as a whole, with over 30 of these in the South Dunrossness area, and nearly 20 in Sandwick. Much of the housing was virtually new, and most of the remainder had been modernised and reconditioned. All houses had mains electricity supplied by the North of Scotland Hydro Electric Board on overhead lines, and a mains water supply. Mains sewage or septic tanks served virtually all houses.

Of the total population, 8 per cent were under school age, 24 per cent were in the age group 5-19, 32 per cent were aged between 20 and 40, 18 per cent were from 40-60, and 18 per cent were over 60. In this latter group 86 people were aged over 80. The division by sexes was virtually even.

While there was a significant degree of unemployment in the area at the end of 1982, there were still 37·5 per cent of the total population employed or self-employed. This figure was spread fairly evenly over the whole area, though Sandwick presented marginally the best picture with 41 per cent employed, and Maywick and Ireland the poorest with 33 per cent. Just over 400 of the people were pensioners, and the main employment scene was still in and around the airport, where there was still work for over 200 people. Indeed, this meant that 20 per cent of all the employed worked at the airport. As was to be expected, workers from South Dunrossness held a majority of these posts, though over 30 still commuted from Sandwick. Next highest employer was Shetland Islands Council which provided over 100 jobs, a significant percentage of these being in the three schools, and this total was closely followed by the total employed in shops, hotels, knitwear etc., which also topped 100. This latter type of work was much more evident in the Sandwick area, where bakeries and knitwear added significantly to the jobs total. In the traditional crofting and farming, where a number of people of pensionable age were still active, and where a number more used it as a part-time occupation, only about 8 per cent of the working population could be said to be making a living from the land, and fishing accounted for only about half of that proportion. The Health Service and Telecommunications each provided jobs for about 25 people, and nine were employed in various capacities as far away as Sullom Voe. Other employment covered a very wide range of occupations. While in South Dunrossness there was a considerable amount of local employment, for much of the area commuting to work was part of the way of life. In the Cunningsburgh area, for instance, 70 per cent of the working population commuted daily, mostly to Lerwick but a few as far afield as Sullom Voe.

Perhaps one of the best illustrations of the change which took place in the Dunrossness area during the 1970s is to be found in the following figures. At the end of 1982 analysis showed that over 700 of the population (25 per cent) had come in from outside Shetland, and a further 9 per cent from other parts of Shetland itself. Maywick and Ireland showed very few incomers, and Cunningsburgh had less than 10 per cent. But in the area south of the Ward Hill—the Sumburgh/Virkie area—incomers from outside Shetland amounted to 38 per cent of the population, while incomers from other parts of Shetland accounted for a further 13 per cent. In this particular area the natives totalled slightly less than half. In Sandwick the figure for people from outside Shetland was 27 per cent, from other parts of Shetland 19 per cent, the natives here making rather more than of half the total. In Dunrossness North the percentages were 27 and 9, with natives forming 64, while in Levenwick it was 36 and 12, with natives totalling 52. In the Quendale, Ringasta and Hillock area the percentages were 32 and 12, with natives accounting for 56.

EDUCATION

After World War II seven schools served the educational needs of the Dunrossness area. One of these, at Sandwick, was a junior secondary school, with a combined primary and secondary roll. The others, at Cunningsburgh, Levenwick, Bigton, Boddam, Quendale and Virkie were all primary schools. All the schools had been built in the period immediately following the 1872 Education Act.

Between the years 1931 and 1961 the Dunrossness population dropped by over 600, and this continuing downwards trend called for a reappraisal of educational provision in the district. The result of that reappraisal was the decision to centralise primary children in the area from Levenwick/Bigton to Sumburgh Head in a new school to be built near Boddam. This centralisation could be effected without it being necessary to transport any of the children for more than a maximum of approximately five miles. The proposal was debated at length both in the Education Committee and in public, and with the consensus of opinion behind it, the new school at Boddam was opened by the Queen in 1969, its roll at the time being 112 children. The old primary schools at Levenwick, Bigton, Boddam, Quendale and Virkie were closed.

Shortly thereafter the Sandwick school became a junior high school. This meant that all the children in the Dunrossness area, including Cunningsburgh, enrolled at Sandwick for the first two years of their secondary school life. Thereafter those who wished to do so transferred to the Anderson High School in Lerwick, a comprehensive school, and the only school in the islands offering a full 5 or 6 year secondary curriculum. Pupils attending the Anderson High from as far south as Sandwick were transported to and from Lerwick daily by bus. The others from farther south were accommodated either in the school hostels or in lodgings paid for by the Education Committee. In 1972 the Sandwick school roll was 100, made up of 45 primary and 55 secondary children. In Cunningsburgh the same primary school continued in use as before.

The coming of oil to Shetland, and the subsequent rise in population, is reflected in the rolls of the schools in the district during the 1970s. Shortly after its opening a rising roll at Boddam necessitated additional accommodation being built. From a roll of 112 in 1969 the number had risen to 222 in 1979—i.e., it virtually doubled in ten years. At Sandwick from 100 children in 1972 the total rose to 210 in 1978, and to 221 in 1981. This last total was made up of 101 primary and 120 secondary children. In Cunningsburgh the roll, which stood at 56 in 1971, had reached 88 by 1979. Here the inadequacy of the old school had been recognised, and a fine new modern school was built in 1977.

At Sandwick the shortcomings of the old school for the rapidly rising numbers had been recognised for some time, and strong pressure from all concerned finally resulted in the building of a new school being commenced, and this work was nearing completion at the end of 1982.

The dramatic rise in the Dunrossness school population during the 1970s was very largely the result of oil-created activity leading to a sudden proliferation of work opportunities at Sumburgh Airport. With the downturn in activity there, an almost immediate outward movement of population took place, and the result also shows up in the school rolls.

In the school at Boddam (Dunrossness Primary School) the roll, from its total of 222 in 1979, had dropped to 160 in 1982. At Sandwick the roll of 221 in 1981 had dropped to 189 by the end of 1982. The former total consisted of 101 primary children and 120 secondary—of whom 25 were in the 3rd and 4th years. At Cunningsburgh where the roll was perhaps rather less affected by the changing employment scene, the roll had nevertheless dropped from its peak of 88 to 70 at the end of 1982.

As 1983 came in, the expectation was that the decline in population and in school rolls was likely to continue. But in Cunningsburgh, with the population relatively stable, and with about 40 children under school age in the area, there seemed little cause for apprehension about the future of that school. In Sandwick there were 53 children under school age. Provided the population decline there slowed down it did seem that the future of Sandwick school was reasonably assured. In the remainder of Dunrossness there were over 90 children of pre-school age. Here the population was more sensitive to the changing employment situation; but, providing the main part of the population movement was over, as seemed possible, the future of the Dunrossness school seemed fairly bright.

COMMUNITY LIFE

The influx of newcomers to the area in the 1970s resulted in greatly increased community activity. Facilities for such activities, both indoors and outdoors, were improved and expanded.

In Cunningsburgh, indoor activities are carried on in the public hall, the village club room and the school hall, while the agricultural society has its own hut which it uses at the time of the annual agricultural show. For outdoor activity there is a sports field, and a multi-purpose, all-weather court at the school. Three churches serve the area.

In Sandwick there are the Carnegie Hall, the Central Hall and Club Rooms, and the social club, while there is also an outdoors playing field. There are three churches.

In the remainder of Dunrossness there are halls at Levenwick, Bigton, Boddam and Virkie, as well as an excellent school hall. The main playing field is at Boddam, near the hall, and the school has a multi-purpose, all-weather court. There are two buildings and congregations of the Church of Scotland, one at a central location near Boddam and the other at Bigton. There is also a Baptist Church near Boddam, Methodist chapels at Scousburgh and Ireland, and a Mission Hall at Levenwick.

Uniformed organisations include 1st Virkie Brownies, 1st Virkie and 1st Sandwick Guides, 1st Dunrossness Boys Brigade, 1st Sandwick Boys Brigade, 1st Sumburgh Scout Troop, and Girls Brigade at Cunningsburgh and Dunrossness. Voluntary organisations are numerous and varied. As well as a toddlers group at Bigton, and playgroups at Cunningsburgh, Sandwick and Dunrossness, there are also youth clubs at Virkie, Bigton, Levenwick, Cunningsburgh (Village Club) and Sandwick. There are S.W.R.I. branches at Boddam, Sandwick and Cunningsburgh, and senior citizens organisations at Dunrossness, Sandwick and Cunningsburgh. There are two well-established drama groups—the Sandwick Drama Group and the Fitful Players from South Dunrossness. There is a Dunrossness Pony Club, a Dunrossness Athletic Club and a Sumburgh Hang-Gliding Club. Badminton clubs are strong at Cunningsburgh, Sandwick and South Dunrossness, while the Southend, Sandwick and Cunningsburgh, have both senior and juvenile football teams. There is a boating club of long standing at Sandwick, while the younger Ness Boating Club has created an impressive marina at the Pool of Virkie.

The whole area is reasonably well served with shops. Cunningsburgh has two, a craft shop and a service garage. Sandwick has two bakeries with shops, along with a knitwear factory and shop. The remainder of Dunrossness has shops at Levenwick, Bigton, Robin's Brae and Tolob, along with a service garage and off-licence at Scousburgh and a butcher's shop at Boddam.

Hotels are also fairly numerous, there being two in the Sumburgh-Virkie area, two at Spiggie, one in Levenwick and one in Sandwick.

Bus services operate to Lerwick from Sandwick and from Sumburgh, but in common with most of the rest of Shetland the family car is the main means of transport.

March 1983

FAIR ISLE

by Anne Sinclair

PHYSICAL BASIS

Part of the parish of Dunrossness, Fair Isle lies 21 miles to the south of Shetland, an isolated stepping stone between North Ronaldsay (Orkney) and Sumburgh Head. Barely two square miles in area, its highest point, Ward Hill, is 712 feet O.D. Bounded by cliffs and geos, the island slopes down less steeply to the shore at the south-west side. It has always been a place to be feared by mariners because, as Mr James Kay, minister of Dunrossness, wrote in 1680 'here are very impetuous Tides'. There is a harbour at the south end, but its use is limited to small boats only, and the main anchorage is on the east side in the North Haven which is now used by *Good Shepherd III*—the mail boat, and by many passing yachts and fishing boats. Although usually a very safe harbour in summer, a north-easterly gale renders it dangerous for all shipping. The island is surrounded by several outlying rocks and stacks, the most obvious being Sheep Craig on the east side—rising sheer for 422 feet on its south face and still attached to the main isle, but only accessible by boat.

The island is effectively divided into two parts—with scattald (i.e., common grazing) on the northern half, while the crofts and arable land are to the south.

HISTORY

Though it is obvious from the tumuli scattered over the island that people have lived there probably since the first recorded settlements in Orkney and Shetland, i.e., 3500 B.C., the first written records to mention Fair Isle (or Fridarey, as it was then known) are the Norse sagas. In the story of Burnt Njal, the viking Kari, sailing from Iceland, makes landfall on the Isle. 'There that man who was David the White took Kari into his house and he told him all that he had heard for certain about the doings of the Burners. He was one of Kari's greatest friends and Kari stayed with him for the winter.' This suggests that the island people were well informed as to the goings on elsewhere, and that they would have had contacts with Orkney, Shetland, Norway and the Faroes. The Orkneyinga Saga tells how Uni was sent to Fair Isle as part of Earl Rögnvald's plan to land in Orkney. When the time was right Uni soaked the warning beacon so that it could not be lit, and the Earl was able to land on Westray without opposition from the Orkney men.

In medieval times a church was established on the south end of the Isle.

Sinclair of Quendale added Fair Isle to his considerable estates in Shetland by 1630, and he and his descendants were to receive all the revenue wrung from the tenants up until the 1750s. This included the rents from 24 households in 4 townships and the rent from at least one 'booth' built at the south harbour for the use of 'an Hamburg Merchant' for trading in dried fish. Fishing was the main source of income for all the tenants, supplemented by the production of fish oil and butter, and the export of feathers gathered on wild-fowling expeditions on the cliffs. When the Quendale estate went bankrupt, Fair Isle was put up for sale, and was purchased by Stewart of Brough (in Sanday, Orkney) in 1770. Many strong links were established with Orkney over the next hundred years and there were several island families who emigrated to Orkney. In the 1850s the runrig system of agriculture and the townships were replaced by single crofts.

In 1866 Fair Isle was bought by J. Bruce of Sumburgh. Because of the severity of the tides and the rough coastline, and after many shipwrecks over the centuries, two lighthouses were built between 1890 and 1892. In the 1914-1918 War many men from the island were in the Armed Forces; and some of them gave their lives.

From 1910 onwards, the Duchess of Bedford and Eagle Clarke paid many visits to the Isle, discovered it to be a mecca for ornithologists, and publicised the fact. This led to the island being purchased in 1948 by George Waterston, a keen naturalist who had first visited it in 1935, and a bird observatory was set up in ex-naval buildings at the North Haven. Subsequently a new modern observatory was built in 1970.

In 1954 the National Trust for Scotland acquired Fair Isle and since then they have instituted many improvements and encouraged the return of young families.

POPULATION

In 1701, Mr John Brand reported that 'Death hath almost depopulated the Isle, the small Pox having lately raged there', but by 1790 the inhabitants numbered 220 and by 1861, 380. On 7 May 1862, a total of 134 people left to begin new lives in Canada, and over the next 30 years the population stabilised at around 220. During a sudden and severe gale on 2 September 1897, seven men were lost at sea leaving 18 immediate dependants, some of whom emigrated. This, coupled with two world wars, and lack of amenities in the island, caused a steady decline in numbers till in 1955 the population was just over 50, and there was talk of evacuation. The islanders, however, refused to leave and, with help from the National Trust for Scotland and the Shetland Islands Council in improving housing and amenities, the population—consisting mainly of young families, many of whom have ancestral links with the island—now stands at 72.

PUBLIC AND SOCIAL SERVICES

Water Supply: Until the 1950s, water was carried by hand to all the croft houses and since that time, pipes have been laid from wells to houses; but it was at first common to have a cold tap only, and no inside sanitation. With the modernisation of the houses, begun in 1959-1960, dwellings now have hot and cold water and inside sanitation. In 1978 a water scheme was commissioned; now the crofts are linked to a main, treated water supply.

Electricity: When the National Trust for Scotland took over Fair Isle in 1954 there was no electricity. Three small private generators were in use in the next years, but in 1962 five diesel generators were installed by the Trust to provide a limited supply (2 kW per house for approximately six hours every day). This scheme was replaced in 1975 by two central diesel generators. Because of increases in fuel and freight charges, a scheme was planned, costing £140,000, to link the existing diesel system with a new aero-generator. Initial funding was offered by the Shetland Islands Council (£60,000) to be followed by the Highlands and Islands Development Board (£38,000) and the European Regional Development Fund (£48,000). The aero-generator was commissioned on 2 June 1982—the first of its kind to operate on a commercial basis in the United Kingdom.

Communications: There were originally three tracks leading from the south end to a point behind the schoolhouse, from where they led to the airstrip and Ward Hill, the North Haven, and the North Lighthouse. Of the original three, two have been kept up since the war and, in the last 15 years, these have been completely tarred except for the airstrip to Ward Hill road. The Shetland Islands Council upgraded and maintain the roads using local labour, and therefore provides a useful additional source of income. Links to the mainland of Shetland are good. Throughout last century the only contact was by sailing boat ('yoal') from the island. A great deal of bartering was done with passing ships; but to get meal supplies—or sometimes to get married—men sailed to Orkney or Shetland. The first mail boat to run regularly *from* Fair Isle was brought to the Isle in 1920. Now *Good Shepherd III*, owned and crewed by islanders, has since the 1960s run to Grutness on the Shetland mainland once a week in winter and twice in the summer months. The pier, built in 1958 by the then Zetland County Council, enables the boat to unload and load in nearly all weather conditions. In 1981 a new slipway was built, the first phase in a breakwater project to enable a fuller use to be made of the harbour.

Since the lengthening and repair of the wartime airstrip, Loganair has operated weekly from Tingwall in Shetland five scheduled flights in summer and two in winter. There are also a good many charter flights from Orkney.

Mail services and telegraph lines were established in 1877, and the island is now linked into the world-wide Subscriber Trunk Dialling system. There are only two houses without telephones.

Plate 3

JARLSHOF, Dunrossness

This is one of the most important archaeological sites in Britain, and has remains from a range of periods from Stone Age to Medieval.

(Courtesy Douglas G. Young)

Plate 4

SCALLOWAY CASTLE

This castellated mansion was built in the 16th century by Earl Patrick Stewart, and commemorates one of the less happy episodes in Shetland history, with the subjugation of the people to the Scottish Crown and to Scottish lairds.

(J. D. Ratter. Courtesy Shetland Museum and Library)

Education: The Society for the Propagation of Christian Knowledge set up a school on the Isle in 1732. A new school and schoolhouse was built in 1880, when responsibility was taken over by local authorities. Fair Isle Public School has always been a one-teacher school. Since 1945 numbers have generally fluctuated between two and 16, with one pupil at its lowest. At the age of 12, pupils go to the Anderson High School in Lerwick, and board there during term time. At present there are eight pre-school children, 11 attending Fair Isle Primary, and seven boarding in Lerwick.

Health Services: From the late 1800s up to 1903, reports on the health of the population were sent regularly by the factor to the County Sanitary Inspector in Lerwick. In 1903, Nurse Payne, the first of a series of Jubilee nurses, was posted to Fair Isle. The original postings were for one year. At present there is a fully qualified district nurse, and the doctors whose practice covers the Dunrossness area visit the Isle on a regular basis. Cases in urgent need of specialist attention are now flown out by air ambulance—a welcome relief to the sick or injured, who used to have to face a three-hour journey on the *Good Shepherd* or, if the weather was very bad, a five-hour journey on the Lerwick lifeboat to reach hospital.

Community Hall: The old school building became the village hall and was used for dances, film shows and Sunday School. In 1980 a new hall was built by the community with aid from the Shetland Islands Council, the Highlands and Islands Development Board, the Scottish Education Department and the National Trust for Scotland. This hall, with all its modern amenities, is now used by the school and play group during the day, and in the evenings it is used for social functions, sports, Cubs and Brownies (a combined pack, at present consisting of 2 Brownies and 4 Cubs), keep fit classes in winter, and as a venue for committee meetings.

Church: A Roman Catholic community till the Reformation, Fair Isle was converted to the Protestant faith, and the Church of Scotland took over for the next 250 years. In 1828, 'owing to some devisive spirit having been introduced . . . by Methodist preachers' (Fair Isle Kirk Session Minutes, August 1828), a Methodist congregation was formed. There is now the Kirk (Church of Scotland, built 1892) and the Chapel (Methodist, built 1886), and they are used on alternate Sundays. The Church of Scotland has a salaried missionary based on the island, while the Methodists have a lay preacher. In the Chapel there are two beautiful stained glass windows gifted in 1936 by 'Thomas Wilson, late of Taft, Fair Isle, in affectionate remembrance of his father and mother, John and Barbara Wilson, and of his grand aunt Barbara Wilson'.

HOUSING

In 1871 there were 28 inhabited turf-roofed houses scattered over the south end of the Isle. These were replaced by slate roofed 'but and ben' type houses between 1890 and 1900, but no more improvements were made till the National Trust for Scotland instituted a programme of modernisation in the late 1950s. The houses now number 21, the school house and the nurse's house included. Thirteen of these have been modernised by the National Trust for Scotland over the last 20 years, using local labour and volunteer camps of young people from schools, universities and organisations such as the International Voluntary Service or the Christian Movement for Peace. There is no overcrowding, and development has meant that more young people have been willing to return to the island. A fish store at the south end is being converted into a hostel and laundry facilities, and two sheltered houses will be built next year.

AGRICULTURE AND COMMERCE

Land use has altered radically over the last half century. The 866 acres of common grazing are still used for sheep, but around the crofts there was formerly a great deal of cultivation, and livestock kept consisted of cows and one or two oxen per croft. The ox was used for ploughing and carting, and each croft had an oxhouse and ox grass (the small field where the ox was kept). What land was not worked using the ox was dug over manually using Shetland spades. The last pony was shipped out of Fair Isle in 1928 and the last ox in 1940. Since 1945 sheep have replaced cattle on the crofts and, despite mechanisation, there is much less ground cultivated. Lambs are exported every autumn, usually Shetland/Suffolk, Shetland/Dorset or Shetland/Cheviot cross breeds. Wool is also sold—mainly to wool brokers in Shetland—but there is a demand for coloured fleeces (Shetland black, grey and 'moorit') by home spinners.

The other main export of the island since the collapse of the fishing industry—due partly to the absence of a safe harbour in which to keep larger boats—is knitting. The name of Fair Isle is synonymous with patterned knitwear. Originally socks and hats were made and bartered for goods, and from the 1880s the women made brightly coloured jumpers for sale. Changes in fashion caused the knitters to alter their designs: more muted shades—the natural colours—came into vogue in the 1950s but, from 10 to 12 hand knitters, the numbers gradually declined. Now there is only one knitter who hand-knits jerseys commercially but, in 1980, Fair Isle Crafts—a co-operative of machine knitters and hand finishers—was set up. Fair Isle garments are knitted on 7 machines and hand finishers sew the garments together. While this enables more people to have the genuine 'knitted in Fair Isle' label, the colour and pattern combinations are chosen by the individual knitters and are, therefore, fairly exclusive.

WAY OF LIFE

Because of their isolated position, the people of the island are motivated to work together, and life, governed to a certain extent by the vagaries of wind and weather, is something of a challenge. All the benefits acquired over the years—running water, electricity, telephone and mail boat, roads and community hall—are serviced by members of the community. There is no significant crime and no uniformed police. They have most of the advantages and few of the disadvantages of modern life, and so the old values still have a place. The people on the island, as it stands at present, look to the future with optimism.

December 1982

THE ISLAND AND PARISH OF FETLAR

Original description by Ian Petrie, 1954
New version by Robert L. Johnson, 1983

PHYSICAL BASIS

Fetlar is one of the north isles of Shetland. It lies between latitude 60° 34′ N. and 60° 38′ N. and longitude 0° 45′ W. and 0° 57′ W. It is separated from Unst on the north and from Whalsay and Out Skerries on the south by waters of the North Sea, while on the west Colgrave Sound separates it from Yell.

The island is irregular in shape; at its greatest length it is c. six miles, while its breadth is generally c. three miles, apart from at the western end, where the peninsula of Lambhoga projects c. two miles in a southward direction.

The island has two deep indentations in its coast line, the Wick of Gruting in the north-east and the Wick of Tresta in the south-west. Three smaller bays, those of Funzie (pronounced Finn-ee), Aith and Urie were the centres of activity when the fishing industry was being prosecuted from the island last century. Fetlar was at a serious disadvantage for fishing and trade owing to the fact that it does not possess a natural sheltered harbour. In the 1830s Sir Arthur Nicolson attempted to provide one at Urie in the north-west; he made a small dock for the shipping of chromate ore and cattle. However the rocks offshore made it unsafe and of limited use.

In general the land is low-lying, the relief consisting of shallow valleys separated by low hills. The highest point is the Vord Hill at 522 feet O.D. Most of the coast consists of cliffs, and at the Blue Banks in the north they reach a height of 400 feet O.D.

Geologically Fetlar is a mixture of metamorphic and igneous rocks. The west end of the island including Lambhoga is composed of gneiss, and this is separated from the rest of the island by a fault line. At Moo Wick near the south-east tip of Lambhoga is a residual deposit of pure kaolin. The remainder of the island consists of shear-bounded thrust blocks of serpentine, mettagabro and phyllite. In the small Hesta Ness block in the north-east, the original serpentine has been completely altered to antigorite and steatite; it also contains bands of pure talc which have been worked in the past.

HISTORY

Fetlar must always have been an attractive island for settlement, and it has remains from a series of past periods, although in many cases insufficient investigation has been done to give definite dates to the various antiquities.

There are numerous cairns, mounds and standing stones, and some at least of those probably date to the Stone and Bronze Ages. Also from this early period is the stone circle at Haltadans near the north coast; it has a diameter of 40 feet, with two earth-fast stones in the centre. The Finnie-gord Dyke, a series of earth-fast stones running in a north-south direction, more or less bisects the island and is especially prominent towards its north end. There are remains of brochs (fortifications, the main period of which is the Iron Age) at Snabrough, Houbie, and at a site just below the old Free Church between Houbie and Aith; there is also one at Brough Lodge, although an observation tower was built on its site in the 19th century.

A mound at the north-west of the Wick of Aith is known as the Vikings' Grave, and there is a tradition that a Viking chief is buried there. The reputed first landing of the Norse was at the Wick of Gruting; and there is abundant evidence of settlement and former cultivation in the valley running south from Gruting towards Aith.

In the later history of Fetlar, of central importance was the acquisition of most of the island in 1785 by Arthur Nicolson of Lochend from the former incumbents the Bruces. The 'haa' or mansion house built by Andrew Bruce in the early 18th century was at Urie; but Arthur Nicolson, who inherited an additional part of the island in 1815, built the mansion of Brough Lodge.

Under Arthur Nicolson, the west end and most of the north of the island was cleared and taken over for a big sheep farm. In 1822, he took over the scattald (hill grazing) of the peninsula of Lambhoga and in doing so deprived the townships of Tresta, Toon and Velzie of most of their hill grazing. In 1839 and 1840 he evicted the thirteen crofters from the Gruting district; and between 1847 and 1858 all the townships of the west end of the island were cleared: the complete list is Colbinstoft, Ruster, Linkster, Uriesetter, Urie, Fografield, Frackister, Oddsta, Hamar, Hamarsness, Odsetter, Scord, Wallspund, Uskister, Sand and Foreland.

In 1826, the landlord had claimed the inheritance to the baronetcy of a distant kinsman which had lapsed 80 years previously, and became Sir Arthur Nicolson. The round house of Gruting is also due to him. It was built in the 1840s, and the stones for its construction were taken from the croft houses of the area.

The other main landowning family in Fetlar in the modern period have been the Cheynes. Their estate earlier belonged to the Earl of Morton, who sold it in 1766 to Sir Laurence Dundas. From 1832 the

Dundases became Earls of Zetland, and the estate was later sold to Sir William Watson Cheyne, the famous surgeon whose mother was a daughter of the Rev. William Watson, minister of Fetlar from 1830 to 1855.

The two large landowning families were never forthcoming in giving land for house sites; in the first half of the present century this discouraged local marriages and was a factor in the decline of population.

In addition to the two estates, a small amount of land is in the hands of crofter owner-occupiers.

POPULATION

The peak population recorded in Fetlar was in 1836 when the number of inhabitants was given as 859. Since that date the population has steadily declined:

Year	Population	Year	Population
1841	761	1911	279
1851	658	1921	224
1861	548	1931	217
1871	517	1941	no census
1881	431	1951	161
1891	363	1961	127
1901	347	1971	90
		1981	104

The first, and arguably the main cause of the decline of the population of Fetlar was the clearing of the west side of the island by Sir Arthur Nicolson, as already described. Hundreds of the people evicted had very little option but to leave the island. These clearances also had a demoralising effect on the people who stayed on, with the result that a large proportion of the young people when they were old enough to seek work left the island never to return. The earlier part of the 20th century did little to stabilise the island population. During the First World War, 10 young men lost their lives; and subsequently a peculiar situation arose where very few couples married. This can be seen in the following table extracted from the Register of Marriage and Births covering the period 1855 to 1981.

Years	Marriages	Births
1855-61	18	90
1861-71	16	105
1871-81	8	92
1881-91	17	78
1891-1901	8	83
1901-11	7	52
1911-21	4	20

1921-31	3	35
1931-41	2	13
1941-51	7	11
1951-61	nil	9
1961-71	nil	6
1971-81	3	19

The upturn of the 1970s can be attributed to the fact that several young Fetlar people having married partners from outwith the island have returned to make their homes there.

PUBLIC AND SOCIAL SERVICES

The Shetland County Council provided a piped water supply from the Loch of Setter to all occupied houses during the latter part of the 1960s. The supply of electricity by submarine cable from the neighbouring island of Yell was installed during the summer of 1982. However prior to the public supply being made available by the North of Scotland Hydro Electric Board, most of the householders had their own private generating plants. The housing estate at Stakkifletts also had its own generating plant.

Medical services are catered for by a district nurse living at Houbie. The doctor from Mid Yell makes consultancy calls every second week, but in the case of emergency he can be in the island within an hour. If the need arises the patient can be flown out from the airstrip by Loganair to hospital in Lerwick or (for more serious cases) on to Aberdeen for treatment.

Education is provided by a one teacher school, which caters for children up to the age of twelve years. Older children must leave the island for the secondary part of their education. It is this which gives concern for the future of the island. If some of these children could complete their school education on the island they would be less likely to leave it afterwards. This could enhance the recent tendency already noted for young couples to make their homes in the island.

The focal point of community activity has been since 1900 the hall at Leagarth. Sir William Watson Cheyne gave the island the use of the hall which was built as part of the house of Leagarth. However the former Free Church building has now been purchased from the Church of Scotland; it is now to be renovated and brought up to modern standards, and will be a community centre owned by the island people themselves. The Fetlar people very generally take part in social gatherings and activities and the new community centre will be a real asset.

CHURCH

From 1709 until 1891 Fetlar was joined with North Yell as a single parish, the minister living at the manse at Tresta in Fetlar. On some occasions there was also an assistant in North Yell. In 1891, Fetlar became a Church of Scotland parish on its own account, having its own minister. Thereafter as the population decreased, the minister's place was later taken by a missionary. Fetlar was linked to the parish of Yell in 1975, and the minister of the joint charge is resident at Mid Yell.

With the Disruption of the National Church in 1843 a Free Church was built at Houbie and continued as such until 1931, when the congregations were re-united following the reunion of the National Church. The congregation continued to use the two church buildings on alternate Sundays until a few years ago. Since then the Tresta church only has been in use. Both manses have been sold and are now guest houses.

COMMUNICATIONS

For a very long period the only service communication was by the steamer *Earl of Zetland* which sailed from Lerwick to the North Isles of Shetland and called at Fetlar three times per week, on Monday, Wednesday and Friday. The main place of call was at Brough Lodge, while every second week a call was made at Houbie, to land more substantial cargo. At both places flitboats were used to convey passengers and goods to the shore.

In 1973 this inter-island steamer was replaced by vehicular inter-island ferries linking Toft on the Shetland Mainland to Ulsta in Yell, and Gutcher in North Yell to Belmont in Unst and to Oddsta in Fetlar. This ferry makes three crossings to Fetlar each day, but is somewhat limited in practice as its main function is to meet the needs of the larger island of Unst. It would be appreciated by the Fetlar people if a more flexible time-table could be arranged, especially at the peak time in the autumn when stock shipments are being made to connect with the ferry at Lerwick for sales at Aberdeen. However the vehicular ferry has been a substantial improvement and has made the island much more accessible, as it is now no problem to make a day trip whenever required to Lerwick or anywhere in Shetland, which was impossible under the previous system. The island also is provided with an airstrip for light aircraft at Turra Field. Loganair, which provides a daily service to Unst from Tingwall, will include a call here if there are passengers for Fetlar. The island is thus far from being isolated.

HOUSING

The standard of the houses now compares favourably with other districts in Shetland. The Shetland County Council in 1968 provided a public water supply from the Loch of Setter, which enabled the people to provide their houses with mains water and sanitation, which are now essential. In 1974 the Shetland Islands Council erected a housing estate at Stakkifletts at Houbie, and this enabled young couples to have homes of modern standard. Also in this estate is sheltered housing for the elderly, where they can spend their latter years in comfort. There are now 43 inhabited houses in the island, including the 15 council houses.

The mansion houses of the proprietors are now standing unoccupied. Brough Lodge, the seat of the Nicolsons, which for a long period was frequented by aristocracy on holiday, is now standing unoccupied and uncared for. Leagarth House, also now unoccupied, was built about 1900 by Sir William Watson Cheyne. Watson Cheyne as he was better known locally, was a noted surgeon of his time, and was a contemporary of Sir Joseph Lister. After his death in the 1930s the house was used as a summer home for members of his family, but for a number of years this has been discontinued.

AGRICULTURE, INDUSTRY AND COMMERCE

The fishing industry plays no part in the economy of the island at the present time. During the 19th century it was actively prosecuted from Urie, Funzie and Aith, Funzie being the chief station in Fetlar for the 'far haaf' ling fishing. However, bad fishing seasons in the 1880s gave the final blow to an activity which was already in decline.

Agriculture is the mainstay of the island. The land is of good quality as is emphasised by the fact that Fetlar has been called the 'Garden of Shetland'. At one time Fetlar was noted for its ponies, which were in demand all over the islands as work ponies prior to the introduction of tractors. A large number were required for use in the island when peat was being fully worked at Lambhoga by all the families from Funzie to Tresta. The peat was transported by large numbers of ponies, in 'kishies' (i.e., panniers which were baskets of straw). Pony rearing sustained a very serious blow when in 1886 a disease, sarcoptic mange, came into the island with the result that nearly 500 ponies died. This was a major catastrophe at the time, causing severe hardship which was made much worse by crop failure and poor fishing seasons. It was during the period of the Second World War that a large number of people found that it was more convenient to import coal for fuel than to work peat at Lambhoga and transport it home. The native Shetland pony is smaller than the type used for work purposes, and it is these that are now to be seen. During the last two decades there was a boom trade in these small ponies, and Fetlar was able to cash in on this with some success. However more recently this has declined, and an important question now is whether to hold on to the pony stock in the hope of an improvement in the market. Sheep are now of much greater importance in Fetlar than in the past, when cattle were the chief source of income from the croft. Owing to the large number of working ponies kept on the scattalds there was formerly little place for the sheep.

A great step forward in the agriculture of the island was made in 1963 when the Crofters Commission reorganised the crofts to give larger, viable units by amalgamating smaller ones, and by the acquisition of the grazing of Lambhoga, Odsetter and Scord for allocation to the newly formed units. Aided by Crofters Commission grants, silage pits and byres for cattle were built, and this gave several crofters a new opportunity. The Farm and Horticultural Development Plan of the late 1970s gave more encouragement to the young men to improve the land by reseeding areas of hill land apportioned to them from the hill scattald. Now more aid is forthcoming from the Shetland Island Council in the form of low-interest loans in their Ten Year Agricultural Plan. This is funded from oil revenues, and is intended to put the holdings on a viable basis and give employment for a much larger number of people than at present.

TOURISM

Fetlar has some activity in tourism, but it is small-scale and specialised in type and there is scope for expansion.

There is a variety of scenery for the visitor, especially on the coast; there is trout fishing in several lochs; and there is much to interest the ornithologist.

For bird-watchers the snowy owls which bred in Fetlar in the late 1960s and early 1970s were of national interest, but unfortunately they have been without a male since then. The red-necked phalarope, which is very rare and which spends only a very short period on land for breeding purposes, is a regular occupant of several marshes in Fetlar. Many other species which are rare farther south in Britain are an everyday sight on the island. Part of the area Stakkaberg and Vord Hill has been designated a Nature Reserve, while the Royal Society for the Protection of Birds has a warden on the island to prevent these rarer breeds from being molested during the breeding season.

THE FUTURE

The number of people is now much lower than at the peak in the early 19th century; in the 20th century decline in numbers and the mounting problems of isolation have been real threats to the community. More recently however, there have been encouraging signs of a real will to survive, and the provision of modern amenities, including vehicular ferries, has done much to lessen the problems of isolation. It is to be hoped that the young people willing to remain on the island will be able to enjoy a secure future, free from the urban pressures which are now felt by so many of the national population.

May 1983

THE BURGH OF LERWICK

Original description by Rev. K. N. MacRae, 1955
New version by Dr T. M. Y. Manson, 1982

Lerwick is the main seaport, the town, the judicial, administrative, educational, commercial and social centre of the Shetland Islands: only the absence of other towns in the archipelago prevents it from being called the capital. With a population of 7,356 in September 1982, nearly a third of the islands' total of 23,307[1] (Health Board statistics), it is situated less than half way up the east side of the long north-and-south Shetland Mainland.

It owes its rise to the splendid deep-water harbour, which is three miles long; the main width is three-quarters of a mile, but it narrows to three-eighths of a mile at the north end. The harbour is effectively enclosed by the island of Bressay, itself six miles long. Originally called Bressay Sound, this haven is now frequently referred to as Lerwick Harbour, a term which has acquired legal status.

The chief life-line of the islands, the passenger and freight-carrying roll-on, roll-off motor vessel *St Clair*, owned by the P. & O. Company,[2] sails thrice weekly from Lerwick direct to Aberdeen and back. Other cargo-carrying vessels sail to and from Lerwick, including one registered in the port. A major portion of the islands' exports go out from Lerwick; but the village of Scalloway, five miles distant on the west side of the island, rivals it in the case of exports of fish products. A great variety of shipping uses the sound: visiting passenger liners and yachts, cargo vessels, supply ships for the North Sea oil industry, fishery protection and other naval ships; above all, fishing boats, both British and foreign, find at Lerwick shelter in bad weather, ample wharfage and marine engineering facilities. One of Shetland's two R.N.L.I. lifeboats lies at Lerwick. A vehicle-carrying ferry provides an hourly service to and from Bressay.

Roads, supplemented by vehicle-carrying ferries, radiate from the

---

LERWICK

Note: The parish of Lerwick includes the Burgh of Lerwick together with the landward area of the district of Gulberwick and Quarff, and Burra Isle. For the purposes of local government and other organisation this parish now has limited meaning, but it still exists as a Census division.

The signals [1] and [2] are explained in the notes on p. 86.

town, bearing the busy motor traffic which distributes goods and carries people all over the islands.

Only in relation to aviation is Lerwick indifferently situated: it is six miles by road from the nearest airfield, a very small one to the west at Tingwall, and is 25 miles north of Shetland's main airport at Sumburgh.

PHYSICAL BASIS

Facing Bressay Sound, the original town rises from the waterfront to a ridge of 100 feet O.D., the top of which is known as Hillhead. At water level at the south end three remaining 'lodberries' or stone enclosures standing in the sea with sea doors for loading and unloading of goods from boats, give an idea of the character of the whole waterfront before the first harbour works with piers and esplanade were built in the 1880s and buried all the other lodberries. Buried also were the underground passages leading back from the lodberries which were used for smuggling.

The buildings that line the inner side of the esplanade also enclose on one side the main shopping centre, Commercial Street; it is paved from side to side, and has shops and offices on each side. Paved lanes with stone dykes and intervening green spaces run up in parallel lines from Commercial Street to the crest of the ridge at Hillhead. Formerly densely populated, then forsaken, these lanes or closes are undergoing a gradual process of rehabilitation and are again becoming inhabited and provided with modern amenities, thanks to both municipal and private efforts.

Facing the north harbour, the north part of the town contains the major concentration of industries along with a mixture of shops and residences.

Practically the whole shore out to the north entrance to the harbour at the Green Head, once lined with herring curing stations, is now covered with wharves and docks, including at Holmsgarth the special terminal for the vehicle-carrying *St Clair*, and there are also four oil supply bases. They are the only visible signs on shore of the great North Sea oil industry. From being in 1970 mainly a fishing harbour, Lerwick Harbour has become one of the main ports servicing the northern North Sea oil fields.

West of the Hillhead crest the land dips, rises again, then undulates in a wide stretch, mainly residential in character, but embracing the Clickimin Loch with its bird islet and its prehistoric broch, built in dry stone. There is also a green belt area to the south, the Ness of Sound where there is a farm.

The present official boundary of the town, fixed in 1965, runs just south and west of the Loch of Trebister to the Green Head, and encloses an irregular area roughly two and a half miles from west to east and three and a half miles from south to north.

HISTORY OF THE COMMUNITY

1. DEVELOPMENT UNTIL THE LATE NINETEENTH CENTURY

Lerwick is not an old town, dating only from the 17th century. In the Norse its name means 'clay bay', and the ground on which the old town stands was not cultivated.

It owes its rise to the usefulness of its harbour as a base for foreign fishing vessels, and to the opportunity its shores gave for trading.

For many centuries the great Dutch herring fleet gathered annually in high summer in Bressay Sound to prosecute the herring fishery which meant so much to the economy of the Netherlands. There is an old saying: 'Amsterdam was biggit oot o' da back o' Bressay'.

Half way between Scalloway and Lerwick there is a hillock called Hollanders' Knowe, where, according to tradition, Dutch fishermen met rural Shetlanders to obtain Shetland knitwear by barter or purchase.

Early in the 17th century, trade was further carried on with the Dutch fishermen by means of temporary trading booths on shore. The authorities in Scalloway, the ancient capital, actually ordered these to be destroyed, claiming that they were the scene of immoral practices.

Gradually, however, permanent buildings took root, and these were not confined to trade with the Dutchmen; more general trade came to play a bigger and bigger part.

War between Britain and Holland twice brought the attention of the Government to Lerwick. Cromwell's government intended to build a fort, but the peace made with Holland prevented the intentions issuing into action. A later war with Holland in the time of Charles II led to the present walls of the fort being built between 1663 and 1665, but construction stopped after peace was made with Holland.

It was not till 1781 that the fort was completed with the erection by the Government of the present buildings inside the walls, the fort being named Fort Charlotte, probably after George III's queen. This was done, however, in response to local protestations about the vulnerability of the islands to seizure by American warships during the American War of Independence.

Already by 1700 the community had grown to 700 and a church had been built. The following year Lerwick and its surrounding area was disjoined from the ecclesiastical parish of Tingwall and made into a parish of its own.

In 1747 heritable jurisdictions were abolished and some time afterwards a sheriff court was permanently established in Lerwick. In 1818 it was made a burgh of barony and a town council with magistrates was elected. These developments show the rise of Lerwick as the main town without any precise date marking the demise of Scalloway as the 'capital'.

The opening of the Anderson Educational Institute in Lerwick in 1862 heralded a great educational advance for the whole of Shetland.

The school was the gift of Arthur Anderson, who was born in the 'Booth' of Grimista, just north of the original Lerwick, and was co-founder of the P. & O. Company. The institute greatly increased the meagre facilities for primary education in Lerwick, and provided for the first time a secondary school for the islands.

In 1875 the County Buildings were erected to provide a home for the Commissioners of Supply (who dealt with rural Shetland), sheriff court rooms and a prison.

2. THE HERRING BOOM

Up to this time the development of Lerwick had been slow. Besides being the county town, it was a fishing and shipping port, with the British whaling vessels calling every year to complete their crews on their way to the Arctic. Sporadic entrepreneurial efforts in the fishing industry did not compare with the regular, massive Dutch herring fishery, which despite setbacks continued to use Bressay Sound as its annual headquarters.

In the latter part of the 19th century the swift rise of the British herring fishery electrified Lerwick. Realising its strategic importance for any British herring fishery, a number of local merchants and others formed the Lerwick Harbour Trust in 1877, and in the 1880s constructed extensive harbour works in perfect time to provide wharfage and shore facilities needed by the great fishery, in which Shetland fishermen and boat-owners took as full a part as their number permitted. In the peak year of 1905 there were 174 herring curing stations scattered around 26 Shetland ports, Baltasound being the top with 46 and Lerwick next with 36, the locally-owned stations in Shetland being 46 in number; there were 1,815 fishing boats of which 1,500 were sail boats including 300 to 400 Shetland ones, and c. 300 steam drifters which were mostly from England; final production of cured herrings in that year was 1,024,044 barrels. This production was more than the combined production of the Dutch and German herring fishing vessels operating at the same time at Shetland.

This industry, well spread about Shetland, was based originally on agreed prices between curers and fishermen. But the emergence of steam vessels requiring water in quantity and of the auction system of selling herring led to a rapid centralisation of the industry in Lerwick. In addition to its harbour works, the town could supply water without stint.

For a number of years Lerwick became Britain's seasonal 'herringo-polis', the herring shoals being at their most dense in summer round Shetland. All the herrings were gutted by hand. All except the mere fraction locally consumed were exported. There was a huge influx every summer of female shore workers from Scotland and Ireland, and of fish curers, buyers and their clerical staffs from all over Britain, and a few foreigners as well. The throng of people on Commercial Street, particularly on Saturday nights, became so great that on the gables of buildings along the street there were affixed 'Keep Right' notices which referred, not to vehicles, but to pedestrians.

One effect of this herring boom was an outburst of private building activity. The handsome stone-built residences along the well laid out streets of what is still called the New Town, west below the Hillhead crest, are one result. Another is the imposing Town Hall in Scottish baronial style, surmounting the Hillhead crest, opened in 1883. It was built by public subscription in the form of shares in a specially formed limited liability company with a capital of £4,000, in 2,000 shares of £2 each. The building was put up by a local builder at a cost, excluding stained glass windows and bells, of £3,640. Few things can more vividly illustrate the decline in money value over the past century.

3. LERWICK IN WAR TIME

The herring fishery, enjoying seemingly inexhaustible markets on the European continent, especially in Russia and Germany, continued to flourish until the outbreak of the First World War in 1914 brought it to an abrupt halt.

During that war Lerwick was a minor naval base and port for the examination of foreign ships arrested by the British Navy on suspicion of carrying contraband goods in breach of Britain's naval blockade of Germany. In common with the rest of Shetland the population suffered heavy war casualties at sea and in the fighting in France and other theatres of operation.

After the war the herring fishing was resumed, but it never regained its pristine vigour and steadily declined as foreign markets for various reasons contracted. The Dutch herring fishers also used Bressay Sound less and less and eventually ceased to come just before the outbreak of the Second World War in 1939.

In that war Lerwick played a more complex role. While it was a naval base on an even smaller scale than in the 1914-1918 war, it was the headquarters of the naval, military and air force commands which, with between 20,000 and 30,000 service personnel in the islands, maintained a state of preparedness for a possible air-borne invasion of Shetland by Nazi forces from occupied Norway, directly across the North Sea.

A symbol of this strategy was the appointment for a time early in the war, to over-all command in Shetland, of Admiral of the Fleet the Earl of Cork and Orrery, who with his staff commandeered the Bruce Hostel which had been built for girls from the rural area attending the Lerwick schools.

Based in an office in Lerwick was the British military command of what the Norwegians called 'The Shetland Bus', the traffic in Norwegian refugees and volunteers coming over from Norway to Shetland, all of whom were kept in a detention camp in the north docks area of Lerwick before being sent to England for security screening prior to being set at liberty. The operational base for the 'Shetland Bus', after being a short time at Lunna, was for the duration of the war at Scalloway.

Under entirely separate command, a squadron of Norwegian motor torpedo boats for three years used Lerwick as the base from which to deliver attacks on enemy shipping in Norwegian waters. Norwegian submarines similarly engaged also used Lerwick as base.

It was always a matter of surprise, in view of these activities, that the Nazis did not lay Lerwick waste by bombing. As it was, there were only two or three small air raids on the town, from which there were no casualties. The very few deaths from war activity were due to the explosion of a British sea mine and similar accidents. On the other hand regular visits from Norway by Germany reconnaissance planes kept the Lerwick civil defence on the alert, and there was a total of 220 air raid warnings.

4. LATER FISHING DEVELOPMENTS

Not long before the war Lerwick had been chosen by the British Herring Industry Board as the location for its pilot fish-freezing factory. After the war this activity was resumed and has since been followed by considerable developments in fish-processing, while the Harbour Trust has provided more shelter for fishing boats, many of which today are expensive vessels costing as much as £1,500,000 each.

There was a move away from herring to white fish, and after the war a modern Shetland fishing fleet was rapidly built, manned mainly by whole time all year round fishermen, as distinct from the seasonal fishermen of tradition. The move away from herring was capped by the international three years' ban on herring fishing in the North Sea on account of overfishing, a ban still in force in the Shetland vicinity in November 1982. The two greatest recent changes in the life of Lerwick have been the cessation, for the first time, of herring landings, and the rise of the North Sea oil industry.

In 1937 a fishing boat from Maalöy in Norway adopted Lerwick as its base for regular fishing activity. It was followed by others from the same home port. The war put a stop to this activity for six years, but it was resumed after the war, by boats not only from Maalöy but from other parts of Norway as well, the waters around Shetland providing much richer fishing grounds for some species than these along the Norwegian coast. The number of Norwegian fishermen congregating in Lerwick became so great that the Norwegian Government bought from the Scottish Episcopal Church a seamen's mission building in Lerwick—it had been a unit of the 'Flying Angel' Mission—and established a Norwegian Welfare Centre for Fishermen which came to supplement, for welfare purposes, the much older Lerwick branch, dating from 1928, of the British Royal National Mission to Deep Sea Fishermen. This Welfare Centre also caters for other Scandinavian fishermen, Danes and Swedes,

Plate 5

RERWICK, Dunrossness (early 20th century)

This shows a traditional type of crofting township at harvest time. The houses are largely grouped, and in the walled enclosures in their immediate vicinity cabbage is grown, while the croft land around is in unconsolidated strips. Some of the houses and outbuildings still have the traditional thatched roofs, and prominent are the peat stacks.

(J. D. Ratter. Courtesy Shetland Museum and Library)

Plate 6. HOUSING AT TOLOB, Dunrossness

This contrast between the new and the old shows the recent housing of the oil era with, on the left, a house more than 50 years old.

and in addition Faroese and Icelanders, while the R.N.M.D.S.F. caters for fishermen of any nationality.

For some years the majority of foreign fishermen using the port continued to be Norwegians, most of them from Maalöy, and in 1956 that town proposed that Lerwick should become its friendship town. The invitation was accepted, and from that time there has been a reciprocal series of official, social, sporting and cultural visits between the two towns.

Unfortunately Britain's decision to join the Common Market in 1972 and Norway's decision not to join it have resulted in the E.E.C.'s fishery limit restricting Norwegian fishing boats in Shetland waters, while the growth in size and power of these boats would in any case have made them less dependent on an overseas base.

5. OIL DEVELOPMENT AND LERWICK HARBOUR TRUST

In the early 1970s just when Shetland's own indigenous industries of agriculture, fishing and knitwear were more successful than they had ever been, it became apparent that owing to its geographical position, Shetland would have to be the main landing-place and distribution centre of Britain's vital North Sea oil industry. It was equally apparent that Shetland would also become host to at least some of the oil supply bases which the North Sea drilling rigs and production platforms would require to service them. The choice of Sullom Voe, 30 miles north of Lerwick, as the place for the great oil terminal itself, was made fairly early in the consultations between the Shetland County Council and the oil-producing companies. Meantime Lerwick Harbour Trust, with foresight reminiscent of its predecessors nearly 100 years earlier at the rise of the British herring fishery, bought in 1972 the Grimista estate, which consisted of 1,500 acres of land inland of the northern shores of Bressay Sound on the Lerwick side. The Trust anticipated a demand for land in that area for the construction of oil supply bases, and believed that whoever owned that land could and would dominate Lerwick Harbour. The Trust not only bought the land—an uncharacteristic action for a harbour authority—but also resolved never to sell any of it. It was only to be leased, and that in portions.

The Trust's foresight was fully justified. In a matter of months fifty applications for the purchase of land were received, and every one was refused.

The Trust then proceeded to lease land for the construction of certain oil supply bases, which, along with the Trust's most recent harbour works, have transformed the shores of the north harbour on the Lerwick side from dereliction to maximum modern activity. The construction of the bases has been carried out by the leasing companies, not by the Trust, but the Trust remains owner of the land, and in time (i.e., when the oil industry is finished), the wharves and other works brought into being to form the bases, will revert to the Trust. Meantime the Trust draws revenue from the handling of goods over the wharves of the oil supply bases as if over its own wharves.

On part of its acquired land the Trust, in conjunction with British Petroleum Development Ltd., has established a small industrial estate of 10 sites, two of which have been taken up, while an interest has been shown in another three. The site lies north of the larger industrial estate of 20 sites, all now occupied, established by the Shetland Islands Council.

The Trust's latest commercial venture has been to attract hotel interests for building of a hotel with 72 double bedrooms with attached bathrooms, and modern amenities including a swimming pool. The first sod was cut for the foundations of this building on 22 October 1982, on land overlooking the terminal where the *St Clair* berths.

The Trust has not confined itself to commercial activities. In the north harbour it has recently constructed a sheltered marina for pleasure boats, which is taking the strain off two more southerly small-boat harbours within the main harbour. These small boat harbours are useful to a more varied class of boat; one is owned by a commercial firm, the other by the Trust.

As the foregoing shows, Lerwick Harbour Trust has played and continues to play a major part in the economic life of Lerwick. Although it includes representatives of the Shetland Islands Council, it is completely independent from that or any other local authority, dealing direct with Parliament through successive provisional orders. Its jurisdiction extends over the whole of Bressay Sound, along both shores to high-water mark and outside the two entrances, to the south up to a straight line from near Bressay Lighthouse to the Ness of Sound on Mainland, and to the north, to straight lines from Score Point (on Bressay), to the Green Holm, thence to Hawk's Ness on Mainland, thus taking in all Dales Voe. The total area is approximately 10 square miles of water.

Much of the shipping using Lerwick Harbour at present is oil-related, and is of many different nationalities. A by-product of this on shore is the establishment, dating from 1978, of a branch of the Norwegian Home Ports Mission to Seamen, catering for Norwegian merchant seamen manning Norwegian oil-supply vessels in the harbour, and also for the crews of Norwegian oil-tankers coming into Sullom Voe. This is not to be confused with the Norwegian Welfare Centre.

6. LAND HOLDING

For over a thousand years the basic land law of Shetland has been the udal law derived from Norway, under which owners of land pay no feu duty to any superior. Under this law the majority of property owners in the old town of Lerwick paid no feu duty to anyone. A few who did were called feuars, though their tenure was never in full feudal form. Collectively, however, the two groups together were called the Feuars and Heritors of Lerwick. With the growth of the town of Lerwick, and in order to put an end to dispute and litigations, the heritors of Sound, west of Lerwick, on the one hand, and the Feuars and Heritors of Lerwick, on the other hand, in 1815, 1816 and 1817, carried out a number of exchanges of properties which gave the Feuars and Heritors of Lerwick title over the ground between the Hillhead crest and the ground to the west terminated by the present Burgh Road, which was designated the official boundary when the town was made a burgh of barony in 1818.

The Feuars and Heritors of Lerwick thus became proprietors of the ground over which any expansion of the town was bound to be carried out, and in 1862, when the need became clamant, they organised the town plan which underlies the well laid out streets of the New Town—St Olaf Street, King Harald Street and Burgh Road. They both feued and sold sites which include those of certain important public buildings, such as the former Lerwick Central School (now a community centre), and the original Gilbert Bain Hospital, as well as the sites of private houses.

The Feuars and Heritors did not, however, retain the money they received as private income: they used it as a common good fund. Right up to the 1970s they annually disbursed grants to applicants, most of them local voluntary organisations, and they also took over from the Town Hall Company the liquidation of the outstanding debt on the building of the Town Hall.

To commemorate the Silver Jubilee of King George V, in 1935 they presented to the Town Council the two fields below the Hillhead crest to the west, to be recreation parks for the community. These lie between St Olaf Street and King Harald Street and had previously been used for grazing sheep. Many years passed, including those of the Second World War (when the fields were used for military encampments), before this project was realised, but in September 1953, three months after the coronation of Her Majesty Queen Elizabeth II, her consort, Philip, Duke of Edinburgh, formally opened the two King George V Fields. The northern one is devoted to children, with swings, chutes and other facilities. The southern one is a horticultural garden with tennis court, bowling and putting greens.

As the feu duties could not be changed, the rapid decline in the value of money and the emergence of lavish government grants diminished steadily the place in the community of the Feuars and Heritors. Then in 1974 the Land Tenure Reform Act, which enabled feuars to redeem their feus, signalled the end of the extremely useful public function which the Feuars and Heritors of Lerwick had for so long carried out. Almost all the feuars redeemed their feus.

7. GROWTH OF THE TOWN

From the time that Lerwick was made a burgh of barony in 1818 until well after the First World War, Lerwick covered a small peninsula about half a mile square east of the Burgh Road line. The first boundary extension, in 1938, went west to take in Clickimin Loch, then north and north-easterly to the north entrance to Bressay Sound at the Green Head, thus taking in the houses and farm of Grimista, overlooking the north harbour. The town then covered an area measuring a mile and a quarter from west to east by two and a half miles from south to north. The second extension in 1965 has already been described. It adds a big area including the Ness of Sound with its farm (the green-belt area), the Geophysical Observatory, and the Sandy Loch, which supplies Lerwick with its water. The westward spread of the town is not even, but it is approaching the eastern shore of the Sandy Loch.

One result of this urban growth has been the disappearance of most of the dairy farming which used to ring the town. Old crofts in the Sound area which used to supply milk disappeared years ago, as also did some small dairy farms practically in the town. The biggest farm to disappear was the farm of Grimista, whose fields are now used for open-air storage of pipes for the oil industry. The only farm left within the latest burgh boundary is the Ness of Sound farm, a dairy one. Apart from it, Lerwick depends for its milk supply on rural Shetland farms, supplemented in winter by milk imported from Aberdeen.

8. Place and street names

The place and street names have a definite Norse appearance. 'Lerwick' has already been explained and is paralleled by the same town name in Norway and Faroe. Grimista is from Grims-stathir, the dwelling-place of a man called Grim.

Scandinavian visitors are often struck by some of the street names—St Olaf Street, St Sunniva Street, King Harald Street, King Erik Street, King Haakon Street—the work mainly of the historically-minded generation who built the Town Hall and adorned it with stained-glass windows which outline the history of Shetland in the long Norse era up to the pawning of the islands to Scotland in 1469.

At the same time the same generation did full justice to the con-temporary British royal family by naming the main pier of the then new harbour works Victoria Pier, two wharves Albert and Alexandra, and a street Prince Alfred.

Political leaders are commemorated in Pitt Lane, Fox Lane and Gladstone Terrace, while local celebrities are remembered in Haldane Burgess Crescent, Anderson Road and Cheyne Crescent.

9. Antiquities and historic buildings

Lerwick has ancient monuments listed by the Royal Commission. The oldest and most notable is the prehistoric Broch of Clickimin (List No. 1246) on the seaward side of the fresh-water loch of the same name, already several times mentioned, which discharges into the sea at the

Bight of Clickimin, the inner end of the wide Brei Wick. It is in a comparatively good state of preservation, though not as complete as the best-preserved of all the brochs which is on the island of Mousa, also in Shetland. The Clickimin broch is of wider diameter than the Mousa one and has moreover outer works peculiar to itself. It formerly had a perfect natural setting away from other buildings at the edge of the loch, but municipal house-building to the east, and still more private house-building nearer to the west, have altered the background adversely. Under the Shetland Islands Council's Lerwick Local Plan a limit has been set to the western house-building and the backdrop of natural hill to the north is being preserved.

The other outstanding ancient monument in Lerwick is Fort Charlotte (List No. 1244) already described. Owing to its completeness it is undergoing a major operation of restoration back to its original state under H.M. Department of the Environment.

Another Lerwick building listed by the Commission in its 1946 Inventory is No. 99 Commercial Street (List No. 1245) dating from the early 18th century, once a house, now part of business premises.

Further south along Commercial Street are other old buildings not included in the Inventory. The Red Cross headquarters was originally the 18th century Tolbooth, and in it Sir Walter Scott and companions were entertained to dinner in 1814, during their visit on board the Lighthouse Commissioners' yacht.

An 18th century house with crow-stepped gables, No. 10 Commercial Street, at present being restored as a private house, was the residence of Patrick Torry, founder of the local lodge of Freemasons (Lodge Morton 89).

What is believed to be the oldest house in Lerwick, dating from about 1690, still inhabited and in first-class condition, is No. 9 Commercial Street, known as the Old Manse because once lived in for a time by a parish minister. Mr Tom Henderson, first curator of the Shetland Museum and ex-Convener of the County, lived in it till his sudden death on 15 October 1982.

On an elevation just beyond the south end of Commercial Street is the building for widows of fishermen and seamen built in 1865 by Arthur Anderson in memory of his wife, who had suggested it. It is near the school he had donated in 1862. For long called the Widows' Asylum or Homes, it was renamed the Anderson Homes when the Town Council took it over and renovated it in 1970.

Just over one and a half miles north-west stands the birthplace of Arthur Anderson, the 'Böd' or Booth of Grimista, of uncertain date. When he was born there in 1792 his father was in charge of it on behalf of the estate owner to deal with the fishermen engaged in the 'haaf' fishing, and to supervise the beach drying of salted fish. The building is being restored and will be made into a historical showpiece through the fund-raising efforts of a voluntary committee, helped financially by individual donors, by the Government, the P. & O. Company, The Pilgrim Trust, the Highlands and Islands Development Board, the Shetland Islands Council, and Mr Fred Olsen, the Norwegian shipping magnate and owner of the Norscot oil supply base at the Green Head.

A late 18th century building of Georgian architecture is Annsbrae House, once the residence of an estate owner. It is owned by the Shetland Islands Council, and is due to be adapted for the accommodation of long-stay mental patients returning to Shetland from mental hospitals in the south.

Under the Town and Country Planning (Scotland) Act, 1972, Section 52, there are a number of Listed Buildings in Lerwick, including those recorded as already stated by the Ancient Monuments Commission. They cannot be altered or demolished without the consent of the Secretary of State for Scotland. One, the Broch of Clickimin, is in category A, and so of National importance. The letter 's' after Category C means 'statutory'. The list is as follows:

Conservation Area

Commercial Street		The Old Manse	C (s)
,,	,,	2-8 (Copelands)	B
,,	,,	10	B
,,	,,	14 (Sea Door)	B
,,	,,	18 (Steamer Store)	B
,,	,,	The Lodberrie	B
,,	,,	Quendale House	C (s)
,,	,,	41-43 (Lochend)	B
,,	,,	47	B
,,	,,	49 & 1-3 Chromate Lane (Seafield)	B
,,	,,	Queen's Hotel	B
,,	,,	Old Tolbooth	B
,,	,,	67 & 1 Church Lane	B
,,	,,	Royal Bank of Scotland	B
,,	,,	1 Hayfield Court, Commercial Street	C (s)
,,	,,	25, 27, 29	C (s)
,,	,,	69, 69A, 71, 73	C (s)
,,	,,	93/95 (Jamiesons)	B
,,	,,	97/99 (White's)	B
,,	,,	101 (Laing's)	B
,,	,,	103 (Peter Barclay's)	B
,,	,,	115/117 (Bank of Scotland)	B
,,	,,	Fort Charlotte	B
Greenfield Place		2-4	B
,,	,,	St Magnus' Episcopal Church	B
Hillhead		St Ringans U.F. Church	B
,,		County Buildings	C (s)
,,		Town Hall	B
,,		Lerwick Parish Kirk (St. Columba's)	B
,,		Annsbrae House & 1 & 2 Annsbrae Place	B
Esplanade		Greig's Kloss & Lodberry	C (s)

Outside conservation area

Anderson High School	C (s)
Böd of Grimista	B
Broch of Clickimin	A
Hay's Dock & Store-House, Freefield	C (s)
North Ness House	C (s)

10. LIBRARY AND MUSEUM

While the history of the Shetland Library goes back to the 19th century, the museum was only opened in 1966, in a new building housing both it on the upper floor and the library on the ground floor. Among the museum exhibits are replicas of the silver objects making up the St Ninian's Isle Treasure, discovered in 1958 during archaeological excavations on the isle by a team of Aberdeen University students under the late Professor Andrew C. O'Dell. Subsequently Aberdeen University lost a law-suit in the Court of Session in an endeavour to get the original treasure placed in the Shetland Museum instead of in the National Museum of Antiquities in Edinburgh, where it now is.

Within the library is a special Shetland Room, containing collections of Shetland and northern books and papers. The biggest collection of books within this room is that of the late Edwin Seymour Reid Tait.

The most important repository of records is the quite separate archives department, established in 1976. It has the most modern equipment and a room where members of the public can consult records.

Two of its collections of papers are quite exceptional. One is Sheriff Court records, kept in Lerwick instead of Edinburgh by special leave. The other is Shetland presbytery and kirk session records kept in Lerwick instead of Edinburgh by special sanction of the General Assembly of the Church of Scotland.

Other notable collections are the Bruce of Sumburgh papers and the Reid Tait manuscript collections, including his comprehensive bibliography of published Shetland material. The best known and most popular local history is *Lerwick During the Last Half Century* by Thomas Manson. It first appeared in 1917 as a series of weekly articles in the weekly *Shetland News*, of which the author was editor and proprietor. Published in book form in 1923, it is in constant demand at the library and second-hand copies fetch big prices at book sales.

Valuable material for Lerwick history is provided in E. S. Reid Tait's *Lerwick Miscellany* and in sections in different volumes of his *Hjaltland Miscellany*.

Arthur Anderson: A Founder of the P. & O. Company is a short biography by the late John Nicolson, published in 1914 and reissued in 1932.

Sir Robert Stout, successively Prime Minister and Chief Justice of New Zealand, who was born in Lerwick in 1844, is the subject of a biography by Waldo Hilary Dunn and Ivor L. M. Richardson, published in New Zealand in 1961.

The Memoirs of Arthur Laurenson by Catherine Stafford Spence, published in 1901, preserves the letters and literary material of a Lerwick man who played a big part in educational and cultural affairs in the second half of the 19th century.

A biographical memoir by T. M. Y. Manson of Haldane Burgess of Lerwick, the blind author, linguist, teacher and socialist, was published in 1979 in the fourth edition of his most popular book of Shetland verse, *Rasmie's Büddie*. Lerwick has its place in many books about Shetland, by both local and southern writers.

11. POPULATION

The figures of population given below for the census years including 1961, are not the official census figures, but the figures produced by the late Dr Robert S. Barclay, an Orcadian specialist in this field who was on the staff of H.M. Register House, Edinburgh. They were published in 1967 in *The Shetland Book*, edited by A. T. Cluness, and issued by the Zetland Education Committee. Just as today the Research and Development Department of Shetland Islands Council has found it necessary to correct official figures in respect of temporary oil industry workers, so Dr Barclay in his time found it necessary to correct some official figures in respect of temporary fish workers and persons on board ship. The figures for 1971, 1981 and September 1982, are based on registrations under the National Health Service supplied by the Shetland Health Board to the Research and Development Department. The figures for the whole of Shetland are here given side by side with those for Lerwick:

Date	Lerwick	Shetland	
1790s	903	20,186	
1801		22,379	
1811		22,915	
			Burgh boundary set 1818
1821	2,224	26,145	
1831	2,750	29,392	
1841	2,787	30,558	
1851	2,870	31,044	
1861	3,143	31,579	Shetland's peak population
1871	3,655	31,371	
1881	3,801	29,149	
1891	4,216	28,241	
1901	4,803	27,736	
1911	5,533	27,238	
			1914-18 war
1921	5,137	24,117	
1931	5,118	21,229	
			1939-45 war; burgh extension 1938

| 1951 | 5,450 | 19,102 |
| 1961 | 5,678 | 17,483 |

Burgh boundary extended 1965

1971	6,127	17,327
1981	7,255	23,130
1982 (September)	7,356	23,307

It will be seen from the foregoing that despite Shetland's steady population decline for 110 years from the zenith in 1861 to the nadir in 1971, Lerwick's population rose on the whole steadily, with one prolonged dip between the two world wars; but that Shetland's dramatic rise by a third in the recent decade 1971-81 was not matched by Lerwick, which rose only by a little over one-sixth in the same period.

These facts suggest that the steady pressure of migration from the rural districts to the town for over a century saved Lerwick from Shetland's general decline, which was due very largely to steady emigration from Shetland rather than to a natural decrease; but that recent increased employment and immigration into Shetland, with ensuing natural increase, has fortunately spread to rural areas as well as to Lerwick, the population of which is now (September 1982) less than a third of the total—a better balance.

The population of Lerwick is mixed. Very few if any of native Shetland stock can trace their ancestry in Lerwick further back than two generations. A great many are themselves actual incomers, from rural districts, from Scotland, England, Wales, Ireland and in individual cases other countries, notably Norway.

Although the detailed 1981 census figures have not so far been published, advance sheets received give the population of Lerwick as 7,147, or 108 fewer than the medical registrations, the males being given as 3,438 and the females as 3,709. The breakdown into age groups, without distinction of sex, is as follows:

Ages	Numbers	Ages	Numbers
0-4	520	45-49	368
5-9	495	50-54	377
10-14	565	55-59	362
15-19	628	60-64	303
20-24	561	65-69	313
25-29	528	70-74	281
30-34	505	75-79	192
35-39	508	80-84	120
40-44	413	85 +	108

Total 7,147

This shows a very even distribution among the age groups. It also shows that there were 2,208 under 20 years of age and 1,014 who were 65 and over, leaving 3,925 aged 20 to 64, the most economically active age group.

PUBLIC AND SOCIAL SERVICES

In 1975, under the national reorganisation of local government, Lerwick Town Council disappeared along with all other town and city councils. The two-tier system of local government was not, however, applied to Shetland; this was thanks to strong resistance from Shetland itself, supported by Orkney and the Western Isles. Each group of islands was given a single authority, vested for most purposes with both regional and district powers. As a consequence, Lerwick is now administered by Shetland Islands Council.

The responsibilities of local government for the whole islands, including constant surveillance over the giant North Sea oil industry, the improvement of roads, and the building of new schools and special housing schemes for a rapidly rising population, has forced the Islands Council to create more departments with bigger staffs than would otherwise have been required, and they are all in Lerwick. No single building houses them all, nor is there any readily identifiable space for one that could. They are housed in nearly a dozen office blocks scattered over the town, while the Council and its committees meet in the Town Hall, formerly the preserve of the now defunct Town Council. All hospitals and the Health Board offices are in Lerwick. There is a massive building that houses central government offices. Add to this a dozen churches, two community centres, a theatre, a cinema, several lesser public halls, a public swimming pool and five recreation areas, and it can be realised what pressure there is on space in Lerwick.

To prevent this pressure destroying the character of the burgh steps were taken in 1975 to create a conservation area in the original town, which the Government designated an outstanding conservation area, while a secondary conservation area has been designated.

Many, though not all, of the public and social services are provided for Lerwick in common with the rest of Shetland, by the Shetland Islands Council.

The design work for council housing, school buildings, roads, streets and street lighting, drainage, sewage, water schemes, burial grounds, is all done in the Department of Design and Technical Services; while the actual varied work is carried out by or under the Construction Department, special contractors being used for school and house building.

As already mentioned, Lerwick's water, both for the population and for industry, comes from the Sandy Loch, just inside the western burgh boundary. In order to cope with the rising demand, the level of the loch was raised by the construction of a new dam in 1974. The water, being peaty, is rendered clear by chemical treatment.

The modern means of power and light is electric, Lerwick getting its share of the electricity generated in the expanding power station at Grimista. This is a diesel station which is run at a loss by the North of Scotland Hydro-Electric Board, and uses diesel oil imported by sea.

Plans to procure power from the much bigger gas-fired power station in the oil terminal at Sullom Voe have so far not come to fruition.

Imported coal, and peat cut in the hinterland of the town or further afield, are still largely used as well as electricity and oil; indeed owing to the rising costs there has recently been a reversion to peat in many cases; but there is no use of any form of North Sea oil.

There is now no piped gas in Lerwick, though there used to be. Some bottled gas is used.

Education is run under the Education Department of the Shetland Islands Council and the Scottish Education Department, with a Director of Education in Lerwick. Since 1975 eleven new schools have been built in Shetland, most of them replacements for older schools. Lerwick's share has been one new additional school, a primary one, and additions to the two other schools.

Of the three schools in Lerwick, one is a comprehensive secondary, and two are of primary status. There is a further education centre, and evening continuation classes.

The comprehensive secondary is the Anderson High School. As the Anderson Educational Institute it was of both primary and secondary levels, right up to University entrance level, from 1862 to 1902, when the Lerwick Central School was opened to cater for primary pupils. It was an educationally selective secondary school from 1902 to 1970, when it became comprehensive secondary and its name was changed. It has been three times enlarged, in 1924, 1964 and again since 1970. It has a school roll now of 1,024 and a staff of 74 full-time and 19 part-time teachers. It takes all post-primary Lerwick pupils and pupils from the age of 14 from the seven rural junior high schools, the course for the first two years being common to all eight high schools. There is some fear that the Education (Scotland) Act, 1981, may undermine this particular system, which was practically wrested from an obdurate Government in the 1960s on strong social arguments. The Act referred to confers on parents the right to choice of school. Already there have been a few cases of parents in Shetland exercising this right. For the change to comprehensive secondary in 1970, the extension to the school was planned for a school roll of 750, so that the school, overtaken by the influx of population due to the oil boom, is grossly over-crowded and is using some 'temporary' huts. To relieve some of the pressure on it, Brae Junior High School has been upgraded to four-year secondary level, with the great help of a brand-new secondary school building opened in 1982.

Attached to the Anderson High School is the Lerwick Further Education Centre with six departments for engineering, machine-knitting, business studies, carpentry and joinery, catering and liberal studies. It has a staff of 14 all told, including the headmaster of the Anderson High School part-time.

Also attached to the Anderson High School are two hostels for rural pupils attending it—the Bruce Hostel for Girls, dating from 1923 but recently enlarged, and the Janet Courtney Hostel for Boys, also recently enlarged, but dating from the Second World War, during which, newly constructed but not under way as a hostel, it was used by the Royal Air Force as operational headquarters for Shetland.

The Bell's Brae Primary School, built in 1957 and enlarged in 1975, has a roll of 492 pupils and a staff of 27.

The Sound Primary School, built in 1977, has a roll of 313 pupils and a staff of 17. As a municipal scheme of houses is being built near to it, the school is due to be enlarged. These two schools replace the former Central School and Infant School.

HEALTH SERVICES

The health services in Shetland are the responsibility of the Shetland Health Board, which is advised regarding public attitudes by the Shetland Local Health Council. The services comprise the New Gilbert Bain Hospital, which has general, surgical and maternity sections; and three geriatric hospitals, the Brevik, Montfield and Old Gilbert Bain. There are 73 beds in the New Gilbert Bain Hospital; of these 44 are for general surgery, 18 for general medicine, and 11 for obstetrics.

The Montfield Hospital was originally built after the First World War as a sanatorium but is no longer needed for that purpose, and has been for many years a geriatric hospital. At the time of writing a very big addition to this hospital is under construction which will enable it to become the one and only geriatric hospital; it will also have a day wing.

When this work is complete, the Brevik Hospital will be converted for nurse training, staff training, staff accommodation and occupational health. It was originally, in the late 19th and early 20th centuries, the Poorhouse.

The Old Gilbert Bain Hospital was the first general and surgical hospital, presented to Shetland in 1902 by the two sisters of Gilbert Bain, member of an old Lerwick family, though himself born and brought up abroad and later resident in Edinburgh. It has been a geriatric hospital since it was replaced by the New Gilbert Bain Hospital in 1961. Its future after closure is uncertain.

There is a Health Centre containing the surgeries of the six Lerwick general practitioners and the chiropodist.

There is one dental practice shared by two partners in Lerwick, and one school dentist who is also the Chief Administrative Dental Officer.

There are two consultant surgeons in the New Gilbert Bain Hospital, which takes in many casualties from ships, fishing boats, and oil rigs and production platforms, these last being brought in by helicopter. For years the Lerwick doctors went out on call by helicopter to the rigs, though their services have been less required since the oil industry appointed their own doctors.

Closely allied to the services provided under the Shetland Health

Board are the services provided under the Shetland Islands Council—a Senior Citizens' Centre; two eventide homes, the Viewforth and the Kanterstead; the Eric Gray Day Training Centre for the Handicapped at Kanterstead; the Laburnum Hostel for the Mentally Handicapped; the Leog Home for Children (especially for children from broken homes); and the Advice Centre for Alcoholics. The Shetland Branch of Alcoholics Anonymous meets in the Eric Gray Centre.

As already stated, Annsbrae House is due to be converted for returned long-stay mental patients.

The Veterinary Surgeon is based in Lerwick.

COUNCIL AND OTHER OFFICES

All the departments of the Shetland Islands Council have public offices in Lerwick, each in a different building. They include—Chief Executive and staff (in the Town Hall); Administration, Finance, Education, Planning, Research and Development, Design and Technical Services, Construction, Housing and Protective Services (weights and measures, sanitation and consumer protection), Leisure and Recreation, Careers Services and Personnel.

In a big new building called Charlotte House on Commercial Road, Lerwick, are housed the local offices of the following central government departments: Department of Agriculture and Fisheries for Scotland, Crofters Commission, Social Security Office, H.M. Customs and Excise, Mercantile Marine Office, Unemployment Benefit Office, Department of Employment (Job Centre).

In yet another building is the Shetland area office of the Highlands and Islands Development Board.

VALUATION

The Assessor and Electoral Registration Officer for both Orkney and Shetland is in Lerwick.

THE COURT

The only court in Shetland is the Sheriff Court in Lerwick, the police court conducted by magistrates having disappeared along with the Town Council in 1975. The Shetland Islands Council decided to have no district court.

Shetland is in the sheriffdom of Grampian, Highland and Islands. The Sheriff at both Lerwick and Kirkwall has been the same since 1968 and lives in Lerwick, travelling regularly to Kirkwall for court sittings there. He had previously been sheriff-substitute at Lerwick since 1961, another sheriff-substitute being at Kirkwall, as had always been the case.

POLICE AND FIRE SERVICES

Lerwick has both the headquarters of the Shetland sub-division of the Northern Constabulary based in Inverness, and the Lerwick Fire Brigade, which is a unit of the Northern Fire Brigade, also based in Inverness.

The Shetland police force, under a chief inspector, is one of approximately 40 officers.

Although there are a very few smaller fire-fighting units in the rural areas, the Lerwick Fire Brigade travels all over Shetland when called.

HOUSING

For a very long time Lerwick has been a magnet for rural people wanting to settle in the town—a world-wide phenomenon—and beginning immediately after the First World War Lerwick Town Council with Government help assiduously promoted one municipal house-building scheme after another, though it never succeeded in wiping out the waiting lists for houses.

In November 1982 there was a total of 2,596 houses in Lerwick. Of these 1,149 were private; 11 were the products of the Hjaltland Housing Association, a non-profit-making Government-subsidised building organisation; 1,317 were local authority, i.e., Council houses; and 119 were houses built by the Scottish Special Housing Association, and administered by the Council.

Not counting kitchens and bathrooms, but taking one-apartment to mean a bed-sitting room, two-apartment a sitting room and one bedroom, etc., the make-up according to apartments was as follows:

Apartments	Private	Hjaltland	S.I.C.	S.S.H.A.	Total
1	4	3	55	—	62
2	66	—	115	—	181
3	258	3	567	60	888
4	348	—	514	59	921
5	219	4	66	—	289
6	105	—	—	—	105
7	44	1	—	—	45
8 and more	61	—	—	—	61
Caravans	44	—	—	—	44
	1,149	11	1,317	119	2,596

The private houses included 66 formerly of Shetland Islands Council and 15 formerly of the Scottish Special Housing Association, or 81 all told, sold to tenants under the Tenants' Rights, etc. (Scotland) Act, 1980. The local authority had been usually, though not always, opposed to the sale of council houses.

Included in the local authority houses are 29 'sheltered' houses in two groups: 20 at Leog, comprising sixteen one-apartment and four two-apartment houses; and nine Brevik Cottages in Burgh Road, old cottages renovated to provide six one-apartment and three two-apartment houses.

Each group includes the house of a warden, with whom all the other occupants are in communication by telephone in case of need.

There is very little overcrowding in Lerwick. A formula based on assumption of 3·5 persons per house suggests less than one person per room.

Most of the houses, both private and council, are of traditional type, the older ones built of stone, a few of stone and brick, and the great majority of concrete block. The council houses include 40 Cruden houses built of steel with concrete panels and 38 Swedish timber houses. There are a few private Norwegian-type timber houses. Most houses have gardens, including many beautiful ones. All the old lane houses had drying greens.

While private house-building has little effect one way or another on the sense of community, council housing down the years has had two opposite effects. Former inhabitants of the densely packed lanes in the old town, who moved or were moved to council houses in the open, miss the very close sense of community which they had in the lanes but have never been able to recapture. On the other hand the two most recent council housing developments are so far west and north of the main town, and so far from each other, that they have created two new communities, as is evidenced by the rise of the Sound Community Association and the North Staney Hill Community Association, each with public-hall facilities. At Sound these are in conjunction with the primary school, though plans have been made for a separate community hall.

Six building societies are now represented in Lerwick. It was an innovation when three of them established their own offices in the town during the oil construction phase. The Shetland Islands Council is empowered to lend and sometimes does lend for house-building when the building societies are unwilling: the council does not normally lend for this purpose. The influence of building societies has thus been on the increase, but whether the influence is continuing to increase or not is uncertain.

Shetland Islands Council at present is continuing the old Town Council's policy of municipal house-building for the town: there is still a waiting list of between 200 and 300. Another chronic waiting list of nearly 150 is that of the homeless under the Housing (Homeless Persons) Act of 1977. This is because during the construction phase of the Sullom Voe oil terminal Shetland became an area of full employment and therefore a magnet to people from the south seeking jobs, many of whom came north without having work arranged. Their plight is probably the worst single problem of the Council's Housing Department. It has permanently housed 150 out of 282 applicants.

INDUSTRY AND COMMERCE

It is never easy to disentangle industry and commerce, and that is especially the case with the biggest factor in the economic life of Lerwick, namely, the activities of Lerwick Harbour Trust. It is mainly through the Trust that a share of Shetland's new indigenous industry, the North Sea oil industry, has been established in Lerwick. Four oil supply bases are at work in the harbour on land leased from the Trust. The biggest of these, one of the bigger ones in Britain, is the nine-berth base at the Green Head, the north entrance to the harbour, established by Norscot Oil Services, a part of the oil division of the shipping line owned by the Norwegian Fred Olsen.

Next in size, just inside the north harbour, is the three-berth base established by the British company Ocean Inchcape Limited. Both these bases are open to business from anyone.

Two smaller bases at Holmsgarth working exclusively for their respective owners are the bases established by Shell U.K. Exploration and Production and British Petroleum Development. The Shell base is the principal bulk supplier to the Brent, Cormorant, Dunlin and North Cormorant oil fields. B.P. have built on their base a large warehouse from which the sea servicing of the Magnus field, the furthest north one, will be carried out from 1983.

The tonnage of goods handled in 1981 over wharves, including both the Trust's own wharves and those of the oil supply bases, can be seen from the following table, the figures being in tonnes.

From Rigs	9,646·3
To Rigs	73,489·4
From Production Platforms	46,317·2
To Production Platforms	312,012·5
From Lay Barges	5,168·7
To Lay Barges	31,593·7
P. & O. Out	34,537·0
P. & O. In	61,336·2
General Out	23,047·6
General In	141,369·0
Oil Related Exports	15,786·0
Oil Related Imports	233,715·4
Total	988,019·5

During 1981, apart from the Shetland fishing fleet, 3,579 vessels entered the harbour, 173 fewer than in 1980, with 1,713,410 net registered tonnage, an *increase* of 90,093 net registered tons over 1980, but with 3,523,830 gross registered tonnage, a *decrease* of 47,934 gross registered tons from 1980.

Plate 7. DELLING TEAMS (probably c. 1900)

The traditional method of working croft land in Shetland was by teams of three or four (which often included women) turning the soil downhill by spade.

(Courtesy Shetland Museum and Library)

Plate 8

TRACTOR PLOUGHING

In the modern period the easier modern methods have been use to turn the soil, although the amount of land now actually cultivated has greatly declined.

(J. Peterson, A.R.P.S. Courtesy Shetland Museum and Library)

The gross income of the harbour trust in 1981 (a record year) was £2·1 million, but that was already passed in 1982 in November. In 1971, the authorised borrowing powers of the trust was limited to £140,000; today they are £7 million, and negotiations are under way with the government to raise them to £10 million.

The fish landings at Lerwick during 1981, shown by method of capture, were as follows:

Method	Arrivals	Tonnes	Value (£)
Pair Trawl under 80 ft.	88	288·92	73,897
Seine Net	883	2,743·75	805,397
Industrial Trawl (all sand eels)	1,384	40,671·55	1,172,342
Light Trawl	925	3,453·13	992,799
Purse Seine Herring	11	828·80	44,228
Purse Seine Mackerel	10	787·40	47,244
Single Boat Pelagic Trawl (mackerel)	1	38·60	2,316
Scallop Dredging	84	24·28	19,871
Creel Fishing	263	4·56	5,858
Shell Fishing by Hand	—	11·63	2,227
	2,265	48,852.62	3,166,179

FOREIGN LANDINGS

Industrial Trawl	1	1·08	299

The weights given are landed weights (as opposed to live weights).

The numbers of foreign fishing vessels using the harbour, which are included in the total of vessels apart from Shetland fishing fleet, were as follows: 117 Danish, 96 Norwegian, 14 Faroese, 13 French, 2 Icelandic, 2 Polish, 1 Swedish and 1 German.

In 1981 the Lerwick section of the Shetland fishing fleet of 124 vessels comprised 10 boats: included were one purse-net/trawler, eight seine-net/trawlers and one trawler. On shore three fish-processing firms run four freezing factories, one of which concentrates on shell-fish. With the continuing ban on herring fishing, no herrings are frozen meantime; landings are now confined to white fish, shell fish and sand eels. Across on Bressay a fish-meal factory takes sand-eels, surplus fish and fish offal; it is mainly Norwegian owned, but there is a minority share of Scottish capital.

In Lerwick a slipway with associated marine engineering facilities provides the fishing boats and other craft with a service of repair and maintenance. There is some building of small boats in the town, but no shipbuilding.

The catching side of the fishing industry has been virtually unaffected by oil development; however the processing factories lost some of their labour for a time, but are now back to their former strength. The knitwear industry has suffered, largely owing to the attraction for women knitters of the high wages offered by the oil industry for domestic work at the two special villages created by the Council for the construction workers at Sullom Voe. As one consequence a knitwear factory specially built in 1949 and at one time employing as many as 30 hand-frame knitters in the building, as well as out-workers, is now a provision merchant's wholesale warehouse. For rather different reasons (declining markets and aging of the workers) weaving, once a small industry in Lerwick, has now quite disappeared. A small knitwear factory using power-driven machinery, is however, active. It is comparatively new.

Yet, as the lists set out below show, there is a great variety of work in Lerwick. On 14 October 1982, the last occasion on which official unemployment figures included (as well as claimants) people registered for work but not claiming benefit, Lerwick's rate of unemployment was estimated by the local Department of Employment office to be between 1 per cent and 2 per cent, when the rate for Shetland as a whole was 6·4 per cent, the national rate was 13·8 per cent, and the rate for Scotland was 15·8 per cent.

Shetland's one weekly newspaper *The Shetland Times*, one quarterly magazine *The New Shetlander*, the largest monthly magazine *Shetland Life*, and one community broadcasting radio, Radio Shetland, are all produced in Lerwick. Newspapers arrive daily by air, weather permitting, and are on sale in Lerwick on the day of publication.

As the appended lists show, there is a great variety of work, recreation and cultural activity in Lerwick. The scale of motor traffic is but one symptom of that. These conditions, taken together with virtual full employment, mean that Lerwick is an exceedingly fortunate town at the time of writing. Life in Lerwick has a very brisk tempo.

At the same time there is hardly such a thing as Lerwick civic pride. Lerwick people think all the time of Shetland, and make no distinction between the other inhabitants of the islands and themselves. Shetland's problems, and its distinctive characteristics, such as the dialect, hold the attention of the people of Lerwick. This has been accentuated by the constant improvements in internal communications, the responsibility thrust on the one council, the formidable nature of the questions posed by the oil industry, and the disagreements in Europe and in Britain over fishery policy.

The following lists, divided in a very arbitrary manner between industry and commerce, show the numbers of firms and shops and organisations in the different categories in Lerwick. The great majority of firms and shops are independent units. In some cases the same shop appears in different categories, but very few are branches of one concern. The oldest firm, however, has branches in several categories.

Industrial firms

Agricultural Engineers	2	Net Manufacturer and Repairer	1
Bakers	2	Newspaper Publishers	1
Blacksmiths	2	Periodical Publishers	3
Builders	15	Oil Company (B.P.)	1
Building Societies	6	Oil and Natural Gas Exploration	
Bus and Coach Servicing	2	Companies	3
Carpenters and Joiners	10	Oil and Natural Gas Field	
Central Heating Engineers	1	Services	20
Contractors, Plant and Machinery		Oil Service Bases	4
Hire and Sale	12	Petrol Pump Filling Stations	4
Craft Product Manufacturers and		Plasterer	1
Retailers	6	Plumbers	2
Development Agencies	6	Post Offices	2
Diesel Engineers	2	Printers	3
Diving Service	1	Radio Broadcasters (Radio	
Electrical Contractors	10	Shetland and Decca Navigation)	2
Employment Agencies	2	Refrigeration Engineers	2
Explosives Engineers	2	Scrap Metal Merchants	1
Fish Processors	3	Security Service	1
Furniture Manufacturer	1	Shellfish Processors	1
Gas Appliances and Bottled Gas	3	Shipbuilders and Repairers	1
Glazier	1	Shipping Companies and Agents	6
Haulage Contractors	6	Taxis	20
Ice Merchant	1	Timber Merchant	1
Knitwear Manufacturers and		Tourist Office	1
Knitted Goods Distributors	18	Travel Agent	1
Marine Engineers	3	Tyre Distributors and Dealers	1
Mechanical Engineers	3	Welding Equipment	1
Motor and Mechanical Repairs	3		

Commercial firms

Accountants	4	Carpet Retailers	3
Agricultural Supplier	2	Caterers	4
Architects	4	Chemists (Dispensing)	3
Auctioneers	2	Chamber of Commerce	1
Bakers' Shops	3	China and Glassware	4
Banks	4	Cinema	1
Bathroom and Kitchen Equipment	3	Civil Engineers	9
Beer, Wine and Spirits (Wholesale)	3	Cleaning and Maintenance	5
Boat and Small Craft Sales	4	Coach and Minibus Hire	1
Booksellers	3	Coal Merchant	1
Builders' Merchants	5	Confectioners and Tobacconists	
Business Consultant	1	(Retail)	10
Butchers	7	Confectioners and Tobacconists	
Cafes	6	(Wholesale)	2
Car and Van Hire	11	Customs Agent	1
Caravan Accessories	1	Cycle Shop	1
Cargo Handling	2	Dairy	1

Delivery Service	1	Jewellery Retailers	5
DIY Shops	3	Ladies' Wear (Retail)	12
Drapers	6	Leather Shops	2
Dressmakers	2	Meat Wholesaler	1
Driving Schools	2	Men's Wear Shops	5
Drycleaners and Laundries	2	Monumental Agent	1
Electrical Retailers	8	Motor Cycle Sales	2
Electrolysis Firm	1	Newsagents	4
Electronic Equipment	5	Off Licence	1
Fancy Goods Retailers	8	Office Equipment and Supplies	3
Fire Extinguishers, etc.	2	Opticians	2
Fish and Chip Shops	3	Paint and Wallpaper Supplies	4
Fish Merchants	2	Painters and Decorators	8
Fish Salesman	1	Photographers	4
Florist	2	Photographic Retailers	3
Frozen Food Wholesalers and		Public Houses	5
Retailers	4	Quantity Surveyors	2
Funeral Undertaker	1	Record and Tape Retailers	8
Furniture Retailers	4	Recording Services	2
Garage Services	13	Removals and Storage	1
Garden Shop	1	Restaurants	3
General and Grocery Stores	10	Sauna and Solarium	1
Greengrocery and Fruit	8	Ship Chandlers	5
Grocery Wholesalers	5	Shoe Shops	3
Guest Houses	4	Solicitors and Estate Agents	5
Haberdasher	1	Sports Goods	3
Hairdressers (Ladies')	6	Stationery Retailers	6
Hairdressers (Men's)	2	Steel Stockholders	2
Hardware Retailers	6	Supermarkets	2
Health Food Shop	1	Land Surveyor	1
Heating Equipment and Solid		Television and Radio	9
Fuel	2	Toys and Games Shops	4
Hotels	5	Valuer	1
Industrial Protective Clothing	4	Warehouse and Storage Services	6
Insurance Brokers and Companies	4	Wool and Woollen Goods Shops	4
Ironmongers (Retail)	4	Yacht Charter	1

COMMUNITY LIFE

As might be expected from a town which is both a busy seaport and the main centre of a whole archipelago of inhabited islands, Lerwick has always had a full social life. Although religious denominations are represented in a number and variety astonishing to visitors, religious observances have never been repressive on the population, and there is today complete freedom with regard to the use of Sunday. Sunday sport, such as football on the town playing fields and golf on the course at Dale a few miles out of town, is common. There is a general cessation of work on Sundays, but it is not absolute and major building contracts are generally carried on seven days a week.

The most marked change in religious observances is the fact that evening services, once the most popular, are now the least popular, and in some cases have been given up.

With regard to alcohol, for twenty years between the two great wars Lerwick was a 'dry' town by local option, though that did not involve complete prohibition. Soon after the end of World War II, however, the community voted to go 'wet' again. Since then, aided by the full employment and affluence of the oil-boom years during the construction phase of the Sullom Voe oil terminal, and the growth of population, consumption of alcohol has soared, and there was for a time a very big increase in the number of petty court cases, many of them motoring offences while 'under the influence'. Although there is not a marked incidence of drunkenness, hardly any social function takes place now, except among groups of abstainers, without a late-licence for alcohol.

In common with the rest of Shetland, Lerwick always did differ from the Scottish mainland in observing Christmas as well as New Year. It is however, a very long time since Old Christmas according to the Julian calendar was observed. The social custom of adult as well as juvenile 'guizing' (visiting friends' houses in disguise), lasted up to World War II, but has now almost died out. The annual fire and guizing festival of Up-Helly-Aa, however, for which Lerwick is especially distinguished, goes on from strength to strength, involving upwards of 800 torch-bearing guizers in varied fancy dress and 13 halls open for the night, after the burning of a Norse longship replica.

Apart from the two fields presented by the Feuars and Heritors, the town's other recreation areas are the Gilbertson Park, used mainly for football, and also now for indoor archery. This was presented by a Lerwick man Robert P. Gilbertson in 1897. The Seafield football and hockey pitches were acquired by the Town Council in the southern green-belt area in 1950. The fields on the east side of the Clickimin Loch were laid out very recently for football, hockey and horse-riding (now popular among girls) under the aegis of the Shetland Islands Council by the Scottish Development Agency. Plans have been prepared and money allocated from the council's oil reserve fund for a comprehensive indoor recreation centre just north of the Clickimin Loch. A camping site, at present entirely lacking, will be established north-west of the loch when drainage and sanitary works have been carried out.

A list of voluntary organisations is appended.

Voluntary organisations

Youth clubs:
    Islesburgh
    Lerwick Congregational Church
    60° North
    Sound

Youth hostel
    Islesburgh House

Uniformed organisations
    1st Lerwick Co. Boys' Brigade
      (with Junior Sections and Anchor Boys)
    1st Lerwick Brownies
    2nd Lerwick Brownies
    3rd Lerwick Brownies
    1st Lerwick Girl Guides
    2nd Lerwick Girl Guides
    1st/2nd Lerwick Sea Scouts
    1st/2nd Lerwick Cub Scouts
    Venture Scouts
    Army Cadet Corps
    Air Training Corps

Mother and toddler groups/playgroups
    Early Birds
    Lerwick
    Islesburgh Creche
    Islesburgh
    Methodist
    North Road Mother and Toddler
    North Road Playgroup
    Sound
    St Olaf

Community centres
    Islesburgh House
    Islesburgh Community Centre
      (former Central School)

Arts and crafts
    Arts and Crafts Committee
    Arts Centre Committee
    Islesburgh House Photographic Club
    Shetland Arts Society
    Shetland Film Club

Drama groups
    Islesburgh Drama Group
    Sound and District W.R.I. Drama Group

Music groups
    Lerwick Brass Band
    Lerwick Orchestral Society
    Lerwick Choral Society
    Lerwick Folk Club
    St Magnus Choir
    Shetland Accordion and Fiddle Club

Shetland Country Music Club
Shetland Fiddlers' Society
Shetland Folk Festival Society

Social and educational societies
Shetland Folk Society
Shetland Civic Society
Community History Project

Community associations
North Staneyhill Community Association
Sound Community Association
Westerloch Residents' Association
Shetland Council of Social Service

Social clubs
Lerwick Club
Royal British Legion
Royal Air Force Association
Territorial Army
Morton Lodge 89 of Freemasons

Sporting organisations

Angling clubs
Lerwick/Bressay Sea Angling Club
Norscot Angling Association
Shetland Anglers' Association

Badminton clubs
St Clements
Sound
Vikings
Islesburgh

Football clubs
Spurs
Thistle
Celtic
Rangers
Banks
Civil Service
Norscot
Post Office
Shetland Islands Council
Oil Distributor

Hockey clubs
Lerwick Ladies Hockey Association
Shetland Junior Hockey Committee
Zetland Team
Anderson High School Hooligans

Boating/sailing
> Lerwick Boating Club
> Lerwick Marina Users Association

Cricket clubs
> Shetland Cricket Association

Miscellaneous
> Clickimin Open Riding Club
> Islesburgh Motor Cycle Club
> Islesburgh Yoga Club
> Lerwick Amateur Swimming Club
> Lerwick Athletic Club
> Lerwick Bowling Club
> Lerwick Indoor Bowling Club
> Lerwick Ladies Darts Club
> Lerwick Rifle Club
> Lerwick Shotokan Club
> Lerwick Table Tennis Club
> Norscot Volleyball Association
> Shetland Archery Club
> Shetland Gymnastics Association
> Shetland Budokai Club
> Shetland Karate Club
> Shetland Netball Association
> Shetland Squash Club
> Viking Car Club
> Viking Judo Club
> Viking Darts Team

Miscellaneous voluntary organisations

Islesburgh Radio Control Club
Islesburgh Dog Club
Lerwick Radio Club
Shetland Flower Club
Up-Helly-Aa Committee
Da Longship Committee
British Red Cross Society (Lerwick Branch)
Shetland Gala Committee
Shetland Pigeon Club
Shetland Bird Club
Aquarist Club
Shetland Norwegian Friendship Society
Rotary Club
Royal National Lifeboat Institution
    (Lerwick Branch)
Lerwick Ladies Lifeboat Guild
Lerwick Deaf Club

Women's organisations

Scottish Women's Rural Institute
(Lerwick Branch)
Eastern Star
National Childbirth Trust
Shetland Women's Aid

Church and religious bodies

Bahais of Shetland
Baptist Church
Roman Catholic Church (St. Margaret's)
Christian Brethren (Ebenezer Hall)
Church of God (Myrtle Hall)
Church of Jesus Christ of Latter Day Saints
Church of Scotland: Lerwick
and Bressay Parish Church (St Columba's)
Congregational Church
Emmanuel Church (Assemblies of God)
Evangelical Church, Garthspool
(Fellowship of Independent Evangelical
Churches)
Lerwick Ministers Fraternal
Methodist Church (Adam Clarke Memorial)
Norwegian Home Ports Mission to Seamen
(Lutheran)
Royal National Mission to Deep Sea
Fishermen
Salvation Army
Scottish Episcopal Church (St Magnus)
Shetland Council of Churches
United Free Church of Scotland
(St Ringan's)

Trade unions

Allied Union of Engineering Workers
Amalgamated Union of Engineering Workers
Association of Broadcasting Staff
British Medical Association
Civil and Public Service Association
Confederation of Health Service Employees
Educational Institute of Scotland
Electrical Power Engineers Association
Electronic, Electrical and Plumbers Trade
Union
General and Municipal Workers Union
Institute of Professional and Civil Servants
Management Staff Association (G.P.O.)
National Association of Local Government
Officers
National Farmers Union

National Union of Seamen
National Union of Teachers
Police Federation
Post Office Engineering Union
Royal College of Nursing
Society of Civil and Public Servants
Transport and General Workers Union
Union of Construction and Allied Trades
    and Technicians
Union of Post Office Workers
Union of Shop, Distributive and Allied
    Workers
National Union of Journalists
S.G.D. of S.O.G.A.T.

Political parties
Liberal
Conservative
Labour

Political movement
Shetland Movement

Defence
Territorial Army (Highland Volunteers)
Royal Observer Corps

ACKNOWLEDGEMENT

The writer gratefully acknowledges help and information from the Harbour Office of Lerwick Harbour Trust and the following departments of the Shetland Islands Council: Research and Development; Leisure and Recreation; Housing; Planning.

NOTES

1. The figures on p. 55 are based on registrations under the National Health Service, used by the Research and Development Department of the Shetland Islands Council. From the 1981 Census the General Register Office for Scotland provisionally estimated the total population at 25,892 but this included temporary construction workers at the Sullom Voe Oil Terminal. The final 1981 Census figures are not yet available.

2. The full name is Peninsular & Oriental Steam Navigation Company, though it probably has few steam vessels now. It is not a limited liability company, being based on royal charter. It heads the biggest shipping group in the world. One of its co-founders was (as stated) a Lerwick man.

November 1982

GULBERWICK AND QUARFF

by James W. Irvine, M.A.

The area included here is that of the distinct communities of Gulberwick and Quarff, and these are described individually below.

GULBERWICK

PHYSICAL BASIS

The town of Lerwick had its boundaries officially extended in 1965, so that the district of Gulberwick is now immediately contiguous to Lerwick on its south side. Gulberwick is now contained by a line running from the eastern shoreline of the Ness of Trebister at the sandy geo known as the Grottie Buckie to the southernmost edge of the Loch of Trebister; thence north-westwards to the south-western shore of the Sandy Loch; thence west and north along the shore of that loch to a point near Gossa Water, thence southwards to the hill Virdalee and from there south-eastwards past the south end of Henry's Loch and down to the sea. The wide bay which indents the coast-line—Gulberwick ('the bay of the gold-bearing lady')—gives its name to the whole district.

Round the bay, or wick, the land rises in a moderate incline on all three landward sides to a height of 200-300 feet. On the lower slopes of the basin thus formed is found most of the best agricultural land and also most of the houses. The higher slopes are mostly peat and heather covered, and are suitable, in the main, only for sheep. The peat, which provides fuel for a number of households, has also been the subject of two peat-processing experiments. The Brindister area, south of the basin, also affords some acres of good arable land which, well-husbanded, supports a herd of dairy cows.

In the main the inhabitants live only a little more than three miles from the town of Lerwick, and there is evidence from as far back as the 18th century of the influence of the town life on the area. With modern communications and transport that influence was becoming much more marked towards the end of the 20th century.

HISTORY

Gulberwick has two brochs. One, the broch of Burland, situated on the brink of a cliff at Brindister overlooking the sea, is of the usual massive dimensions, with the only entrance on the seaward side. A prominent landmark, it occupied a position of great security. The other, smaller broch, occupies a defensive position on a small island in the middle of

Brindister Loch. Its diameter is only about 50 feet, its walls are only 8 to 10 feet thick, and they probably rose to a height much less than the fairly common 40 feet. In other words, this latter is a broch much smaller than the usual size, with its chief interest lying in its very unusual situation. The 'Hollanders' Knowe' has an obvious connotation. Situated half-way between Lerwick and Scalloway, near the south road joining the two, the 'Knowe' was the scene of busy barter activities between the Dutch fishermen and the Shetlanders in distant days when Dutch fishing boats exploited Shetland waters in their hundreds.

POPULATION AND HOUSING

With Gulberwick forming part of the Lerwick (Landward) District until 1967 when Gulberwick and Quarff became a district of county, it is difficult to establish exact population figures for Gulberwick alone over the years. But, in common with the rest of Shetland, it reached its peak population soon after the middle of the 19th century. Then, and for many years thereafter, the people's livelihood was wrested in the main from both the land and the sea.

By 1931 Shetland's population had declined by over 10,000 during the preceding seventy years. In Gulberwick itself by 1940 the population was down to 90, inhabiting 33 houses. Virtually all of the houses were old or becoming old. For the next 30 years there was little change in the population level and little new housing, but the percentage of elderly people steadily increased. In the early 1970s the oil boom began and almost immediately life in Gulberwick began to be transformed. By 1982 Gulberwick's population had more than doubled, and was made up as follows:

Age	Male	Female
80 and over	5	4
60-80	8	8
50-60	7	7
30-50	42	39
20-30	13	13
In higher education	11	7
In primary school	20	15
Pre-school children	10	11
	116	104
Overall total	220	

These 220 people inhabited 67 houses. Of these, 45 were new or fairly new, 14 had been reconditioned, and only eight could be classed as old. Among the householders were 17 who had come from outwith Shetland, and 21 who had come from other parts of Shetland itself. Ten houses had only a single inhabitant (in most of these the occupant was elderly), while 36 of the houses had three or more inhabitants. The overall average was just over three people per house. Virtually all of the houses were owner-occupied, and there was no council housing. A feature of the population was that over 80 per cent were under fifty years of age, with 45 per cent being actually under thirty.

OCCUPATIONS

In 1982 the working population numbered 89, which included 33 women. While over 20 people were still making a living from agriculture in 1940, by 1982 the number of active agricultural units was down to five, providing work for only eight people. In 1982 one stone quarry was operative in the district, and there was one small distributive business, but only about 10 per cent of the working population had employment in the Gulberwick area. Among the others there was a wide spread of employment. Oil-related work accounted for 10, shop-workers 12, electrical and mechanical engineering 11, Hospital Board employees five, teachers nine, other Shetland Islands Council employees 10, clerical workers seven, and plant hirers three. Other employment included bricklaying, diving, joinery, pharmacy, fishing, seafaring, and other occupations.

EDUCATION

Prior to the passing of the Education Act of 1872 the only education provided in the district was provided in a small building situated down at the shore. However, the census of children carried out by the new School Board in 1876 showed that Gulberwick needed school accommodation for 60 children, and this was duly provided two or three years later in a new one-room school with schoolhouse attached.

That school remained in operation until 1947. In the school's early days the roll was over 50; 30 years later it had dropped to under 30; and in 1947 the then Education Committee, with the roll down to five, decided to close the school. The Gulberwick children were then transported daily to the Quarff School, but even with this addition the Quarff roll only reached 11.

For nearly 30 years this arrangement continued unchanged. While the number of Gulberwick children fluctuated slightly, the numbers never rose sufficiently high to warrant the reopening of the Gulberwick School. However, the coming of the oil industry caused a rapid population increase. A new primary school was built at Sound (now within Lerwick burgh), and Gulberwick parents were given the choice in 1977 of sending their children either to the new Sound School or to Quarff School. The 1982 figures showed the dramatic change which had taken place. There were 30 Gulberwick children at Sound school, and five at Quarff—a total of 35 primary school children. There were a further 21 pre-school children in the area.

In the early days any child going on to secondary education attended the Anderson Educational Institute in Lerwick, but in the 1920s Lerwick Central School was given intermediate secondary status, and, after World War II, the entry of Gulberwick and Quarff children to either secondary school was regulated by the county-wide control examination.

In 1982 all children of secondary age from Gulberwick and Quarff attended the Anderson High School, a fully comprehensive school, and the only school in the islands offering a full five or six year secondary course. In that year, Gulberwick children of secondary age attending the Anderson High numbered 18.

COMMUNITY ACTIVITIES

For a long time the venue for community activities was the old hall which stood on a site near the school. It had reached the end of its useful life, however, and in 1946 the community purchased a large 90-foot long wooden hut surplus to the needs of the departing Services authorities. This hut was re-erected on a central site near the school, and well-maintained by the community, served the social needs of the people for over 20 years. The empty school-room housed a full-sized billiard table.

In 1969, as a result of much hard work by the people and the purposeful co-operation of Shetland Education Committee, the new Gulberwick Community Centre was opened. A commodious complex, the best of its kind in Shetland at the time, it incorporated the old school and schoolhouse, along with a spacious new addition.

Within the building the numerous community organisations and groups meet. These include the badminton club, the bowling club, snooker and table tennis activities, the 500 club, the play group, and there are frequent very well attended social evenings. There have also been numerous weddings, both of local people and of others from further afield, and the hall has even been honoured by a visit from the Queen.

THE CHURCH

Down the road from the hall is the church. Built towards the end of the 19th century, it has survived the ups and downs of social and educational provision. Over the years its congregation, with a declining population, has frequently been small, but its fabric has been well maintained, and it has always had a healthy women's guild. It is part of a linked charge of Lerwick, Bressay and Gulberwick Parish Churches, and is served by the ministers from the Lerwick Church of Scotland.

PUBLIC SERVICES

In 1982 every house had an electricity supply, which had been provided in 1950 by the North of Scotland Hydro-Electric Board on overhead lines from its diesel-powered generators at its Lerwick power station. Similarly a water supply is available to everyone, but no public sewage system has yet been provided, most of the houses being dependent on septic tanks. There are no shops. The main road runs just above the line of houses, and the Sandwick-Lerwick bus service serves the Gulberwick area. However, 90 per cent of householders own at least one car, and where there is no car it is usually because of the advancing years of the householder. Lerwick Health Centre with its panel of doctors serves the Gulberwick area, though the district nurse has her base at Cunningsburgh, 10 miles to the south. A home help service is provided where necessary, while meals on wheels are provided for two or three of the older residents.

WAY OF LIFE

In 1982 the importance of the sea and the land to the lives of the people of Gulberwick has shrunk to minor dimensions compared with a century previous. The proximity of the area to the town of Lerwick has always been of importance to the district's inhabitants; but it has become much more important from 1970 onwards. Indeed, as we approach the end of the 20th century, Gulberwick has become virtually a dormitory suburb of the town. Only three miles from Lerwick, with an excellent new road providing first-class access, the age of the car has brought the journey to town down to five minutes, and has made commuting to even more distant work-sites such as Sullom Voe an accepted part of the way of life. Although a town suburb in many ways, it has its own live church, its own excellent and active community hall housing a variety of local organisations and activities, its own healthy and younger generation. The district still has much to offer in its own right.

QUARFF

PHYSICAL BASIS

Quarff is 'a low-lying place surrounded by hills'. Located between Gulberwick and Cunningsburgh, its northern boundary runs from Whal Wick on Clift Sound up to the hill Virdalee, where it joins the Gulberwick boundary and then runs south-eastwards past the south end of Henry's Loch and so down to the sea. On the south side, starting at a point on the West Cliffs, it runs eastwards in a fairly straight line over the South Brae of Quarff and out to the east sea near Scarf Taing.

On both the north and south sides of the Quarff area the ground rises to a height of over 700 feet, with a fertile valley lying in between, the valley stretching for two miles east to west right across the Shetland Mainland. While this valley provides a considerable acreage of good arable land, the hill slopes are peat and heather covered and suitable in the main only for sheep. Most of the houses are built at either end of the valley—Easter Quarff and Wester Quarff—and, in days gone by, the main livelihood of the people was derived from the valley crofts, although up to the early years of the twentieth century the men of Wester Quarff pursued a considerable summer herring fishing. In later years, in common with many other areas of Shetland, the Merchant Navy provided employment for many. The main road from Lerwick to Sumburgh passes through the area, with branch roads serving Easter and Wester Quarff.

POPULATION AND HOUSING

Quarff forms part of the electoral district of Cunningsburgh, Quarff and Gulberwick; in 1967 it became a district of county along with Gulberwick. Separate population figures for Quarff are difficult to establish, but there is no doubt its population reached a peak just after the middle of the nineteenth century. From then onwards it declined until by 1940 it was less than 80, after which it was fairly stable and in 1961 it was just over 80. However, the coming of oil in the 1970s had an effect on the Quarff numbers, to the extent that, by 1982, the total was 131, made up as follows:

Age	Male	Female
80 and over	1	1
60-80	12	12
50-60	7	6
30-50	20	20
20-30	5	7
In higher education	5	6
In primary education	9	8
Pre-school children	6	6
	65	66
Overall total	131	

From this it can be seen that, while nearly 20 per cent of the inhabitants were aged over 60, 40 per cent were in the 30-50 age group, and the remaining 40 per cent were under 30.

In 1982 the population inhabited 46 houses. Twenty per cent of these were occupied by people who had come in from outside Shetland, and a further 30 per cent of the houses by people who had come into the district from other parts of Shetland. Thirteen of the houses had only single inhabitants, the majority of them elderly, while 23 houses had three or more people residing in them. The average occupancy rate for

Plate 9. SIXAREENS AT FETHALAND, Northmavine (c. 1885–1890)

Formerly the main fishery of Shetland was the "haaf" fishery for ling and cod, operated with open boats such as these from outlying points on the islands to minimise the distance to fishing grounds. Fethaland, at the northern tip of the Shetland mainland, was a leading "haaf" station.

(J. D. Ratter. Courtesy Shetland Museum and Library)

Plate 10

MODERN PURSE-NET FISHING BOAT

Included in the modern Shetland fleet are steel-built vessels such as
these, which in favourable conditions can catch hundreds of tons of
herring or mackerel in a single night.

(Courtesy Research and Development Department, Shetland
Islands Council)

the area was just under three people per house. Nearly 40 per cent of the houses were new houses, while most of the remainder have had extensive reconditioning schemes carried out. There were virtually no houses in poor repair. A public water supply was available for all the houses, but there was no public sewage system with the result that most householders utilised septic tanks for sewage. Electricity, carried on overhead lines from the North of Scotland Hydro Electric Board's diesel powered generators in Lerwick, had been available since 1950. There were no council houses, and, with the exception of a few croft houses, the remainder were owner-occupied.

OCCUPATIONS

Of the total population over 35 per cent were in employment in 1982, and, of that number, 14 were women. While agriculture was providing a living for only five of the working population, a further eight senior citizens were deriving some income from crofting. Six workers were in clerical posts, four in shops, two worked as teachers and a further three were otherwise employed by Shetland Islands Council. Hospital Board and other health workers accounted for five, oil and oil-related work employed three, the building trade two, woodworking two, the Post Office two, and shipping one. The remainder pursued a variety of occupations. But of the total working population only one in seven had work in the Quarff area—the others were commuting, in the main to Lerwick.

EDUCATION

Before the 1872 Education Act a measure of teaching was provided in the little old school which stood near the main road, beside the road leading to Wester Quarff. Then, in the years 1878 and 1879 a new school was built, a little way above the old school, and thus situated about mid-way between Easter and Wester Quarff. Soon after it opened the roll had risen to over 30, including, in those days, a few from Fladdabister to the south. Soon thereafter, however, the Cunningsburgh School became the venue for the Fladdabister children. By 1900 the roll was down to 24, and, by 1947, when the Gulberwick School was closed, the roll of the two schools thus combined amounted to only 11. The coming of oil brought a resurgence, and by 1974 the total had increased to 23. In 1982 the roll stood at 22, including five children from the Gulberwick area. The increased roll necessitated extra accommodation being built at the school, and a second teacher was appointed in what had hitherto been a one teacher school.

Secondary education is provided for all Quarff children of secondary age at the Anderson High School in Lerwick, a comprehensive school, and the islands' only full five or six year secondary school. These children use the daily school transport provided by the Islands Council. In 1982 the number of such secondary children from Quarff was 11.

SERVICES

The Health Centre in Lerwick with its panel of doctors is used by the Quarff people, and district nursing services are provided by the nurse based in Cunningsburgh. Meals on wheels and home help services are provided as required. The main Lerwick to Sumburgh road runs through the area, and the Sandwick-Lerwick bus service is used by the residents. Over 80 per cent of households own at least one car, and travelling time to Lerwick on the excellent new road is no more than ten minutes.

COMMUNITY ACTIVITIES

The Public Hall, situated a little way west of the school, was built in 1927, and houses a number of community activities and organisations such as social evenings, badminton, 500 Club and Youth Club. As well as a Church, there is a Church hall, and Quarff is served by the same Church of Scotland minister who serves the remainder of the south Mainland of Shetland. The Quarff Church and manse were provided by a Parliamentary Commission set up in 1823 to establish 43 new churches in remote parts of Scotland. The Commission's grant for the purpose was £50,000, and the Quarff Church and manse, designed and planned by Thomas Telford, was completed in 1829 within the permitted maximum ceiling of £1,500. A feature of the church were—and are—the six large iron-framed windows, each glazed with countless small diamond-shaped panes. The ravages of time and corrosion have made it necessary to replace the windows, and the bill for this work, in 1982, was expected to be £12,000, eight times the total cost of the buildings in 1829. The church houses an active women's guild. Near the church is another very old building—the lodge. There is record of workers at the building of the church having lived at the lodge, and there is little doubt that this well-maintained building must have a place among the oldest inhabited buildings in the islands.

WAY OF LIFE

Quarff's population has risen considerably as an indirect result of the coming of oil, but good roads and the age of the car have meant that most workers are commuters. With Lerwick only ten minutes away, shopping, entertainment and other activities are within easy reach in the town. Nevertheless, a fairly active community life continues to exist in Quarff itself in the hall, the church and the school. The public hall, situated a little way west from the school, was built in 1927 and houses a number of community activities and organisations. These include social evenings, badminton, a 500 club and a youth club. The population has a strong younger element, which, given economic stability for the islands, augurs well for the future. The influx of people from other areas may well give strength to the way of life of the area.

November 1982

BURRA ISLE

by John H. Goodlad, M.A., M.Litt.

PHYSICAL BASIS

Burra is located off the west mainland of Shetland and consists of two separate islands which are connected by a small bridge. West Burra is the larger island, being some $5\frac{1}{2}$ miles in length by less than one mile in breadth, while East Burra is only about four miles long by less than one mile wide. Given the rather indented and elongated shape of the two islands it is not surprising that the total area of Burra is less than five square miles. In contrast to the adjacent mainland, both islands are of low relief. The topography is, however, extremely rugged and barren, even by Shetland standards, and there is consequently little arable land.

LOCAL HISTORY PRIOR TO 1945

A survey of the history of Burra, in common with most of Shetland, is very closely linked to the history of the fishing industry. The fishing industry has always been of particular importance to Burra, however, because of the lack of suitable arable land on the islands, and due to the position of Burra adjacent to valuable fishing grounds. This proximity to prolific fishing grounds, including the 'Burra Haaf', meant that Burra fishermen could return daily from these areas in relatively small open boats. As a result of this locational advantage, Burra never developed the standard two or three day trips characteristic of the larger 'sixaereens' which went line fishing for ling, cod and tusk during the 'Shetland haaf fishing era'. However, during the latter part of the nineteenth century a large number of Burra fishermen ventured much further, since several cod smacks which fished as far away as Rockall and Faroe were based on the islands.

Towards the end of the nineteenth century, Burra crews were amongst the first Shetland fishermen to invest in decked sailing vessels to fish for herring. The success of this fishery throughout Shetland resulted in a rapid decline of the 'haaf' and 'cod smack' fisheries. When the herring fishery declined after the First World War, most areas in Shetland experienced the consequent unemployment problems of a declining industry. In contrast, Burra succeeded in maintaining a strong fishing industry throughout this period. Burra fishermen had retained their line fishing skills during the herring boom, and had developed a line fishery for haddock during the early part of this century. Through a combination of drift netting for herring during the summer and autumn months, and setting haddock lines during the winter and spring, fishing remained important and Burra fishermen were amongst the first in Shetland to abandon crofting and become full-time fishermen. This development was accompanied by the growth of Hamnavoe as a fishing village around the sheltered natural harbour of that name in West Burra.

Despite the considerable recession experienced in Shetland fisheries during the 1930s, fishing maintained its importance for the economy and employment prospects in Burra. As a result, Burra was able to retain a stable population of over 700 during this period despite the considerable decline in Shetland's total population. Hamnavoe continued to expand at the expense of the more scattered townships throughout Burra and also at the expense of the smaller islands to the south (Havra) and north of Burra (Oxna, Papa, Hildasay etc.) which became depopulated during this period.

BURRA FROM 1945 TO 1972

1. FISHERIES

Following the Second World War, Burra maintained its position as a leader in the Shetland fishing industry with the acquisition of several modern 'dual purpose' vessels. These boats were about 70 feet in length and specifically designed to drift net for herring and to fish for white fish species (haddock, whiting and cod) by means of the seine net. This development resulted in the eventual demise of the 'haddock line' fishery by the early 1950s. By the mid 1960s there were a total of some 12 such dual-purpose vessels in the Burra fleet together with several smaller full-time boats fishing for white and shellfish. This fleet provided full-time employment for well over 100 fishermen throughout the year on a well defined annual pattern. The herring season lasted from May to August, with the total Shetland fleet being based in Lerwick for most of this time. The Burra crews generally remained in Lerwick for the duration of the fishing week (Monday to Saturday), commuting to Burra at the weekends via the daily ferry service from Scalloway to Hamnavoe.

Burra fishermen had two holiday periods, the first immediately prior to the herring fishery when the fishing gear was checked and made ready: 'riggin oot' took about two weeks. The second break occurred immediately after the end of the herring season when the drift nets were dried, mended and stored away for the next season. This period usually lasted some four or five weeks and was often associated with considerable celebrations especially if the fleet returned from Lerwick ('comin-roond') after a successful herring season. For the remainder of the year the fleet fished for white fish which was either sold in Aberdeen (by consignment on the steamer to Aberdeen, or by direct landing in Aberdeen following a week's fishing), or in Scalloway where fish processing activities had been developed from the early 1960s onwards. By 1972 all but two of the Burra fleet were based in Hamnavoe—being anchored when not in use in the voe itself since the pier (although substantially enlarged in 1956) could not be used for berthing in adverse weather conditions.

2. POPULATION

Despite the varied fortunes of the fishing industry during the post-war period, the Burra fleet continued to provide full-time employment for somewhat over 100 men on the islands. As a result, Burra succeeded in retaining a remarkably stable population throughout the 1950s and 1960s in contrast to the continued decline of the total Shetland population at this time. In 1951 the total population of Burra was 648, while in 1961 it had actually increased by five to 653. Even more important than the actual population figure itself was its relatively well balanced structure, with a large number of young married couples with families confident of an economic future based on fishing in Burra. This again contrasted with the general Shetland situation at this time with many young people leaving the islands. Although the total population had declined to 565 by 1971, this did not represent any significant trend of depopulation since the age structure of the islanders remained better balanced than in most other areas in Shetland.

3. EDUCATION

Throughout the post-war period, Burra was served by two primary schools—those at Bridge End and Hamnavoe. The Bridge End school was the original school serving all Burra (predating the development of Hamnavoe) and was conveniently located on a small island where East and West Burra are joined by bridge. However, with the growth of Hamnavoe during the early part of this century, the school roll at Bridge End had declined to around 20 pupils by 1950. This school roll remained remarkably stable at about 20 until Bridge End Primary School closed in 1972.

In contrast, the Hamnavoe school roll was much higher, especially since there tended to be more young couples with families in the village. In addition to its role as a primary school for the Hamnavoe area, it also provided secondary schooling up to the age of 15 for all Burra. In 1948 the school roll at Hamnavoe was 61. This school population decreased slightly during the 1950s but had increased to about 100 by 1965. This high level was not maintained however, and numbers fell back somewhat to between 50 and 60 in the period prior to 1972.

While the Hamnavoe Junior Secondary School undoubtedly provided a good standard education it did not present pupils for school leaving certificates, and those parents wishing their children to receive a more academic training had to send them to the Anderson Educational Institute in Lerwick. In addition to the then necessary 11 plus examination this necessitated lodging in Lerwick all week and returning home only at weekends, and only a minority of Burra pupils attended school in Lerwick. Throughout the 1950s and 1960s around 10 to 20 pupils regularly travelled to Lerwick. While most boys leaving the Hamnavoe school at 15 years of age obviously went to the fishing, those completing an education in Lerwick often found work in the town while quite a few proceeded to take university degrees at various Scottish universities.

4. Housing

In the immediate post-war period all housing remained privately owned, most being owner-occupied. Because of the development of the fishing industry, and the full-time occupational specialisation of most men, new housing tended to be built in well defined hamlets. Burra, therefore, lost its distinctive Shetland crofting settlement pattern during this period. The main concentration of housing was obviously at Hamnavoe but smaller hamlets were also found at Freefield and Papil in West Burra.

Despite strong pressures for the provision of council housing, the first council housing scheme was not completed until the mid 1950s with 16 Units at Glenburn in Hamnavoe and 4 Units at the Toogs (near Freefield). Although a considerable number of private houses were built in Hamnavoe and elsewhere in Burra during the later 1950s and 1960s, there was a continued demand for further council housing during this time.

The standard of housing improved significantly during this period, partly as a result of smaller families and improved earnings. Provision of water and electricity to all Burra households was completed by the early 1950s and obviously made a considerable difference to living standards.

5. Transport

The physical limitations of such a small island community enabled most people to walk from place to place, and precluded the need for public transport, although lorry and car transport could be hired from the local shops (three in Hamnavoe, one at Freefield and one at Papil) if the occasion merited. By the mid 1960s a considerable number of private cars had been brought into Burra which obviously considerably changed the mobility of people within the island.

Transport from Burra to Scalloway on mainland Shetland was provided by ferry. The main ferry service which made the 30-minute crossing from Hamnavoe to Scalloway 3 times per day was usually provided by a 40 foot vessel (the *Tirrick*) or else by a slightly larger vessel (the *Hirta*). Both boats were operated by a Hamnavoe man living in Scalloway. A smaller ferry (the *White Launch*) ran on a more irregular basis from Bridge End to Scalloway. Both ferry services connected with a service bus from Scalloway to Lerwick and thereby enabled residents of Burra to make a daily return trip to Lerwick for a few hours' shopping or business.

6. COMMUNITY LIFE

In the late 1960s Burra remained what it had been for most of the century—a relatively prosperous, self-contained fishing community with a stable population. There was a considerable degree of inter-marriage within Burra, thereby maintaining the predominance of the surnames which characterised Burra such as Inkster, Goodlad, Laurenson, Ward, Henry, Fullerton, Christie, Pottinger, Cumming and Jamieson. Of those marriages involving a partner outwith Burra a significant number consisted of Burra-Whalsay marriages reflecting the degree of interaction between the two main fishing communities in Shetland. In the post-war period somewhere over twenty Whalsay brides made their homes in Burra while a lesser number of Burra women married into Whalsay.

Religious activity within Burra was exceptionally varied for such a small population, with the Church of Scotland, Baptist and Methodist denominations being represented throughout the islands. Social activity was very much self-contained within Burra with football matches, concerts, whist drives, S.W.R.I. activities and various dances being held on a regular basis in addition to the several island weddings usually taking place each year. Instead of a family drive on Sundays, most families went for boat trips during the summer months to the nearby uninhabited islands in their small open 'Shetland model' pleasure craft. Up to the mid 1960s Hamnavoe also hosted an annual sailing regatta each summer. Christmas was a much more important festival in Burra than New Year. By the late 1960s the traditional rivalry between Hamnavoe and the other areas of Burra had virtually disappeared, helping Burra maintain its distinctive identity as an island community.

BURRA FROM 1972 TO 1982

In 1972 Burra was connected to the Shetland Mainland with the building of two bridges: a causeway and bridge from West Burra to Trondra and a bridge from Trondra to the Shetland Mainland near Scalloway. Although the Burra community was by no means united on the desirability of a road connection with the Mainland, the majority of islanders had been arguing for a bridge for several years. The completion of this link in 1972 has had a profound effect on most aspects of island life during the past ten years.

1. TRANSPORT

The building of the bridges suddenly transformed Lerwick, from being several hours distant by ferry and bus, to being just 12 miles by road from Hamnavoe—a journey taking only some 20 minutes by car (which was the result of a purpose-built modern road through Trondra linking the two bridges). In other words Burra was transformed from being a separate island grouping to an appendage of mainland Shetland. The ferry service was replaced by a direct public bus service from Hamnavoe to Lerwick, via Scalloway. Given the high per capita level of car ownership in Shetland the greatest effect was of course the increased mobility afforded to car users in Burra.

2. FISHERIES AND OTHER ECONOMIC ACTIVITIES

One of the main effects of the bridge to Burra was to provide alternative employment opportunities outwith the fishing industry for the islanders. By the mid 1970s quite a number of fishermen had taken the opportunity of leaving the sea to find alternative employment ashore, mostly in Lerwick. An increasing number of school leavers also began to serve apprenticeships on mainland Shetland (as joiners, electricians, builders, etc.) rather than follow their fathers to sea. In addition, a significant number of Burra men also found employment at Sullom Voe, both in the construction and operational stages. The bridge also provided, for the first time, employment opportunities (in shops, canteens, hospitals, etc.) for many Burra women. In 1982 it was estimated that up to 40 men and about 20 women commuted daily outwith Burra for employment. In addition about 20 men were also employed at Sullom Voe, again commuting daily.

Despite these developments, the fishing industry remains the major employer in Burra. In 1971 a small white fish freezing plant was built at Easterdale on West Burra. Although the factory has had a varied history (it is currently owned by the Shetland Islands Council and rented to a Scalloway fish processor) it continues to employ over 20 full-time staff (mainly women) and thereby provides a valuable contribution to the island's economy and employment.

The last ten years have seen the demise of the traditional drift net fishery for herring and the development of the more efficient purse-seine vessel. Although the first Shetland purse-seiner was purchased by a Burra crew in 1968, all subsequent purse-seine vessels have been based elsewhere in Shetland. Instead the Burra men concentrated on seine-netting and trawling for white fish for the whole year, although a few vessels have recently participated in the industrial fishery for sand eels during the summer months. A total of 11 seiner-trawlers are currently owned by Burra partnerships and provide employment for over 80 men. A further 20 Burra fishermen are involved in six separate vessel partnerships based in Lerwick and Scalloway. Most of these vessels represent recent acquisitions to the Shetland fleet and illustrate the widening geographical distribution of fishing vessel crews, presumably as a result of the increased mobility of Burra fishermen due to the bridge connection. A further consequence of this increased mobility is that the entire Burra fleet is now based in Scalloway, where a new safe harbour and fish market complex has recently been completed. Although certain units of the Burra fleet still use the pier at Hamnavoe when weather permits, and although two vessels can still be seen moored in the voe at weekends, the majority of Burra boats are now based permanently in Scalloway with the fishermen commuting to and from their vessels by car. Another indication of this integration of Burra and Scalloway fishing interests was the emergence of West Side Fishermen Ltd., a fish selling cooperative based in Scalloway with membership from both Burra and Scalloway.

3. POPULATION

The proximity of Burra to Lerwick (which encouraged ease of communication and daily commuting to Lerwick) together with the general increase in the Shetland population since 1971 has resulted in a considerable increase in the total Burra population. By 1974 the population of Burra had increased to 672; by 1976 to 743; by 1978 to 797; and by 1981 the total population of Burra was recorded as 848. This increase in population is in part the result of a significant number of non-Burra (and often non-Shetland) families and individuals moving into Burra to live, although working outwith Burra. More important, however, has been the return of many families of Burra or part-Burra origin who had previously lived outwith the islands and have taken the opportunity to return as a result of the building of the bridge. It is worth noting that not all of these 'incomers' have taken employment outwith the fishing industry, and quite a number are actually employed in the fish processing plant and several non-Burra men are now working partners in Burra vessels. Out of the total 1981 Burra population, it is estimated that upwards of 500 (58 per cent) now live in Hamnavoe.

4. EDUCATION

The connection of Burra to mainland Shetland by the bridges resulted in a major re-organisation of education within the islands. Upon completion of the bridge, the Bridge End Primary School was closed and the pupils transferred to the Hamnavoe School, which lost its secondary education component and became a primary school only. All secondary school pupils were then taken by bus to the Scalloway Junior High School where, after two years, they can decide either to proceed to the Anderson High School for a full academic education, or to remain at Scalloway. Immediately after this re-organisation took place in 1972 there was a total Burra primary school roll of 55 at Hamnavoe, with a further 25 or so attending the secondary school at Scalloway. In addition to this about 15 pupils attended the Anderson High School in Lerwick (now being able to commute daily rather than lodging in Lerwick during the week). Corresponding with the general population increase over the last ten years the school population has also increased considerably. By 1976 the Hamnavoe Primary School roll had increased to 65; by 1978 to 95; and by 1980 to 103. Partly in response to this increased roll, a new primary school was built at Hamnavoe in 1980. The current primary school roll at Hamnavoe now stands at 108. The number of Burra pupils attending the Scalloway Junior High School has also increased and it is estimated that 40 Burra pupils currently travel to Scalloway. In addition a further 15 pupils travel directly to Lerwick to attend the Anderson High School.

5. Housing

In 1974 a further 30 council house units (of Scandinavian design) were built at Hamnavoe. In 1978 13 council house units (including several sheltered housing units for the elderly) were built at the Toogs. In addition to these schemes private house-building has continued over the last ten years. During the last few years it has become increasingly difficult to secure a new site in Hamnavoe for house-building because of congestion. As a result several of the older cottages are being renovated within the village itself. The potential of many of these cottages has particularly been recognised by several of the incoming families. The importance of Hamnavoe as a centre of population was reflected in the provision of street lighting in 1980.

The housing provision within Burra is currently a total of 270 units. Apart from 63 council units, the remainder are mostly owner-occupied. Of the total about 150 (56 per cent) are in Hamnavoe.

6. Community life

With the advent of the bridge to the mainland, Burra is no longer an island community. Probably the major change in community terms has been in the mobility of its younger generation. Unlike the teenagers of the 1960s, Burra youth of the 1970s travelled outwith the islands for entertainment at weekends. The much greater mixing of younger people which has resulted, has led to a very different pattern of marriages, with two Burra partners becoming the exception rather than the rule. The marriages with non-Burra partners, together with the various incoming families which have moved into Burra, has resulted in a much more varied and less close-knit community.

Increased mobility has not only had an influence on the younger generation, as the older Burra residents now generally seek entertainment and social activities (e.g., music, night classes, sports, restaurants, dancing, etc.) on the mainland. Scalloway is particularly popular in this respect. Much more shopping is now done in Lerwick than previously, and most Burra families make at least one major shopping trip to Lerwick each week. As in most areas, church attendance has declined, and this has resulted in the Burra Church of Scotland parish being merged with the Tingwall parish on the Shetland mainland. The local Baptist Church has, however, remained fairly active and retains a resident minister.

Despite increased interaction with the mainland of Shetland, Burra continues to retain something of a separate identity with certain social activities continuing to take place within the island, such as those of the local football and pool teams and the S.W.R.I.

January 1983

THE PARISH OF NESTING AND LUNNASTING

by P. B. A. Hunter

PHYSICAL BASIS

The parish of Nesting and Lunnasting lies towards the north-east of the Shetland Mainland; it is bounded to the north-west by the parish of Delting, and to the south-west by that of Tingwall, Whiteness and Weisdale, while its eastern boundary is the sea. Included in the civil parish are the islands of Whalsay and Out Skerries, which are separate for nearly all administrative purposes, and for which separate descriptions are given. The mainland part of Nesting and Lunnasting has a considerably indented coastline; its greatest length is 14 miles, and its breadth varies from one to five miles. The land is hilly or undulating, but in relatively few places does it exceed 500 feet in height; and small lochs are fairly frequent. For the great part, the land is fairly gently sloping, apart from the cliffs on the more exposed parts of the coast which can reach 100 feet in height.

HISTORY

Like the rest of Shetland, Nesting and Lunnasting has a long history of human occupation. However details of the earlier period are known only in an outline form, as very little detailed archaeological investigation has been carried out in this parish.

In the parish is one of the main concentrations of Neolithic houses in the islands, and this could indicate a relatively big farming population as early as 3000 B.C. Continued occupation is likely through the prehistoric period, and this is also suggested by the five Iron Age brochs which have been recognised.

At a later stage, the strong effect of the Vikings is evidenced by the place-names, which are almost completely of Scandinavian derivation. As well as the more obvious settlement names like Kirkabister ('church farm'), not a few other settlement names have been derived from topographic descriptions. These include Laxo ('trout burn'), Vassa ('loch isthmus') and Neep ('peak-shaped headland').

After Shetland had come under Scots rule, the main estate in

Nesting was that of the Bruces of Symbister, while Lunna was the estate of the Hunters. The earlier Statistical Accounts show the interest of both these estates in the fisheries, and they created many 'outsetts' (new holdings outside the hill dykes) as holdings for fishermen.

Traditionally this area, like virtually the whole of Shetland, depended on a combination of crofting and fishing for its livelihood. Also important and essential in traditional life was the use of peat fuel.

As most crofters depended directly or indirectly on their own produce for a substantial part of an adequate food supply, crofting activities were conducted with a routine and in a thorough manner which entailed careful planning coupled with hard physical work. Spring operations were preceded by preparation of sufficient fertiliser to apply to the land. Many crofters sited a compost heap near their out-houses so that byres could be emptied at regular, or not so regular, intervals. Native cattle stocks were considerable on most small crofts in relation to the limited acreages of the holdings. From seven to ten animals would have been the average per croft in the early 20th century. During February the accumulation of byre manure was dispersed to the 'rigs' by means of wheelbarrows or 'kishies' (straw baskets), depending on the accessibility of the cropping land. A good heavy layer of approxi-mately 8 or 9 feet square was put down as a foundation on which was placed a layer of earth dug from the nearest available source; and if at all possible a heavy layer of seaweed, transported by barrow or kishie, was spread on the earth. This succession of byre manure, earth and seaweed was repeated four or five times, and this produced a good compost. The making of several of these per croft was a commonplace part of early spring work. By the third week of March operations on the land com-menced in earnest. The now integrated compost provided the balanced fertiliser for the different plots of land, and barrowfuls were liberally spread over the land to be cultivated. Central to the 'voar' (spring) work was 'delling' (delving) by the Shetland spade which was the general method of tilling the land. Usually three, and sometimes four, persons per 'peat' starting from the right hand side of each row performed this work. (The word 'peat', here meaning the area cultivated at one time by a delling team, is unfortunately liable to confusion in the light of the common use of peat as fuel). Delling was done in unison, each person digging in the spade, then 'breaking' (i.e., jerking the earth and turning the underside up and with a few well aimed 'skelps' to smooth the new earth). This exercise was repeated many thousands of times before the voar was completed. Seed, mostly the Shetland type of oats which had been thoroughly winnowed, was sown each day to allow harrowing by one of the family to complete the day's routine. This was an arduous task as the 7-inch iron teeth embedded in the wooden harrow measuring about 4 × 6 feet required a degree of physical strength to operate. On most crofts these daily activities would last for three weeks.

The next stage was planting potatoes which was somewhat less arduous. One member of the family, usually an agile youthful member undertook the work of placing the potatoes in rows whilst the delling operations continued, taking special care to cover each seed. Planting cabbage from home grown seed of the previous year and sowing turnips heralded the end of four or five weeks of hard spring work.

The next stage was peat cutting—an operation which has not changed over the years except for the timing and transport arrangements. There was a degree of urgency in getting peats cut by early May as many menfolk were expecting to obtain seasonal work, e.g., fishing and other ancillary work during the fishing season. Again the method of curing peats has not changed over the years, but while the wheelbarrow and kishie were the main modes of transport then, today we see tractors, land-rovers, vans and trucks and all types of vehicles engaged in the work. Where peats were some distance from houses small carts pulled by the native Shetland ponies provided slow but adequate means of transport. It was common practice to stack part of the year's supply of peat on the banks. These stacks were meticulously built and covered with 'flaws' (turves) to protect the 'blue' peat underneath and additional flaws were placed at the end of the stack so that the open face could be covered each time a small supply was taken off, mainly by kishie— kishies which had been made during the winter months. The production of the kishie was a planned event commencing in summer when certain areas where 'floss' (rushes) thrived were visited, sometimes at a con- siderable distance from dwellings, and uniform bundles were cut, brought back and dried for several weeks in the 'but' end of the house ready for twining during winter evenings. Straw was then selected and prepared for kishie making. This was a pastime which the older men enjoyed although a fair amount of physical effort was required. The satisfaction they obtained on completing this modest work of art was sufficient reward for their efforts. Several kishies could be made during a winter; some were retained for family use and some presented to neighbours and friends as gestures of kindness without thought of monetary reward.

Sixty odd years ago inshore fishing with small boats was part of the relaxation crofters enjoyed, and it was a red letter day for youngsters when allowed to accompany their elders. Apart from being a relaxation, this fishing provided a component of their staple diet for part of the year. Surplus requirements were salted or dried for winter and spring con- sumption. Haddock and whiting could be caught on handlines baited with mussels, until modern fishing methods employed by larger boats gradually thinned out the stocks.

In more recent history, Lunna was the base in the Second World War from which the 'Shetland bus' operated in its earlier phases. This was the operation conducted by Norwegian fishing-boats whereby contact was maintained with the resistance movement when Norway was under German occupation.

POPULATION

It is not actually possible to state the population of the mainland part of Nesting and Lunnasting at the Census enumerations in the earlier 19th century, as at that time the available figures include Whalsay and Skerries.

However by the peak date of Shetland population in 1861 Mainland Nesting had a population of 1,754, but its subsequent history has been one of decline until recent years; in 1901 it was 1,403, and by the 1971 enumeration had sunk to 380. The strong turn-around induced by the oil boom is shown in the 1981 figure of 510. While out of this total 99 were over 65 years, the fact that the strongest age group proportionately was between 20 and 40 years (with a total of 164) and that there were 109 children below 15 years are welcome signs of a rejuvenated population for the future.

PUBLIC AND SOCIAL SERVICES

EDUCATION

From the later 19th century, under the Education Act of 1872, there were three schools in Nesting and Lunnasting. Halfway between Freister and Vassa the South Nesting School was situated and served the whole district of South Nesting which included Catfirth at one end and Gletness, Eswick and Skellister at the other. From early school days only one form of transport prevailed—that of shanks mare. The odd lift in a cart or gig, or on the crossbar of a cycle, would have caused excitement and delight no mode of present day transport could generate in a youngster sixty or seventy years later.

There were also schools at Laxfirth and Brettabister, which served the North Nesting area but with the declining pupil numbers of the present century, these were closed soon after World War II, and the children of the area transported by mini-bus to South Nesting School.

In the early 1920s about sixty children attended the two-teacher school at Vidlin. In comparison with present day facilities it would possibly be an understatement to say conditions were extremely primitive. The mid-day meal was mainly of biscuits (often broken), buns, twopenny scones or plain homebakes, and was washed down by cocoa served on a communal basis. Water had to be fetched from a nearby well. Toilet equipment (one would not dare use 'facilities') was about as unhygienic as can be imagined. A couple of pails housed at either end of the playground—one for the girls and one for the boys—were provided for these purposes, without any provision for hand washing. To digress, one cannot help wondering if the former conditions were as primitive and unhealthy as has often been assumed: in this day of education in hygiene and of up-to-date facilities, one constantly hears of gastric upsets in a way that was formerly little known.

Both South Nesting and Vidlin are now two-teacher primary schools, and recent extensions at both schools have improved facilities and include canteen facilities for the supply of mid-day meals. Most pupils are now brought to school by motor transport.

At the 'junior high' stage of education, pupils from Lunnasting now go to Brae in Delting parish, and those from Nesting to Scalloway. For senior secondary education all pupils go to Lerwick; pupils from South Nesting (which is within reasonable commuting distance) travel daily, but those from North Nesting and Lunnasting are boarded in Lerwick.

MEDICAL PROVISION

Nesting and Lunnasting formerly shared with the parish of Delting the services of a doctor stationed at Voe. In the 1920s his mobility was enhanced when he acquired a motor cycle, and later he progressed to a car. His area was wide-ranging as was his professional skill; and he invariably displayed characteristics which endeared him to patients and non-patients alike. Whatever professional or other pressure he was subjected to, his attitude was cheerful and constant; and he responded immediately to calls, irrespective of details supplied. It was not until the 1930s that district nurses were appointed to give some assistance to this hard-working physician; this allowed the extending of more home care to patients.

Now there are two doctors based at the health centre at Brae whose practice includes Nesting and Lunnasting. There is also a district nurse resident in Nesting and a health visitor based at Vidlin.

CHURCH

The main building of the Church of Scotland is centrally placed in Nesting between Brettabister and Housabister and was built in 1794; at Neep there is the rather elaborate manse for the resident minister, built in 1770, but which has now been sold. There is also a church at Lunna, and services are also held in Vidlin Hall on occasion. The distance people formerly walked to church can be instanced by the twelve-mile return journey from Laxo to the Lunna church.

There have also been Methodist chapels at Vassa in South Nesting, and at Vidlin; and there is a Baptist chapel at Vidlin. The chapel at Vassa is still regularly used for services and Sunday school classes, and caters for members of any denomination. There has always been a happy atmosphere of co-operation between the different denominations in Nesting and Lunnasting.

In the organisation of the established church Nesting and Lunnasting are now part of a linked charge with Delting; and the one minister resident at Brae now is responsible for six different churches.

Women's guilds are active in both Nesting and Lunnasting.

Plate 11

M.V. FYLGA, INTER-ISLAND FERRY

Communications within the islands have since 1970 been greatly
improved by the provision of drive-on ferries between the bigger
islands. These ferries take buses and trucks as well as cars.

(Courtesy Michael T. Peterson)

Plate 12. M.V. ST. CLAIR (III)

Throughout the modern-period the main service transport to and from Shetland has been provided by cargo-passenger steamers such as this. This vessel operated the service from 1960 to 1977.

(Courtesy Shetland Museum and Library)

Plate 13. M.V. ST. CLAIR (IV)

This steamer is drive-on for vehicles and takes passengers. It has operated the service to and from Shetland since 1977.

(Courtesy P. & O. Ferries)

During the early part of this century Sunday was a regular day of rest. Degrees of observing the Sabbath varied from the most rigid to the rather more casual, but there was general recognition. Work-a-day clothes were set aside and both sexes normally donned their 'shifting claes' which could be termed their second best for general wear. The few casual menfolk generally wore their new or newly washed dungarees. Dark shirts used on weekdays were replaced by light shirts and practically no work of any description was undertaken. A supply of peats and water sufficient for the weekend was brought in on Saturday and almost the only permissible activity as far as the older generations were concerned was attending to their livestock—the accepted works of necessity and mercy. It is true that this rigid observance could at times become rather boring and the more adventurous souls exercised a degree of latitude in attending to animals by methodically searching the hills for straying sheep or just observing the well-being of the other members of the flock. During spring months when conditions were favourable, the smell of burning heather would filter back from a miniature fire on the more distant hills, and this pleasant aroma was not entirely welcome as part of Sunday observance. For the minister in his manse at Neep, peat fuel and other general services were provided by part-time staffing arrangements from the area. Ministers also formerly had the use of glebe land as part of their remuneration. More recently, when labour had become less easily obtainable the agricultural land was separated off, and as a result ministers found that providing comfortable living conditions severely taxed their modest income.

TRANSPORT

Before motor vehicles were introduced goods were transported by sea, and as in all Shetland districts the male population were skilled in handling craft from small boats to the sail-boats engaged in herring fishing, and many had sailed the seven seas at various times of their lives. One would tend to assume that the comparatively short distance from Lerwick to Nesting would have been undertaken in a rather casual manner, although there must have been many occasions when the local expertise in handling small sail-boats was tested when sudden changes in weather conditions overtook these small craft. Until the early part of this century goods were delivered to and collected from Lerwick in an open sail-boat which had to cross an exposed stretch of sea. While the crews who manned the boats were capable seamen, it was naturally a worrying time for the womenfolk who, when conditions became un-favourable, kept a constant watch for the boat to appear in view at the expected time. In one of the houses there is evidence of this habit and of a partial solution to the continual wandering outside to get a view from a vantage point. A younger member of one of the families (incidentally there were 26 residents in three thatched-roofed houses living within a few yards of each other) was a time-served mason; he decided to take remedial action and he cut into the three foot thick wall and fitted a window twelve inches square, providing a view of the bordering coastline, so that their anxiety could at least continue with a degree of comfort.

By the inter-war period, road transport had superseded sea links although the small motor-boat formerly used to bring up goods to Billister was still in demand as a ferry to the island of Whalsay at times when the regular steamer sailings of the *Earl of Zetland* did not suit. When motor transport was first introduced passengers were accommodated—possibly fitted in would be a better description—according to space, and departure times were irregular. Eventually applications were made for licences to operate public service vehicles. Regular times for uplifting passengers at different stages were fixed. Vehicles were required to be maintained in good condition and drivers were required to obtain PSV drivers' licences. A single fare for a journey of 20 miles was 3/6d. and return fare 6/6d. From Nesting three public service vehicles operated. The most appropriate was a Chrysler seven-seater. The other two vehicles contrasted in the extreme. A Model T fifteen cwt. van meticulously maintained, plied between South Nesting and Lerwick for several years, while a small Singer seven cwt. van (adapted to meet licensing requirements) with four seats served the needs of North Nesting.

More recently, increased prosperity has meant that most households have become substantially self-reliant for transport. New improved roads have now been provided for a wide range of motor vehicles of all descriptions owned by local residents. The sight of a pedal cycle is now unusual as a mode of transport. Ferry piers have been provided at Laxo and Vidlin to accommodate the Whalsay ferry, which can carry ten or eleven vehicles and about 60 passengers for the thirty minute passage.

POST OFFICE

There was in the early part of this century a post office at Skellister in South Nesting together with a sub post office at Brettabister in North Nesting. Three postmen served South Nesting. The sub-postmaster at Skellister collected mail bags at Catfirth, first by pony and trap and later by motor van, and undertook mail deliveries from Brettabister to Neep, in addition to delivering mail bags to the sub post office at Brettabister for distribution to the remainder of North Nesting from Billister and Laxfirth to Dury. Deliveries were thrice weekly—the distance covered on foot would have amounted to at least twelve miles per journey, as the postmen wended their way to and fro among croft houses. This was a considerable undertaking, quite apart from the steady flow of parcels and bags of yarn from mainland mills that also had to be carried. The supply of postage stamps was within the remit of their official duties and they were always willing to provide any additional services cheerfully, often no doubt being required to stretch their imagination to accommodate neighbourly messages and requests, e.g., a setting (i.e., about a dozen) of eggs, a bottle of milk, etc.

There are now three sub post offices, in North and South Nesting and at Vidlin. One postman delivers mail in Nesting and another in Lunnasting; both now use motor vans.

SHOPS

In the early part of this century, with more limited transport and a higher measure of local sufficiency, there were several shops. In South Nesting, there were three shops quite close together—two at Freister and one at Vassa. In North Nesting the general merchant's shop at Billister was a hive of activity. This shop was well patronised by visiting customers from Lunnasting and even Whalsay, as the site was near the seashore and access was provided by a rubble pier which facilitated small boat operations. The firm also served part of Lunnasting with groceries, etc. from a horse-drawn van. However this shop closed in the late 1920s and for several years North Nesting was served by vans from South Nesting and Lerwick; this included weekly rounds from Lerwick butchers' shops. In 1935 a small general shop was opened at Grunafirth in North Nesting, and this followed what had become the usual pattern of providing van deliveries to surrounding districts. This shop has now changed to a self-service and delivery store. The original shops in South Nesting have been closed down, but in the last year a new venture initiated by four young local men has been launched at the Catfirth/Freister junction. The partners have building, motor repairing and clerical experience and they are undertaking house building and repair work and motor maintenance, in addition to providing a self-service general merchant's business.

The shopping pattern has changed considerably as better transport has increased opportunities for regular visits to Lerwick. This has encouraged bulk buying from supermarkets and stocking of the now common deep freezes.

HOUSING

During the present century the standard of housing has improved very substantially. The traditional thatched roofs gradually gave way to ones of tarred felt and other materials, and walls were often raised up to two feet to give more headroom. In building, Nesting and Lunnasting could claim time-served masons which reflected credit on the expertise of their work in providing dwelling houses; and as time went on concrete was used to build new houses or extend old ones. The outbuildings were a credit to the handyman/crofter who provided himself with steadings meticulously planned and built as dry-stone buildings.

Despite gradual house improvements however, modern housing amenities were substantially lacking until 1955. Eventually government departments became alive to the fact that rural dwellers were entitled to the provision of modern facilities. Both Nesting and Lunnasting were supplied with electricity, and a water scheme followed. The provision of a water scheme, which made mains water available to practically all croft and cottar houses, was instrumental in encouraging residents to provide themselves with all modern conveniences, in which they were helped by government grants; and this renovation signalled the revival of interest of the young people. The installation of water and electricity provided welcome employment, and road improvements also provided extra jobs. In addition to the provision of modern amenities, grants from the Department of Agriculture stimulated the building of new houses and the extension of existing ones.

In the 1970s, the oil-boom has also considerably affected housing and living conditions. Undoubtedly this opportunity accelerated the provision of accommodation on both a permanent and temporary basis. A feature of temporary housing was the widespread siting of caravans to provide housing for personnel from outwith Shetland who had come to Sullom Voe either in connection with their professional or technical roles, or as participants in a massive labour force of a wide range of trades. The general progress of developments is now a matter of national and local history. Derelict areas became overnight hives of activity. Nesting and Lunnasting quickly adjusted to the opportunities on offer. During recent years the result of substantial earnings was reflected in the general progress of repairs and improvements to living accommodation and in the erection of new houses in both districts. These developments were wide ranging, and were either directly financed by individual earnings or partially provided by Department grants from government sources and Council grants and loans. The welfare of those unable to benefit from the new opportunities prevailing was not neglected. The Social Work Department of the Shetland Islands Council functioned actively to ensure that lack of funds was not an obstacle to providing improved facilities and extended living conditions to residents who qualified as a result of advancing years or adverse circumstances. Council houses have been provided at South Nesting and Vidlin for general needs, and sheltered houses have also been built at Vassa and Vidlin.

AGRICULTURE AND EMPLOYMENT

During the modern period there have been considerable changes in crofting activities, and their overall importance has declined. Much less land is now cultivated, and there has been a run-down in cattle stocks together with an increase in those of sheep.

However from the 1950s there have been important developments in crofting with the help of the generous grants of the Crofters Commission. These have aided land improvement, fencing, the building of access roads to outlying parts of holdings, the building of new steadings, and other improvements. Initially the Crofters Commission appeared to aim at crofting becoming a full-time occupation but it soon became apparent that crofters on smaller units still require some form of ancillary employment in order to obtain reasonable living standards.

During the 1960s improvement was sustained. Interest was aroused in developing the fishing industry and this provided welcome ancillary employment. Several small boats engaged in lobster fishing. As a result of adverse weather conditions preventing one lobster fisherman being able to gain access to Lerwick markets, he improvised an emergency water supply in miniature tanks to keep his catch alive. The result kindled his enthusiasm and he went on to build modern tanks at Vidlin capable of housing many hundreds of lobsters.

During the late 1960s and early 1970s a steady pattern of improvements continued. Details leading up to the impact of the oil era need not be repeated here. Nesting and Lunnasting were within comfortable commuting distance of Sullom Voe, and practically overnight job opportunities of all kinds became available. Previously undreamed of pay packets were earned by people of all age groups and of both sexes.

Both Nesting and Lunnasting have enjoyed the benefits of ample employment opportunities and improved living conditions in the 1970s, but there are now signs that the crest of the wave is passed. It is to be hoped that as the wave subsides the improvements made will be consolidated and that opportunities will be provided for the steady development of traditional and new industries for established local residents, and for the several families from outside Shetland who are now permanent and welcome members of the community.

SOCIAL LIFE

Until the early part of this century, social life consisted mainly of gatherings in private houses and sometimes in school buildings. The main time for this was the festive season; stories containing wit and humour were exchanged, and fiddle music and dancing added to the enjoyment. Before World War I, community halls were built at Benston in Nesting and at Vidlin in Lunnasting, and both have since been used for a variety of purposes. At the Benston Hall, locally organised concerts were occasionally presented. Contributions from talented local musicians were frequent, and sketches were presented which portrayed a depth of thought, a sense of humour, and on occasion good-natured and subtle references to amusing or slightly embarrassing situations of topical local interest. These sketches were always produced and accepted as good clean fun, never causing offence to individuals. One local producer of sketches and poems was gifted in this respect and his productions were in demand from all parts of Shetland.

The public hall at Vidlin was opened in 1913 after an enthusiastic effort at fund-raising for the purpose. Overcrowding did not appear to hamper the talents displayed by the residents. It may be noteworthy to mention that one boy of eleven attended a wedding in Vidlin Hall in 1913. Guests aware of his musical talent persuaded the modest boy to 'spell' the official fiddler during his break time; and when hoisted on to the platform he performed to the delight of guests. Incidentally seventy years on the modest fiddler is a household name throughout Shetland, and the father of an equally talented son.

More recently both the Benston and Vidlin halls have been extended and modernised.

There are active branches of the W.R.I. in both Nesting and Lunnasting, and Nesting has a mothers and toddlers group.

There is a badminton club in South Nesting, and several years ago South Nesting and Girlsta (which is in the neighbouring parish of Tingwall, Whiteness and Weisdale) successfully revived a local Up-Helly-Aa festival.

THE ISLAND OF WHALSAY

by Henry A. Stewart

PHYSICAL BASIS

The island of Whalsay is administratively linked with Out Skerries; formerly it was also linked with Nesting and Lunnasting on the Shetland Mainland, but for most purposes was separated in the middle of last century. Whalsay is six miles long by an average of two miles broad. The origin of its name is Norse, but the meaning is disputed. It has been rendered 'island of the hill' or 'island of the whale'. The nearest part of the Shetland Mainland is two miles west of Whalsay, and the nearest ferry pier is five miles distant, at the west head of the South Voe of Lunnasting: this voe on many maps is erroneously named 'Dury Voe'. In contrast to the above distances in statute miles, sea-faring inhabitants of Whalsay normally give distances in nautical miles. There are several rocks and islands around Whalsay; starting from the west, and in a clock-wise direction, the main ones are as follows, the derivations of the names being given in brackets: Unerim (Arnorr's holm); Brusim (Brusi's holm); Littleim and Kettlim (little holm and Ketill's holm); Skurim (Skori's holm); Little Linga (little heathery isle); West Linga (west heathery isle); Wadrim (ram holm); Holms of Skaw (holms of the point); Nista (north-most isle); Mooa (narrow isle); Holm of Isbister (holm of east farm); East Linga (east heathery isle); Grif Skerry (skerry adjacent to deep sea); Rumble (probably, round rocks); Holm of Sandwick (holm of sand bay).

There is danger of confusion with the rock names between Rumble and the headland of Moull of Eswick in Nesting. On the Admirality

Chart they are named Muckla Fladdacap, Muckla Billan, Litla Billan and Haerie; but the Whalsay names for them are respectively Muckle Fladdacap, Peerie Fladdacap, Haerie and Ooter Vooder. In this age of radio communication, sailor beware!

Cliffs are comparatively high on the east side of Whalsay, where they face the open North Sea; but on the west side the shores are lower and more accessible. There are only two sizeable inlets, both at Symbister in the south-west. There are un-manned lighthouses, at Symbister Ness and Suther Ness. The bedrock of Whalsay is mainly gneiss and the land is undulating with generally smooth slopes; the highest point on the island is the Ward of Clett at the extreme south end with a height of 393 feet O.D. There are eleven small lochs on the island.

HISTORY

Discovery of several ancient sites of 4,000 to 5,000 years of age or even more, have been made since the 1920s by a Whalsay archaeologist. The most complete of these are at Pettigar's Field in the north-east of the island, and at Water Hammers near the south end. There is evidence of farming at such sites, but no evidence of defence. The latter came more than 2,000 years later with the building of the 'brochs' of the Iron Age period. Three such brochs, or other fortifications—at Loch of Huxter, Broch Skeo at Symbister, and da Brochs at Brough—have been almost cleared of stones. There is a handed-down tale that a woman from the township of Brough who had tunnel vision could see from the top of the broch sails spread on the Grif Skerry, almost five miles away; and in this way she could tell which fishing boats were ashore at the 'lodges' used on Grif Skerry. This if true would give a good indication of the height of the broch, as the sea on the east side of Whalsay (and the Grif Skerry) is cut off from view by the intervening hills. The stones of Huxter Broch were used to build 'plant crubs' (small circular enclosures for cabbage seedlings); those of the Broch of Symbister were used to make an artificial beach; and the houses of the township of Brough were built from the local broch.

Whalsay at one time had several local lairds or small landowners, but these were ousted by the Bruces of Muness in Unst, who first established themselves in the house of the deposed laird of Symbister, Colbyn Ormsson. The Bruces later built the 'Auld Haa' (old hall) near the same site, and finally built the 'New Haa' (new hall), now Symbister House School. The lairds before the Bruces appear to have been crofter-fishermen themselves but under the new lairds a class-conscious society developed, with the overwhelming majority of the islanders leading a serf-like existence; and ministers, teachers, doctors and henchmen in more or less that order applied rules of discipline. Punishments for indiscipline varied in severity. Last century punishment was invariably exile, the culprits being forbidden ever again to show their faces in Whalsay. The effects of this treatment are in evidence to this day in the fawning attitude of some of the older people to the successors of the once-important hierarchy.

The crofts of Whalsay became grouped into 'toonships' (or townships), which have remained as centres of population. From south to north they are as follows, the derivations of the names being given in brackets:

Symbister	(south farm)
Clett	(a rock)
Sandwick	(sand bay)
Huxter	(mound farm; named from pre-Norse mounds)
Sodom	(formerly South Hammister; south harbour farm)
Skibberhoull	(skipper hill)
Hammister	(harbour farm)
Treawick	(wood [or wreck] bay)
Marrister	(horse farm)
Isbister	(east farm)
Brough	(borg, or fort)
Shallister	(tent farm)
Vatshoull	(loch hill)
Skaw	(point)

The biggest crofts in Whalsay are of about 10 acres in size. Peat for fuel is still cut in large quantities, and within living memory was also transported to nearby Out Skerries. 'Casting' peats was a communal activity for the people from Out Skerries, and when they came they were helped by scores of Whalsay people.

During the 19th century, Whalsay men depended almost entirely on their crofts along with fishing in open boats. Some men, however, got permission from the laird to join the mercantile marine or to go to the whaling at Greenland. Many men were pressed into the Royal Navy, and two hiding places where men concealed themselves from the press gang can still be traced. One is at Leeans and the other at Eastermuir: however in the latter case continued digging at an encroaching peat bank may soon see its end. Stories of press gang activity have not been well recorded, but it is known that many men were taken off 'sixerns' (thirty-foot open boats) while at sea. By 1900 the sixerns had been replaced by fifty-foot decked sail-boats which fished with long lines at a range of 30 to 40 miles in April and May for the bigger white fish; and the same boats from June to October fished for herring with drift nets. Strange as it may seem, small four-oared open boats ('fowereens') were used in the dead of winter to catch the demersal fish (especially haddock), which were found close inshore while the pelagic herring were 'outshore' (now called 'offshore').

POPULATION

Due to the income derived from whaling, Faroe cod fishing and the home fishing with decked boats, population grew towards the end of last century, and by 1911 had reached a figure of 1,042. There was a subsequent sharp fall in numbers during and after World War I, when the prosperity of the herring fishery declined markedly. After World War II, however, the island built up a modern fishing fleet, and renewed prosperity saw the population recover to its present level of 1,064. These developments were considerably helped by the building of a small harbour at Symbister. There have been few instances of families moving in to the island, but there are many cases of men and women marrying into Whalsay.

The future population now very much depends on decisions made at the E.E.C. level on fisheries policy. However, experience of recent decades suggests that it is in this island that advances in fishing are most likely to happen in Shetland.

PUBLIC AND SOCIAL SERVICES

Postal deliveries are made four times weekly.

Since World War II a mains water supply has been installed and there are now two sewage schemes which provide for part of the island; similar schemes are planned for the remainder, and will replace the septic tanks now in use. There is a weekly refuse collection.

Whalsay is now joined by submarine electric cable to Nesting on the Shetland Mainland, and hence to the grid system which is supplied by the generating station in Lerwick. There is no public lighting other than at the two council housing schemes of Tripwell and Harlsdale.

Roads are mostly single track, and are surfaced with tarmac, but the number of vehicles is now such that they need widening and resurfacing.

There is a policeman on the island.

EDUCATION AND HEALTH SERVICES

Symbister House, formerly the seat of the lairds, was converted into a school (both primary and junior secondary); the latter part is now a junior high. The numbers of pupils and teachers now necessitates an extension to the building.

There is a doctor on the island, who also serves Out Skerries; there is also a district nurse.

The social worker for the North Mainland area is resident on Whalsay, and is also responsible for Out Skerries.

Facilities at Symbister House are used by visiting dentists both from the Education Department and the Armed Services; between them they provide for the needs of the island.

Chiropodists and physiotherapists visit regularly.

VOLUNTARY ORGANISATIONS

For the very young there is a play school. There are Boy Scouts and Girl Guides organisations.

W.R.I. and Women's Guild are organisations of long standing, and there are frequent meetings of various kinds organised under the auspices of the Church of Scotland. There is also a Young Mothers' group.

Activities in music, drama and art are organised by both the Education and the Hall Committees; these committees also organise many sporting activities. There are on the island two halls and a football field.

TRANSPORT

Whalsay has a roll-on roll-off ferry service from 6.45 a.m. to 6 p.m. connecting every two hours with Laxo on the Shetland Mainland. Supplementary trips can be arranged and schedules are often slightly changed. There is an airstrip, and a scheduled air service links with Tingwall on the Shetland Mainland.

CHURCHES

There is a very old church at Kirkness, and another church at Saltness; both are of Church of Scotland denomination. Occasionally there are visits by various other religious groups, and one such group is converting an old house into a manse.

HOUSING

In Whalsay a young married couple normally gets the tenancy of a council house, but when savings allow a new house is built. The new house is generally built on land belonging to relatives of the couple concerned. There are five groups of council houses, and there are two small groups of sheltered houses looked after by a caretaker. The total number of householders is 260.

There are no serious cases of overcrowding, and until recently there was no substantial waiting list for houses. Other than the council houses, homes are almost invariably owned by the people who live in them. Old croft houses have been adapted to modern requirements. Most old houses are of two storeys, although ceilings are often low. Ribbon development, although frowned on on the Scottish mainland, is approved of on Whalsay, and has led to a fair-sized housing scheme being built in what was a lonely area, with every house having a view of the sea and seashore. The idea of council houses being built facing each other does not appeal to the people.

AGRICULTURE, INDUSTRIES AND COMMERCE

Since the 18th century, fishing has been the main source of income, while the yield from crofts and from knitting served in poor seasons to prevent earnings from 'slipping through the back door'. Greenland whaling, codfishing at Faroe and the Merchant Navy were also comparatively good sources of income which led to improvements in houses and in croft husbandry.

The decked sail-boat, which was the main fishing vessel employed at the start of this century, was superseded by motor-boats and steam drifters. The herring fishery became the main activity, but this suffered a serious recession in the inter-war period with the disorganisation and partial collapse of the continental markets on which it mainly depended. Shetland herring could generally find a market on the continent, but in Whalsay there was a recurrent problem of herring being dumped when catches exceeded curing capacity. During World War II a beginning was made in the use of the ground seine for catching white fish, and subsequently fishing was viable and prosperous: a renewed fleet of dual-purpose (herring and white fish) boats was built up with the help of government grant and loan schemes. However in the later 1960s the advent of the purse-seine for catching herring fairly rapidly led to serious depletion of the stocks. This technique was adopted in several countries, but the big fleet of Norwegian purse-seiners, fishing for the market for meal and oil rather than human consumption, was mainly responsible for the over-fishing of the herring. Subsequent restrictions on pelagic fishing (mackerel as well as herring) have been imposed while the British fleet of purse-seiners has risen to about 50 vessels, of which Whalsay has nine. Most of these are manned by Whalsay crews, but one has men from Out Skerries and Vidlin (on the Shetland Mainland) as well as Whalsay. The modern organisation of pelagic fisheries compels these vessels to engage in them wherever and whenever they are permitted, and results in their operating as far away as Cornwall as well as in the Minches. The purse-seine is a productive and efficient technique and if controlled is not waste-ful, and the most modern Whalsay boats are steel built, some of them over 100 feet in length. It is possible that boats of this size could also be used to supply the white fish market in winter.

In addition to the purse-seiners there are eleven boats concentrating on white fish, and three scallop-dredger/long line boats. These boats are of a range of sizes, but are smaller than the purse-seiners. There are now 190 full-time fishermen who operate in the winter as well as the summer, in contrast to the 38 full-time men of the late 1940s. There is also on the island a white fish factory which employs up to 90 people.

Lacking on the island for the purse-seine fishermen are pelagic fish processing factories, cold stores and net stores. While provision of such facilities would involve considerable investment, it is suggested that this would be a better alternative than uprooting the fishermen and getting them to operate from other bases. The fishing tradition in Whalsay is well established, and the men have shown that they can hold their own with the best; and to maintain development now, innovations in shore-based facilities are very important. The very active Whalsay Community Council could play a valuable part in this.

Work on the crofts is now largely performed by tractors except in inaccessible fertile corners where older methods of husbandry may still be employed. The produce of the land is of high standard, and is frequently divided by the crofter among his relatives. A former dairy farm (in effect, a unit composed of several crofts) has now been turned over to the rearing of beef cattle.

There is a small knit-wear industry.

The first chalet has now appeared to cater for tourists, but there is no guest-house or hotel.

It is planned to open the old Hanseatic trading 'booth' at Symbister to visitors as a museum. The large membership of the new boating club at Symbister has led to this building being used for diverse communal activities.

WAY OF LIFE

The young people are very conscious of being part of a fishing community. Many boys are on fishing boats during their summer school holidays, and most try to get a berth on a boat when they leave school. Girls tend to be employed in the fish factory.

Occasional dances and weddings provide ample festive events. A relatively new practice is to go off the island for annual holidays, although the older members of the community see little necessity for this, and find that the island itself has enough to offer. Older people take part in the various social and sporting activities; although life is busy, it is seldom boring. The annual regatta is a main focus of interest, and recreational fishing from small boats or on lochs gives great pleasure to older men.

Whalsay people think that they are 'different' from elsewhere in Shetland. Some very distinguished visitors have recognised the unusual spirit and community solidarity of the island.

March 1983

OUT SKERRIES

by Rev. Thomas C. Bogle, B.D., Dip.R.Ed.

PHYSICAL BASIS

Four miles north-east of Whalsay and Scotland's nearest point to Norway, the Out Skerries—sometimes referred to nowadays as the Outer Skerries, usually in letters from London—are not so called because of their remoteness, despite being due north of Whitby and consequently Scotland's easternmost speck of land; the name in fact derives from the Norse 'Oust', i.e., east.

The Out Skerries are a tiny group of three isles, Bruray, Housay or

West Isle and Grunay or Grönay, together with over 20 named rocks, on the largest and farthest east of which stands a lighthouse. The total area is said to be 660 acres. All three islands are inhabited. Housay, the largest, is joined to Bruray by a bridge built in 1957 and most of the inhabitants actually cross the North Sea daily. The isles are heavily indented by the sea. From Mioness in the south-west to Bound Skerry in the north-east, is three miles, and from Vogans Point to Stoura Stack is one and one eighth miles. Neatly placed in the midst of the isles is a deep water harbour. The Out Skerries are near good fishing banks and the community continues to rely on fishing for its livelihood. An article once said that the outstanding feature of the Skerries landscape was the sea. In a full force 10 south-easterly gale the sea fills not only the ears with its thunder and the eyes with its fury, but the mouth and the nostrils too, for shelter is a luxury. The thin soil and rocky landscape in addition make crofting very unrewarding.

Grunay and Mioness (a long finger of land joined to the West Isle only by the remains of a collapsed cave, the 'Steig') have a granite base. The southern edge of West Isle is of fragmented limestone and the northern half is of gneiss. Perched on the hills are glacial erratics, the largest of which is called Gutcherabon. When the late John Stewart of Whalsay started to collect Shetland place-names he found around 1,500 here because the miniature landscape with tiny mountains, 'pocket hand-kerchief' rigs and even a twenty-yard long esker, encourages naming.

HISTORY

There is a variety of antiquities on the islands, and in recent centuries a number of wrecks have been particularly prominent events.

There is a stone circle called the Viking Battle Pund where according to tradition Vikings fought to the death in combat; and there are two other stone circles, one on either side of the West Voe. All over the North Hill are mounds of stones shaped like seven-foot long upturned boats; these are by tradition pre-Christian graves. There are also lengths of ancient walls made of giant stones which have served no need in modern times. Overlooking the West Voe are ancient 'skeos', used into the present century for drying fish.

In the folk memory of the Out Skerries, the first incident on record is the wreck of a Spanish horse-carrier from the Armada which sank at a narrow channel mouth called the Rett. Later two Dutch East Indiamen, both with wages aboard, were wrecked. The *Carmelan* (or *Kennemerland*) sank in the South Mouth on 12th December 1664 with only three survivors. The drummer boy was buried near the present fish factory with his drum, and according to tradition the people were drunk for weeks on the barrels washed ashore. The story also goes that our first hens flew ashore then.

De Liefde sunk with its treasure on November 6th 1711, hitting

Mioness and throwing the man in the crow's-nest ashore—the sole survivor. Both of these were going 'Achter Om'—i.e., the long way around
the British Isles, avoiding the enemy ships and wrecks in the Channel.
They were en route for Java. In the present century, the *North Wind* was
wrecked in 1906 with a cargo of wood; and by 1907 every house had a
wooden floor, and most had wooden roofs. In 1912 the *Advena* also sank at
the Out Skerries.

In former times, the visits of the press gang to get recruits for the
Royal Navy were a traumatic experience. It seems that all the men were
in danger of being pressed, and when the gang appeared the men would
hide in the cave known as the Pieds Hoose or Pictshouse, until a white cow
appeared on the brow of the hill—the sign that the coast was clear. The
old village was on Housay and is reputed to have had round houses and
circular ash-pits, but was abandoned partly because the sea could not be
seen from it. The site was converted to arable land in the 1920s, which
here were a time of poverty and hunger. By the time of World War I many
men were in the R.N.V.R.; this gave some supplement to their income at
a time when existence in the isles was still fairly precarious. It was not
until World War II that good fish prices allowed the community to reach
prosperity and an adequate standard of security.

POPULATION

The maximum population was 165 in 1891. The present total is 88,
showing a remarkably small decline for a remote island community. Of
these 53 are on Housay, 32 on Bruray and 3 on Grunay. Included in this
are three non-Shetland households—the two teachers and their families,
and three Lancastrians on Grunay.

The future of the community has its problems as there is a marked
reluctance of girls to marry into Out Skerries, and there are a dozen
bachelors ranging between 16 and 50 years. On the other hand, the
young people—especially the girls—are attracted by the employment
opportunities and amenities of the towns.

SCHOOL

The first school was erected in 1844, on a site which is now in the present
churchyard. The present incumbent is the 16th missionary headmaster to
be appointed. A new building was erected in 1896 to be both church and
schoolroom, and at the maximum there were nearly 40 children in the
school. In 1965 a new modern school was built. It is inevitably small and
has two full-time teachers and 14 pupils; this includes a primary department with 10 pupils and a secondary department with at present four,
including two about to sit O-grades in English, Arithmetic and History.
This, the smallest secondary school in Britain, exists because the parents
adamantly refuse to send the children away for education, claiming that

would lead to the death of the community. In 1978 the Scottish Education Department after a 30-year long struggle recognised that Skerries School was of junior secondary status and now the pupils study subjects as diverse as home economics and computer graphics.

CHURCH

The old school building was re-opened in 1967 as the church after extensive modernisation by the congregation. On most Sundays two-thirds of the population are present at the service.

COMMUNITY HALL

A modern community hall, which replaced a former war-time service hut, was opened in 1981 at a cost of £109,000. The cost of this was largely borne by the Leisure and Recreation Department of Shetland Islands Council, and this did mean that the community got some indirect benefit from the oil boom. Some help from the same source also came to the Toddlers Group, the Brownies, the Youth Club and the Playground Association.

TRANSPORT

In 1957, the contractors built a concrete bridge from Housay to Bruray using some of the excavated rock from the water scheme. They also blasted a new road from Bruray pier to the church on Housay. Four years later the roads were tarred. The following year the first motor car arrived; there are now 19 of varying ages. Most show, since the M.O.T. test does not apply, the signs of terminal rust—silencers missing, bonnets lashed on with nylon rope and doors that refuse to open. An airstrip has been built on Bruray. There is no scheduled service from this airstrip but the Shetland Islands Council subsidise flights on a 'taxi' basis for the inhabitants. There are some other chartered flights for visitors and some ambulance flights. However the basic life-line is the M.F.V. *Spes Clara*, a 35 year old converted fishing boat based in Whalsay and run by the Construction Department of Shetland Islands Council. It leaves for Lerwick twice weekly at 8 a.m. carrying passengers, mail, and up to 30 tons of goods. It returns in the early evening, weather permitting. Now it makes a trip to Whalsay on Sunday afternoons by request which means relatives can come here for a week-end. A new boat is on order specifically designed for the route.

VISITORS

Most of our visitors are relatives of the isles population. Very few tourists travel here except for those who want to claim to have been on as many islands as possible. There are two exceptions to this. The first is the bird watchers who come here twice yearly to look for rare Scandinavian migrants and incidentally provide amusement for the locals. The second is the divers who come most summers to look for treasure on our wrecks. They are now barred from diving on the *Carmelan*, as it is an archaeological treasure in itself. After a hard-fought court case, only one group—largely students—is allowed to dive on the *Liefde*.

HOUSING

The post-war period has seen some new house-building, along with extensive house modernisation, using the government grants available. Five council houses were completed in 1967. Since 1977, two new houses have been built, nine houses have had their windows renewed, mainly by double-glazing, and all but the house on Grunay have full modern bathroom and sanitation facilities. Every house now has a telephone, and every house is connected to an electricity generator. Although mains electricity is due to be installed when a cable is extended from Whalsay, no-one intends to part with their generator. Fresh water was a major problem for years, as there is no running water and in dry summers most of the springs run dry. In 1957 the SIC built a reservoir to hold 300,000 gallons of rain water running along channels on Bruray Hill, but that was soon not enough. Water tankers had to be hired in the driest summers to replenish the reservoir. In 1979 a large tank holding a further 300,000 gallons was added to the scheme.

AGRICULTURE, INDUSTRIES AND COMMERCE

Crofting is difficult and limited on the Out Skerries. Most of the croft land is on Housay, and is largely artificial; an area of 12 acres on the sheltered part of the island was many years ago made cultivable by the practice of 'flaying'—i.e., cutting turf on the hill and mixing it with seaweed to make what is called the 'infields'. There are 13 very small crofts, unfenced but marked by 'met' stones. Some potatoes and cabbage are still grown, the former a traditional black strain; and some mutton and eggs for home use are produced, but the last cow went in 1969.

Fishing continues to be the main employment and despite problems continues to be fairly prosperous. There are at present three vessels ranging from 40 to 80 feet, with a total of 13 fishermen; and another man is building a boat for himself and his sons. There is a factory which freezes white fish and which employs six men and eight women, some of them part-time.

Skerries women also still largely knit by hand and sell the products.

This community, however, has had little direct benefit from the modern oil boom.

Despite their small numbers, the community continues to support two shops.

Plate 14

COMMERCIAL STREET, LERWICK (c. 1925)

The original development of Lerwick was along the sea front, and the main street behind the shore-side buildings is a secondary development which is noticeably irregular. On it pedestrians and vehicles are still unsegregated.

(J. D. Ratter. Courtesy Shetland Museum and Library)

Plate 15

HERRING YARD, LERWICK (c. 1890)

From the late 19th century till after World War II, the main activity
of Lerwick was the herring fishing, which at one time attracted
hundreds of boats from all parts of Britain, and continental vessels as
well. At the peak there were 30 herring curing yards in Lerwick and
another 22 on the island of Bressay opposite.

(J. D. Ratter. Courtesy Shetland Museum and Library)

WAY OF LIFE, AND THE FUTURE

The main reason for the Out Skerries being inhabited originally was the fishing opportunities, when it was important to cut down the distance to fishing grounds in the days of the rowing-boat. Fishing has continued to be their main source of income, unlike other more favourably situated parts of Shetland. Life was for long a struggle, but the prosperity of the fishing during World War II set the community on a path of progress. There is a Shetland saying that Skerries people are never idle, and despite the problems there is a will to survive rarely exceeded in remote communities.

October 1982

THE PARISH OF NORTHMAVINE

by Andrew Ratter, B.A.

PHYSICAL BASIS

Northmavine has a tortured geological history. Just about everything that can happen to a rock has happened here at some time during the past 400 million years or so. As a result there are three main kinds of rock; volcanic, intrusive and metamorphic. That is to say, rocks that were molten when they came to the surface, molten rocks that cooled before reaching the surface and rocks of various kinds that have been altered by compression and heating.

Along the Yell Sound (east) side of the parish, rocks that were laid down as orderly, layered sediments have been squashed by huge pressures, distorted by the inner heat of the planet, and repeatedly split and smashed into pieces by enormous geological forces moving in the earth's crust. The Geological Survey map of Northmavine looks like a well-used collection of plasticene, with all the different colours twisted and confused in no discernible pattern. In fact there *is* a pattern to this apparent chaos, but it has taken geologists over a hundred years to make sense of it and many details are still uncertain. What is certain is that, if we had no other evidence from other places, the state of the north Mainland's rocks would be ample proof of the immensely long process of mountain building which created the mighty Caledonian range that once stretched from Scotland to Scandinavia, in the days before Greenland drifted away to join the North American continent and the volcanoes of Iceland erupted to fill the gap.

The broken schist rocks of Ollaberry and district, for example, were once simple sandstones and mudstones, laid down in wide rivers, lakes and shallow seas. Their present convoluted banding gives some indication to the non-geologist of the power that formed these metamorphic rocks over an unimaginable length of time. In places you may find traces of the relatively undisturbed Old Red Sandstone, 350 to 400 million years old, but this rock itself is made from sand that was produced by the erosion of even older rocks by wind and water.

From Fethaland at the north end of the parish down to Mavis Grind at its south end this jumble of shattered and twisted rock borders the much larger area of granite and associated rocks that form Muckle

Roe, Ronas Hill and the knobbly landscape on the southern side of Ronas Voe. Some 350 million years ago this granite was forced up from inside the earth in a semi-molten state but it was overlain by thousands of feet of other rocks, long since eroded away, so that it must have cooled into its present form far below the surface.

To the west of these intrusive rocks are lavas and compressed ashes in the volcanic series around Eshaness. These rocks are probably even older than the granites to the east. The volcano that ejected them is of course long gone. The lavas form magnificent cliffs, the rock standing near vertically where eroded by Atlantic storms.

There is one other major class of rocks in the parish, the ancient gneisses around Uyea, north of Ronas Hill. The gneiss comes to the surface only in an area of a few square kilometres. This rock appears to have been even more severely compressed than the schists, but never heated or deformed quite enough to become semi-molten like the granite (which it resembles in the minerals that it contains, though not in its appearance). The origins of the gneiss appear to be connected with the building of the Caledonian mountain system. The rocks from which the gneiss was made may have been part of an even older part of the earth's crust which was disturbed by this mountain building.

Over the aeons of time all these old Northmavine rocks have been invaded by veins of minerals which crystallised and solidified out of high-pressure vapours and liquids moving up from the depths. The backbone of the parish has been further disturbed by geological faulting—the cracking and splitting as the earth's crust heaved. The most remarkable of these faults are: the Melby Fault, which emerges from St Magnus Bay and runs from Breiwick to Ronas Voe, separating the Eshaness volcanics from the granite intrusion; the Walls Boundary Fault, a major dislocation on the earth's surface which runs under Sullom Voe near Brae, emerges at Sullom village, and passes under Gluss Voe to run past the Skerries of Skea before disappearing beneath Yell Sound. The rocks have been displaced along this fault, which is believed to be a continuation of the Great Glen Fault which splits Scotland along the line of Loch Ness; thirdly, there appears to be a major fault the line of which has been gouged out by ice to form Ronas Voe, the only proper fjord in Shetland.

Given the complexity of the raw materials, it is hardly surprising that the sea, the glaciers and the burns modelled such a distinctive shape for Northmavine over millions of years. By the time the first humans appeared on the scene, a mere 5,000 years ago, most of the solid geology had been covered from view, except along the exposed coastlines which were to puzzle the early geologists when they arrived in Shetland in the 18th and 19th centuries.

Local ice caps and (possibly) sea ice overriding the islands from the east, had plastered much of the land and seabed with stony clay and glacial sands, obliterating the earlier soils and peats in all but a few places. Here and there the melting ice left better quality material to nourish the plants which quickly colonised the barren surface to form the soil and peat of today.

On the exposed upland, notably Ronas Hill, soil and peat never had much chance to form. Here rare arctic-alpine flowers have survived into the present century, being too small for sheep to remove them totally. On the lower slopes and in pockets of valley land there was probably a good covering of grasses, heather and shrubs. Our ancestors, unfortunately for this natural vegetation, brought with them fire and grazing animals. On some islands in the lochs can now be seen the remnants of the post-glacial vegetation, though even here damage has been done by sheep wandering across the ice in hard winters and 'eating the place out' when they got stranded by the thaw. On some steep slopes and cliff ledges a more lush vegetation also survives.

Five thousand years of heather burning, poorly controlled grazing, and the cutting of dwarf trees and peat for fuel have left a ravaged landscape, the details of which are largely man-made. Yet for the early settlers Northmavine was probably an easier place in which to make a living than it became by the 18th century. Undisturbed fish, seabirds, wild berries and grass meadows must have been considerably more productive than today. Settlement could well have begun on a basis of fishing, hunting and gathering, and at a later stage the knowledge of farming came in leading to organised cropping and stock raising, which produced supplies of grain, meat and milk.

Even with modern fencing, drainage, fertilisers, seeds and veterinary knowledge, agriculture and animal husbandry are difficult. The climate and the poverty of most of Northmavine's soil are only two of the reasons. People themselves have created the other problems. The constant battle against over-grazing and soil exhaustion forced the crofters, many generations ago, to limit their livestock numbers and practise crop rotations.

The physical geography of the parish is not all negative however. The work of the sea and the ice have made good beaches for launching small boats, and also several natural harbours where larger fishing vessels may shelter safely during winter gales.

The hundreds of lochs still support trout which, along with the spectacular coastal scenery, attract visitors whose holiday money helps the local economy to a small extent.

A supply of fresh water from Roer Water and Eela Water was a fortunate thing for the new oil terminal at Sullom Voe, even if another scar on the landscape was created in the piping of it to Calback Ness. The granite heights of Collafirth Hill proved useful for the military when seeking a relay station site for their signals. Iron ore occurs at Clothister, which supported a mine for a time. The beaches of Northmavine still furnish sand for building work and agriculture, and may yet be harvested again for seaweed manure when imported phosphates become too expensive.

The Northmavine folk could indeed have a worse place to set themselves down. Given a few thousand more years of glaciation and they might have been living on an island, separated from the rest of Shetland by an ice-scoured chasm through Mavis Grind (The gate on the narrow isthmus). Nature is not always unkind.

HISTORY OF THE LOCAL COMMUNITY

The history of the 19th century in Northmavine was a history of population growth, development of fishing through the 'haaf' (i.e., the deep sea line fishing) and a continuation of the subdivision of the crofts which had led to the steady decline in agricultural methods noted by Shirreff in 1812.

Duncan's *Zetland Directory and Guide* for 1861 states that while eighty years previously the use of ploughs had been general in Northmavine, at that date spade cultivation was universal.

This growth in population, coupled with decline in agriculture and the fact that through the truck system and debt bondage the merchant-lairds managed to expropriate all (or almost all) of the men's income at the fishing led to the need for a new source of income, to allow the people to survive. That which provided this was not new, and was in fact the exploitation of women's labour through an expanded knitwear production. That this was a very old craft goes without saying, but it underwent substantial development and specialisation in the 19th century. In Northmavine, in fact, the form that it took was concentration on woollen undergarments. The argument could be made that all, or almost all, of the income above and beyond the money gathered for the rent (which was most of the croft's product), came from this source. This income took the form of truck, goods being given for the final product, a system which did not die out entirely till World War II. A linguistic relic of the labours of crofting women lingers in the dialect word 'cockramin' (cock-crow meat). When I was told of this, the teller explained that as a child she had heard this word, and I asked its meaning. It was explained as tea and oatcakes eaten by women at four in the morning after they had been sitting up all night carding and spinning. Had this practice been occasional, it would not have led to the coining of a special word.

Change in these oppressive circumstances was gradual, following upon the Napier and Truck Commissions at the end of the 19th century; these slackened the grip of the merchant lairds on the population, although the last member of them retained his grip until 1923, 40 years after the First Crofters Act! It must be said that this is a much later date than in other parts of Shetland.

In the time since then, lack of planning in the economy, a consequence of the whimsical and storm-driven nature of small-scale entrepreneurial capitalism surviving anachronistically in a backwater, has meant that local employment in the private sector has been mostly temporary and often ill paid. This has meant that in the first half of this century, the fishing industry disappeared with the decline of first the 'haaf' fishing and then the herring, both associated with lack of investment in bigger boats. Subsequently those men who sought employment did so away from the community, at sea and at the Antarctic whaling. Women continued to work despite being ill paid; they were engaged in knitting in the home, and on the crofts.

Ownership of the land in Northmavine is vested in crofting estates (now combined as one estate), with a small number of larger farms, these being cleared crofting lands; and there are a few crofter owner-occupiers.

In 1855 the Gifford family of Busta was by far the largest of these estate owners, holding 751 merks of land at a rental of £1,031. Ten smaller landowners then held the other 410 merks piecemeal. In 1931 the Busta Estate was still the main landlord, though the old established Gifford family had vanished, and by 1981 the Shetland Islands Council was the only estate owner, apart from Lochend estate and the owner-occupiers. This local authority ownership has existed since 1974 when the Busta and Ollaberry estates were purchased by them from A. Cussons and Co., the soap manufacturers. Time will tell whether there has been real improvement in estate management.

There are no comprehensive collections of estate papers referring to Northmavine. What would have been the largest and oldest collection of such papers, those of the Gifford family of Busta, were donated to H.M. Government for paper pulp during World War II. These would have contained material from as far back as 1567 when Mr John Gifford was church reader in Northmavine. The rise of the family from this period was steady, and they owned most of Northmavine at various times, until upon the death of Arthur Gifford in 1856, the estate became insolvent and fell into the hands of creditors.

Such records and papers as do refer to Northmavine are all in the Shetland Archives in Lerwick, or the Scottish Record Office in Edinburgh.

POPULATION

Between 1755 and 1790 the recorded population of Northmavine rose by 77 per cent, a tremendous increase even within a European context where everywhere populations were increasing. This increase continued, although more gradually up to 1871, when the number of people living in the parish reached 2,602.

This increase was due in part to smallpox vaccination, and also to the rise of the 'haaf' fishery with the accompanying subdivision of land-holdings by the merchant-lairds to increase the supply of crofts for fishermen. This being so, with the decline of the 'haaf' fishing, where the open 'sixareens' could not compete with the larger more modern boats for which capital was not available, in the century from 1871 to 1971 the population showed a steady decline; it was 1,997 in 1901, and reached a low point of 696 in 1971.

The following decade, 1971-1981 took in the construction of the oil terminal at Sullom Voe and its attendant ramifications, and led to some increase, with the population in 1981 recorded as 748.

PUBLIC AND SOCIAL SERVICES

As far as amenities are concerned, a public electricity supply came to Northmavine in 1959, and a water supply in 1969. More recently, in the late 1970s a weekly refuse collection was instituted.

Public education began with the formation of a school board in 1873 following the 1872 Act. This body established schools at North Roe, Collafirth, Eshaness, Urafirth, Ollaberry and Sullom, and levied a rate to support these. The school buildings were complete by 1880. The functions of the school board were taken over by the Education Authority for Shetland in 1919. Of the six schools mentioned, three now survive— at Ollaberry, North Roe, and Urafirth.

At present, Northmavine is served by one doctor and two nurses, one of the nurses serving as a health visitor. There has been a doctor in Northmavine since 1844, first at Ollaberry, then in Hillswick. This doctor, in earlier days, was rowed to the Island of Yell to attend cases there.

Until the arrival of the National Health Service, a local club levied a household medical fund, plus a fee per visit. In 1912 this was one shilling per visit, and ten shillings per annum. The County of Shetland was the last in Scotland to appoint a schools medical officer.

Northmavine is well supplied with community organisations, encouraged and assisted by money from the Shetland Island Council's department of Leisure and Recreation, but based on an increased awareness of community and identity among the people of the parish which has accompanied the oil era. In some ways the past few years, to those who knew the prevailing gloom of the 1950s and early 1960s, have been a time of renewed optimism, confidence coming with prosperity.

A list of community organisations is as follows:

> Hall Committees: North Roe, Ollaberry,
>   Lochend Central, Hillswick, Sullom and
>   Gunnister
> Ollaberry Sport Association
> 2 Sailing Clubs
> 2 Badminton Clubs
> Happy Hour Club
> Ronas Drama Club
> Northmavine Up-Helly-Aa Committee
> Northmavine Fiddle and Accordian Club
> Hillswick Women's Guild

North Roe and Ollaberry Women's Guild
North Roe and Ollaberry S.W.R.I.
2 Playgroups
3 Youth Clubs
North Roe Photographic Club
Northmavine Sheepdog Trials Committee
Northmavine Community History Group
'Nortaboot' Editorial Group
Collafirth Hill All Ranks Club
Ollaberry Boating Club
Community Council
Cattle Compensation Group

These groups, along with various night classes, for the most part have a far wider basis than their brief might indicate. They have a very important social function in that they promote gatherings, especially during the winter months without much regard to sex and age differences, and hence do more than anything else to promote activities and general community awareness.

HOUSING

An examination of the valuation roll for the parish for 1981 reveals that the croft house is still the most common form of dwelling in Northmavine. Of houses mentioned, 240 could be described as croft houses, 103 as other dwellings, (including residential caravans), and 72 are local authority and Hjaltland Housing Association houses, the former of these including a proportion of sheltered housing. The local authority and association housing has all been built since 1970, in response to some extent to the demands of the oil industry, or rather the construction industry serving the oil industry.

Housing, by and large is of a reasonable standard, due to improvements made in the post-war period, with the help of crofting and local authority grants. Croft houses are owned by the crofters, irrespective of who owns the land, and hence people were and are willing, with the availability of money, and latterly of water and electricity, to extend their own houses. The houses are normally 'two up and two down' cottages, with bathrooms, kitchens and extra bedrooms. Quite a number of houses of the standard 'modern' type have been built over the last decade. These by and large blend ill with the landscape.

A glance at the number of houses and the population would indicate that overcrowding is not a problem in the parish, but it should be stressed that there are numerous people living in residential caravans, which are not suitable because of the climate. There are others living in substandard accommodation who would wish to move into local authority housing, should it be made available.

The other significant point is that most local authority housing estates are not at all environmentally appropriate in a parish with a traditional settlement pattern of scattered crofts.

THE CHURCH

At the end of 1982, Northmavine is, apart from Unst, the only Shetland charge not to be linked or united with another. It still uses five church buildings: the Parish Church at Hillswick, built in 1869, to replace the kirk built in 1733 in the middle of the old churchyard at the same place; the former Congregational chapel (1865) at Sullom; the former United Free Church at Eshaness (1871); the Church of Scotland mission chapel at Ollaberry (1865, and built on the site of the old Ollaberry Church), and the Church of Scotland mission chapel at North Roe (1870). The manse at Hillswick was built in 1768, and enlarged later. The glebe is now immediately south of the manse, and extends to 43 acres. There is a Methodist chapel in North Roe (1878), and an excellent relationship exists between Church of Scotland and Methodist congregations in the parish.

In the first 80 years of this century, Northmavine has had eight ministers, but only twice has there been a lengthy vacancy. Two of the ministers stayed for nineteen years, and one for eighteen. The most obvious pre-Reformation ruins are the outline walls of the Cross Kirk, in the churchyard at Eshaness.

Though the congregation uses five church buildings, at the end of 1982 its roll was limited to 113. In 1983, the congregation will be aid-receiving from central funds, the amount approved being up to 72 per cent of the stipend. The average age of the members is high, and church attendance, placed against national averages, is good. Church offerings amount to little more than 50 per cent of the congregation's running expenses. The fact that the congregation, though heavily aid-receiving, is still able to cope financially, is evidence of the support the Church receives from the wider community, through sales of work and donations. In 1982 the congregation's biggest single contributor was the Women's Guild, with its branches in Hillswick, Sullom, and Ollaberry with North Roe.

The congregation enters the 1980s with a number of difficulties. The lack of a secondary school in the parish has made it difficult to attract children older than those of Sunday School age: the village halls have now in many ways supplanted the church and church socials as the centres of community life; the congregation's buildings are all falling into disrepair, and small numbers and rising costs make it difficult to justify retaining five church buildings. Though neither constituted as a union nor a linkage, the congregation is much divided into five areas, which struggle to maintain their independence, and resist united worship. One unifying factor is the existence of a Northmavine choir. The hidden congregationalism within the parish is almost certainly the inheritance of fairly recent history: this includes the building of mission chapels in the 1860s and 1870s, and then the deployment of lay missionaries along with the minister. In 1940, when Sullom was in Delting ecclesiastical parish, and had a missionary as well as the minister in Hillswick, there were missionaries in Eshaness and Ollaberry. As late as 1960 there were missionaries in both Ollaberry and Sullom. The last missionary was withdrawn from Sullom in 1976. To survive as a church community into the 1990s, the congregation will have to learn to reunite itself, and find some way of bridging the gap between village hall and kirk.

AGRICULTURE, INDUSTRY AND COMMERCE

At the present day employment is mainly provided in Northmavine by fishing, crofting and knitting, together with employment by the local authority, and in the oil industry at Sullom Voe. Of these, the fishing and fish processing are a product of the late 1960s and the 1970s, as the oil industry (including construction and catering and now work at the Sullom Voe oil terminal) are of the 1970s and 1980s. The local authority has also expanded its workforce over the past decade. Crofting has altered its form and scale somewhat due to the schemes of grants and subsidies for extension of holdings and for various agrarian improvements.

Knitting, principally a cottage industry, has never died out, and undergoes periodic fluctuations. It is marked by payment at piece rates which constitute an extremely low hourly rate to the knitters, a highly skilled and almost exclusively female workforce.

Although it has been stated that crofting has altered to some extent, and this has certainly led to some increase in potentially full-time crofters, crofting is still predominantly accompanied by other employment. The distribution and scale of the crofts is in fact a commentary on the history of the community.

All in all the development which has taken up the slack in the economy and so far has protected Northmavine from recession is the arrival of the oil industry, as all of the other employments—fishing, knitting, and crofting have been in sectors which have traditionally suffered from the vagaries of the market.

There is a very limited amount of other employment. A few people are engaged in 'jobbing' building, and some in small-scale plant contracting, but these are one man operations, and nothing on any scale has ever developed. The tourist industry, due to distance, expense and lack of imaginative organisation is quite irrelevant to the economy of this community.

WAY OF LIFE

The term 'way of life' is one which is heavily over used while its meaning is imprecise and consequently it is difficult to employ it satisfactorily.

In Shetland the term has been used over the last century in an idealised or over-idealised manner. Its origins are associated with the sustained period of growth and relocation of the native bourgeoisie in the late 19th century. It has persisted since and the main body fostering it today is the Shetland Movement.

The consequence is that when 'way of life' is mentioned, there are conjured up stereotype images of a living wrested from the sea, Viking ancestors, and cruel and oppressive lairds (who are all gone now!).

The importance of relocation also requires comment. Until the late 19th century, the ruling class in Shetland was scattered round the islands (though for some, town houses were a feature) and was numerically small and localised, thus necessarily entering into personal relationships with their communities.

The wealth brought by the herring boom of the late 19th century changed this state of affairs. The new town in Lerwick was built, and the new and invigorated bourgeoisie was able to draw close together. In these circumstances was born a mythology of a Shetland way of life.

This mythology is easily recovered from amongst the publications of the time and its signature was intriguingly both a heroic view of the past and a re-assessment of the present in terms of status and value. For the view of the present we must examine the selection of exceptionally patronising 'humorous' books which came out, and of which Joseph Gray's *Lowrie* is typical. It consists of a collection of newspaper pieces, and describes the results of a half-witted and hidebound crofter's misunderstandings of the modern world, in which the Lerwick haberdasher felt at home. At the same time Up-Helly-Aa was being invented, and the weekly *Shetland Times* devoted the best part of a page a week, ably abetted by correspondents, to creating a myth of race and blood, of a glorious Scandinavian past.

This may seem irrelevant in a description such as this, but I want to make it clear that we are entering an area where the waters are muddy, and I want future researchers who may use this book to be aware of the fact. Life for the people of Northmavine has probably over the last hundred years followed much the same course as in a crofting community in the north-west of Scotland. Norse place-names do not a Scandinavian influence make.

The same forces which have dominated recent history apply all over the north of Scotland, with differences of detail. The fishing industry in Northmavine collapsed largely because of the existence of a ruling class unwilling to invest to modernise, and its resurgence in the late 1960s and 1970s was made possible by central government policy relating to investment and loans. The hosiery industry has been perpetuated by the ability to guarantee its work force.

In recent years the possibilities for work paid at the usual modern rates for women at Sullom Voe produced a lull in knitting. Now that the oil-related work is finished, hosiery is picking up again but is still very poorly paid. The changes in crofting have been caused and shaped by crofting legislation and the Crofters Commission, the function of which extends throughout the crofting counties.

In the end, I suppose, we know our own communities best, and each possesses its own uniqueness. Why should affection and loyalty be conditional on assertion of 'historical and geographical uniqueness' (whatever these may mean) and on claims for 'a unique way of life'?

February 1983

THE PARISH OF SANDSTING AND AITHSTING

by James P. Nicolson, M.A.

PHYSICAL BASIS

The parish of Sandsting and Aithsting lies on the West Mainland of Shetland, adjoining Weisdale for much of its eastern boundary (which lies just west of the Weisdale or Skalla hills), and bordering part of Delting parish in the north-east. From the innermost end of Gruting Voe the boundary on the west with Walls and Sandness runs northwards to West Burrafirth including all of that community save the isolated Snarraness. These are still the parish boundaries but for electoral purposes West Burrafirth has recently been linked with Sandness, while Bridge of Walls, Gruting and part of Selivoe have become part of the Walls area. Those changes, though in the interest of more equitable populations, have nonetheless aroused opposition as they pay no regard to other factors such as geographical, historical and social links.

Eric Linklater has described this area as 'a bewilderment of land and water' and such it certainly is. Both to the north and to the south it is deeply indented by long voes; there are West Burrafirth, and Brindister, Clousta and Aith Voes in Aithsting, while Sandsting, sometimes locally referred to as 'the south neuk' is a peninsula formed between the long arms of Bixter and Gruting Voes. But adding to the confusion of land and sea are the many lochs usually formed in peaty areas and liberally distributed throughout the parish. There are no rivers but the Burn of East Burrafirth is perhaps the longest in Shetland; it has spectacular falls at Ramna höl and in spate carries a considerable volume of water.

The terrain is very undulating but there are no high hills in this area, the highest ground being close to the eastern boundary. All the hills are rounded and generally covered in peat, though in some areas land reclamation has seen the heather replaced by grass.

There are a number of small islets or holms lying offshore, some of which may support a few sheep; but the most significant islands are Vementry and Papa Little, both lying to the north of Aithsting, and both of which were inhabited till last century. These islands help to form Swarbacks Minn, an important naval anchorage in the First World War and guarded by the two 6-inch guns still standing sentinel on the island of Vementry.

The most interesting geological feature of this area is undoubtedly the Walls Boundary Fault, possibly an extension of the Great Glen Fault, which bisects this parish and the line of which is perhaps most apparent near Garderhouse, and less so at South Gardie in Aith. To the west of this fault the rocks are mainly of Old Red Sandstone but there are metamorphic schists along the northern coastline and in the isle of Vementry while at Clousta volcanic rocks are to be found. The rest of Aithsting to the east of the fault is composed mainly of metamorphic rocks, usually well covered in peat. In the Reawick and Skeld areas a most attractive red granite occurs with fine cliffs and pleasant red sands.

The voes previously mentioned, and others such as East Burrafirth, Sand Voe, Selivoe and Skeld Voe, with a few lesser indentations in Sandsting such as Reawick, Westerwick and Culswick, are generally the areas around which settlement has taken place. It may not always have been so in prehistoric times, but more recently the most easily cultivated land has been found around the voes; and of course sheltered harbours and beaches over which a boat could be drawn were essential for the pursuit of the fishing vital to these communities. Sea routes were for centuries the most convenient means of transportation and, for example, close links were established between Reawick and Scalloway, helping in the development of the former as a commercial centre in Sandsting.

There are therefore a great number of small communities each with its own sense of identity which go to make up this parish, which in area is one of the largest in Shetland being over eleven miles long from north to south and seven miles in width. By road it is a journey of over twenty miles from Culswick to East Burrafirth at opposite ends of the parish. These communities, the settings of which are perhaps bleak and desolate in a winter gale, nevertheless have each their own individual attractiveness.

HISTORY

The western part of this parish and the neighbouring area in Walls and Sandness have proved fruitful areas for excavation by archaeologists in recent years, and there was settlement in this area from about 3500 B.C. onwards. Some Neolithic houses have been discovered particularly in the Gruting area, including what may well have been the site of an early temple at Stanydale.

Early settlement in the islands was in the era prior to the conditions which resulted in much of the islands being covered by peat and obviously the changing climate must have altered the pattern of settlement of this area. Remains of dykes under the peat cover and stretching for quite considerable distances, particularly in the area near the present parish boundary with Walls and Sandness, suggests the early population was of such size as to need territorial divisions. Respect for their dead obviously figured highly in the culture of these early peoples, as can be seen from a number of burial cairns usually placed in prominent places, with perhaps the best example in this area being on the isle of Vementry.

A later group of settlers, who have left a great deal of evidence of their settlement, but regarding whom there is still considerable mystery, were the broch builders. Numerous sites of brochs are to be found—at West Houlland, Westerskeld, Skeld, Tumlin, Clousta, Brindister, East Burrafirth and West Burrafirth; and until last century there was the broch second only in state of preservation to that on Mousa, at Culswick. Culswick was to suffer the fate which had undoubtedly befallen the others in previous centuries: it provided a relatively easy supply of building materials. These brochs situated as they were either on hills, promontories or on small islets were undoubtedly defensive structures. They are probably from the early centuries B.C., and having fallen into disuse perhaps 500 years before the arrival of the Norsemen, by whom they were built and for defence against whom are still matters of conjecture.

It has been suggested that Christianity penetrated to the Northern Isles before the coming of the Norsemen, and indeed the name Papa Little may indicate that island to have been occupied by priests. Monks, desirous of an austere life probably occupied Kirk Holm near Sand, but one shudders at the self sacrifice of the individual who it has been suggested occupied a cell on the extremely exposed Burgi Stack near Culswick.

A great impact was of course made on this area as on the whole of Shetland by the coming of the Norsemen from the eighth century onwards. Norse language, laws and culture were established, apparently wiping out virtually all traces of previous inhabitants. Every voe, headland, farm and hill received a name of Norse significance which in most cases continues in use to this day, though some of the names when written have been corrupted by anglicisation. Aith is still pronounced 'eid' (meaning isthmus) by most of the inhabitants, and Effirth should correctly be 'Aefirth'. The pattern of settlement created by the Norse is well illustrated from the place names in Aith: Biggins, the central dwelling area would probably have been occupied first, with perhaps under the udal system land being shared by all children and thus split up by heredity. Other steadings were probably later established round the centre—Nesthouse, Uphouse and Southtown; then in a final stage North Gardie and South Gardie settled on the outskirts.

There is little written evidence from the Norse period relating directly to this area except one reference in the Orkneyinga Saga to Borgarfiord as the place where one Thorbiorn was slain by Earls Magnus and Haakon in the early 12th century. Presumably this event took place at or near the broch at Hebrista, West Burrafirth.

Little change probably resulted immediately from the transfer of sovereignty from the Danish to the Scots government in 1469, but by the seventeenth century Scots lairds were emerging, building up their estates and subjugating a people who had under udal law enjoyed a certain amount of freedom. Though ministers, dependent as they were on the lairds for patronage and stipend, were rarely critical of their masters, the writer of the Old Statistical Account for this area draws attention to the unscrupulous use of the law to evict small land owners from their property, and notes that no udallers were by this time left in the district.

Much of the land came to be owned by heritors resident outwith the parish, but probably the oldest dwelling still inhabited today was built at Sand in 1754 for Sir Andrew Mitchell of Westshore. The 'Haa' of Sand, still an imposing if sombre building, incorporates stone removed from Scalloway Castle for use in its construction.

Even relatively small landowners were regarded with some awe by the local populace in the 18th and 19th centuries. When Samuel Hibbert the famous geologist was visiting West Burrafirth he was guest of the laird of Fogrigarth, one Robbie Doull. Hibbert notes that when approaching Robbie Doull on his 'high seat' he passed through a double rank of servants. Many of these were in this case probably kinsfolk of the laird but were nonetheless obligated to him.

The Rev. Patrick Barclay in the Old Statistical Account indicates that, with the first 'haaf' (deep sea) fishing skipper in the parish still alive at that time, the large-scale prosecution of the fishing was comparatively recent. People had previously been able to obtain sufficient profit from their sheep and cattle to pay their rent, or if they desired had been able to hire their services as fishermen in other districts on their own behalf. But by subdividing tenancies and creating outsetts (new intakes) the lairds created units that were incapable of providing even a bare livelihood and ensured the dependance on them of the tenants. These tenants were obliged to fit out a share in a sixareen and land fish exclusively to their laird who in the late 18th century had assumed the role of merchant.

In defence of the lairds it has been stated that outsetts were necessary because of the natural increase in population taking place. This is partly explained by the increasing control of diseases such as smallpox which could (as in 1740) decimate a small village such as Culswick; but inoculation had virtually eradicated smallpox by the end of the century. There is no doubt that the lairds encouraged early marriage by making land available in order to ensure a ready supply of fishermen. Bitterness was inevitable from the system involving short-term leases, rental in kind, and the truck system which virtually ensured the tenant's continued indebtedness to the laird.

Some men were able to opt out of fishing by joining the Greenland whalers which called at ports in Shetland to supplement their crews; but in addition to the dangers of that hazardous occupation, their families might well have to suffer a penalty from the laird in the form of a rent increase.

As fishermen and whalers, Shetlanders were highly regarded for their ability as seamen and as such were prime targets for the press gangs, active during the Napoleonic Wars and at other times. John Nicolson in his story of Kirkcaldy's Sword tells of an incident involving the press gang at Clousta, in the course of which a naval officer named Kirkcaldy and

Plate 16

SUMBURGH AIRPORT, Dunrossness (1980)

This shows the new terminal built by the Civil Aviation Authority to handle the vastly expanded traffic of the oil era. The numbers of helicopters as well as fixed-wing aircraft testify to the great activity in servicing the oil industry.

(Courtesy Civil Aviation Authority)

Plate 17

SULLOM VOE OIL TERMINAL, Delting

The tank farms and tanker jetties are clear. The scale of the terminal
may be gauged from the fact that the sea frontage on the south-west
of Caldback Ness (foreground) is one mile long.

(Courtesy British Petroleum Co. Ltd.)

one of his intended victims perished on the Loch of Setter at a spot still called Kirkcaldy's Bight.

By the mid 19th century lairds were taking less interest in the fishing, only one proprietor (according to Rev. John Bryden, writing the Statistical Account of 1841) letting his lands on a fishing tenure. In other areas merchants were becoming increasingly involved in fishing, especially in Reawick where James Garrick was very much in the forefront. Sloops were purchased second-hand from the Mainland of Britain and fitted out for cod fishing, which was to develop at the expense of the 'haaf' fishing for ling in the second half of the nineteenth century. Faroe was the favoured place of operation, but Rockall and even Iceland were not beyond these cod-fishers; and beaches at Reawick and Skeld were a bustle of activity, providing work splitting and drying the fish for those too old or too young to be involved in the actual catching.

Apart from their official purpose the cod fishers also took advantage of their trips to Faroe to indulge in smuggling. Despite the diligent attention to duty paid by numerous excise officers, many stories abound of the successes of this feature of the voyages, with peat stacks and corn 'skroos' accommodating the illicit goods.

It is, however, all too easy to place too much emphasis on the lighter side when in reality conditions were extremely harsh. Perhaps particularly was this so for the women, who in addition to bearing the large families common in those days had, with men engaged in fishing, to attempt to eke sufficient from the croft to maintain the family throughout the winter. Primitive agricultural practices frequently resulted in poor crops, and it was not uncommon for example for the rotten potatoes of one year's crop to be eaten in order to ensure that there were sufficient good seed left for the following year. The fisherman who earned sufficient to pay his rent was content for the time being; the one who did not might well face eviction.

Small wonder then that on hearing of the lands of opportunity overseas many decided to emigrate, particularly to New Zealand but also to Australia and North America. There were no clearances as such in this area, and indeed during the 1850s a number of families evicted from neighbouring Weisdale moved into Aithsting. However years of poor fishing and the insecurity of tenure resolved many, often the younger and more able members of the community, to search for pastures new.

The high emigration rate of the 1870s was partially halted by the Crofters Holdings Act of 1886 which did bring about substantial improvements for crofters, with the right to fair rents and security of tenure. But, having links with relatives abroad, and with the economy generally depressed, further emigration was inevitable and continued throughout the first half of the 20th century.

POPULATION

The Census enumerations from 1801 to 1981 are given in the following table:

Year		Year	
1801	1,493	1901	2,393
1811	1,617	1911	2,100
1821	1,884	1921	1,871
1831	2,194	1931	1,552
1841	2,478	1941	no census
1851	2,603	1951	1,225
1861	2,670	1961	957
1871	2,806	1971	873
1881	2,702	1981	995
1891	2,562		

The population figures for Sandsting and Aithsting over the last 200 years have risen and fallen in a similar pattern to those of Shetland as a whole. From the 911 of Dr Webster's count of 1755, numbers had increased to 1,493 by 1801 and for the first half of the 19th century a steady increase took place, there being a slightly steeper rate of increase than that for Shetland as a whole, and peaking slightly later. This perhaps was due to the successful cod fishing and curing taking place at Skeld and Reawick.

From the maximum population of 2,806 in 1871 a steady decline set in. This was steeper in the initial stages than for Shetland as a whole, largely due to the limited extent in which this parish participated in the successful herring fishery prosecuted from the 1880s till the First World War. Shetland's Roll of Honour shows the numbers who paid the highest price for their country in that conflict, but despite these sad losses, the population figures show that other factors (especially emigration), resulted in a greater rate in decline of the population over most of the modern period.

The decline continued through to the mid 20th century reaching the figure of 873 in 1971 but by the 1960s there were signs of a levelling off. The 1971 figure was only 15 fewer than that of a mid-decade census carried out in 1966 and it seemed that with some local industries thriving there was a new faith in the communities. But though there was much concern regarding rural depopulation it was felt that the only feasible way to arrest the decline was by development of 'holding points', so that even within the parish considerable demographic changes were taking place. Villages such as Aith and Skeld were growing, with successful industries expanding and services such as shops, schools and council housing being concentrated; but for the more peripheral areas such as West Burrafirth, Culswick and Sandsound such services as had existed were often discontinued.

The 1981 Census figures of 995 confirms that the tide has turned. While the rise in this parish has been much less than in other areas more directly affected by oil development, it must still be regarded in part as oil-related. With oil-related employment now past its peak, further developments in local industries will be required.

PUBLIC AND SOCIAL SERVICES

Twentieth century advances and a positive approach on the part of the local and other authorities have brought improved services to rural areas such as this. Electricity reached this area during the 1950s, providing initially mainly lighting, but in an area where there are no butcher shops and no milk deliveries deep freezes and fridges have come to assume perhaps a greater importance than to the city dweller. Water supplies serving most of this area were provided during the 1950s and 1960s while the scattered and sparsely populated West Burrafirth area have hopes of a supply being provided during this coming financial year.

Unfortunate as regards both these utilities have been the residents of the so-called 'end' houses to which public supplies were not extended. To the residents of such houses the cost of obtaining these amenities often became prohibitive and tended to lead to depopulation of these most remote dwellings. In cases of considerable need, however, the Social Work Department of Shetland Islands Council have shown a willingness to lend assistance.

Social provision has been in recent years to a very high standard. The provision of sheltered housing, as has been noted, keeps within the area people who might otherwise have had to move into an eventide home. The meals-on-wheels service is an important one ensuring vital nourishment in the diet of those in need, and the home-help service provides necessary 'back-up' to the medical and nursing services.

Roads have suffered in recent years from a need to concentrate resources towards the areas in Shetland most affected by oil development. The main route to Lerwick is adequate only in parts, there having been lengthy delays to major improvement schemes in recent years. The road from Bixter to Aith was re-surfaced in 1981, but generally only minor improvement works have been carried out to the roads in this area. There is a feeling in the community that more resources should be made available, particularly for up-grading the main roads from Bixter to Walls, from Bixter to Voe and from Parkhall to Skeld, but also to ensure that the many side roads are adequately maintained. It is recognised, however, that with a substantial mileage of roads in this area (perhaps 70 or 80 miles of council roads together with another 20 miles of private roads), improvements on the scale hoped for would be extremely costly.

For a time after the Second World War bus services operated to Lerwick from various communities (Aith, Gruting, Westerwick and Reawick), though not always on a daily basis, but since the end of the 1960s only the Reawick service has remained. Such a service as can be operated economically is inadequate for the needs of many, particularly for those who have to travel to work; indeed for most people the motor car has become essential. However, as more people come to have their own vehicles the less viable becomes the bus services; and it is only through local government subsidies that such services can be maintained. These services are essential for the older and less well-off members of the community, and it is gratifying to see that in some respects services have been extended in the last two years. With Community Council support a feeder service operates to serve the Aith and East Burrafirth areas one day per week, while an occasional service is provided by the Social Work Department, particularly to assist the elderly to visit Lerwick.

At one time each small community was able to support at least one shop (and sometimes more). West Burrafirth, Clousta, East Burrafirth, Reawick, Westerskeld and Gruting each had their general merchants, but though there are still six shops in this parish (at Bridge-of-Walls, Skeld, Aith, Bixter, Sandsound and Tresta) providing a valuable service to their communities, one suspects that trade may not be sufficient to ensure the continued viability of some of these establishments. During the decades immediately following the Second World War mobile shops or vans were extremely popular, operating from the more successful local shops, and even from Lerwick stores; but high operating costs and strict regulations led to most of these being withdrawn. Now fish is the only commodity supplied in this way.

Like some shops, post offices too are under threat of closure. Services are still provided at Aith, Tresta, Bixter, Reawick, Skeld and Bridge-of-Walls but the post office at Garderhouse closed last year; and the Post Office has made it very clear that unless local offices are substantially used they are likely to face the axe. It is perhaps inevitable that services should be concentrated in the larger communities; but it is nonetheless regrettable when services are withdrawn from the smaller, more remote areas which inevitably lose part of their vitality.

CHURCHES

At the time of the last Statistical Account in the 1840s the Church of Scotland did not quite enjoy the unchallenged position it had held at the time of the 1790 account. Inroads had been made by the Methodists and the Independents: both these groups had built chapels at Sand. The Methodist chapel built close to the beach with an unusual floor of rounded beach stones was to suffer severe flooding in the exceptional tides and gales of 1900, but the Independent or Congregational chapel continued in use well into this century.

The Church of Scotland was situated near Semblister at a spot, perhaps not surprisingly in those days before proper roads, more accessible by the sea than by land. This impressive galleried building had in 1780 replaced the pre-Reformation chapel at Sand which had seen use successively by Catholics, Episcopalians and finally Presbyterians. The chancel arch of this latter building is still standing in the old churchyard at Sand.

A much greater trauma than the successes of the Methodists and Independents was to be suffered by the established church when in 1843 the Disruption caused splits even in this remote part of the nation. But the end result in this extensive parish was an extension of religious provision to areas previously remote from the central church. Established churches were to be provided at Sand and Twatt, while Clousta was to be the main centre of the Free Church which also had a mission in Aith. The roles of Aith and Clousta were to be reversed, however, by the time of the reconciliation of the Free and established churches in 1929.

In the meantime other dissenting churches had gained strength in various other parts of the parish. The Methodist church in Aith is now ruinous, but a considerable following was built up at Tresta, Westerskeld and Gruting where the churches established are still in use. A fine Congregational church was constructed at Reawick and a Baptist chapel provided at Sand, both of which are also still in use though there is now no resident minister serving either.

For a few years following the turn of the century the Salvation Army operated a mission at Hestinsetter but this was discontinued after the First World War. Much longer lasting however has been the Brethren sect which has now been in existence in this area for over a century and which maintains a gospel hall at Selivoe. In Tresta, however, a small chapel of the Exclusive Brethren has closed in recent years.

There is little doubt that virtually all religious denominations have suffered from diminishing membership and declining support, especially during the most recent decades. Funerals and marriages are still religious ceremonies required by most; but for many, regular church attendance is no longer an intrinsic part of their way of life. With fewer contributing, and escalating costs of maintaining buildings and ministers, inevitably services have had to be reduced.

Particularly in the Church of Scotland rationalisation led first to ministers being withdrawn from Twatt and Clousta, and then eventually in the 1970s to these churches being closed and the latter being disposed of. The resident minister was withdrawn from Aith in 1971 and finally in 1979 Sandsting and Aithsting was linked with Walls and Sandness under the charge of a single minister with a lay reader, both resident in Walls and Sandness. Services are conducted each Sunday at Sand and Aith with occasional services in the non-denominational chapel at Culswick. A non-denominational chapel at West Burrafirth in which, as at Culswick, services were held by Methodists and the Church of Scotland, has been unused in recent years.

With the Methodist minister almost certain to be withdrawn from Gruting this year this entire parish will be without a resident minister of any denomination.

EDUCATION

The first parochial school in this area opened at Twatt in 1802, and by 1834 a survey of education referred to seven other schools of varying types; these included S.P.C.K., adventure and General Assembly or subscription, but only those at Gruting and West Burrafirth were still in existence in 1873. Other early schools at Sand, Sandsound, Arg (Skeld), Wart (Reawick) and Hestataing (East Burrafirth), were short lived for though there was a demand for education, many of these early schools faced continuing problems of finance.

The 1872 Scottish Education Act had great significance for Sandsting and Aithsting as for the rest of Scotland, and resulted in the setting up of school boards to ensure the provision of education for all children from five to thirteen and the making available of finance for the building of new schools. Within the next few years new and substantial schools were built at Skeld, Sand, Sandsound, Clousta, Gruting, West Burrafirth and Twatt. However in a widely scattered parish such as this, some children still had to walk considerable distances, carrying with them perhaps a piece of coarse meal bread for lunch and a peat to contribute to the heating of the school.

Children from East Burrafirth usually attended the school at Gonfirth in the parish of Delting, but in the early 1900s a side school was established to accommodate the younger children of this area. Aith, however, was a growing community and in response to demand for a school there a wartime hut was moved from Vementry in 1922 to provide education for those who had previously had to walk to Clousta or Twatt. This temporary building was to be replaced by a permanent one in 1935.

A variety of legislation amended the 1872 Act, and in 1918 control was taken from the school boards which were replaced by Education Authorities. The most significant Act was that of 1946 which made provision for secondary education till the age of 15, as compared to the elementary education previously provided. Aith, its numbers increased by the closure of East Burrafirth side school in 1945, and itself the largest of the elementary schools, was designated a junior secondary school and temporary buildings were erected to provide accommodation for the secondary classes and for the school meals service. Transport was to be provided for secondary pupils from the Skeld, Sand, Sandsound and Twatt areas but within a matter of days Twatt primary school closed and those pupils were also transferred to Aith.

The late 1940s was a time of falling rolls, and the Twatt school roll with the older pupils removed was now in single figures, even including those who would otherwise have attended Clousta school which had closed previously. West Burrafirth school suffered a similar fate at this time, its pupils being transported to Happyhansel Junior Secondary in Walls.

The post war 'bulge' helped to alleviate the situation for a time in other areas, but in the 1960s Education Authority policy was again that of closure of small schools; in 1965 Sandsound and in 1968 Sand schools were finally declared non-viable, the pupils of the former being transferred to Aith while those of the latter were given the option of going to Aith or

Skeld. Under threat, a spirited defence of Gruting school was conducted and, though small, Gruting still operates as a single teacher school. Skeld, from being also a single teacher school became firmly based as a two teacher primary during the 1970s but, though still in this category, its roll has dropped in the past few years. If the present policy of Shetland Islands Council is maintained, this school is scheduled for replacement in the late 1980s.

Secondary education was a matter of considerable controversy in Shetland in general, and in the Westside in particular in the late 1960s. The Secretary of State had proposed that all secondary education be centralised in Lerwick but this had been strongly opposed, and instead the principle of junior high schools was established with all pupils remaining in their area junior high for the first two years of secondary education; and thereafter they either remained in their local school for the one (soon to become two), further year of compulsory schooling, or were transferred to the Anderson High School in Lerwick for a course leading to 'O' grade examinations. Thus was replaced the system which had dominated education for much of the previous 20 years, whereby only the small minority of pupils successful in 11 plus examinations were transferred to Lerwick at the age of 12 for a course leading to certificate examinations.

Only one junior high school was designated for the Westside however, and strong claims for it were pressed by both the Walls and Aith communities with, perhaps understandably, strong feelings generated for a time. It was ultimately decided that Aith should become the junior high school, with secondary pupils being transported from as far away as Sandness; but a further 13 years were to elapse before a new school building was provided. This building is however an extremely fine one, fitting pleasantly into the area. In addition to providing excellent education facilities, it also has a fine gymnasium, a training swimming pool and includes in its grounds a multicourt, a newly constructed hockey pitch and the football pitch (provided as a result of community effort in the early 1970s) but now taken over by the Education Authority.

HOUSING

Houses in this area were formerly primitive. Only those of the laird and minister (and later of the merchant, schoolmaster and doctor) were substantial buildings with slate roofs and large windows. Home to the crofter till the early years of this century was normally a long low stone-built building with a thatched roof and only one entrance leading first into the byre before one gained access to the dwelling part. The floor was usually earthen with the fire in the centre of the 'but' end and no chimney, the smoke escaping through a hole in the roof. The crofter may have been as comfortable, however, as the resident of the 'Haa' or the manse with its high ceilings and draughty rooms.

By 1900, however, improvements were taking place; fires were placed at the gable end of rooms with built-in chimneys; doors giving access to the dwelling only were made; and if a windfall should arrive in the form of a wrecked ship with a cargo of wood it was accepted gladly to provide flooring and roof timbers. Members of a family would often return from years at sea or other work outwith Shetland with sufficient finance to make substantial house improvements, but for the most part improvement was carried out to the original croft dwelling, perhaps involving heightening to create 'one and a half' storey houses with attic-type bedrooms and felt roofs replacing the thatch.

The inter-war years saw a few substantial dwellings built, usually of mass concrete as compared to the stone used previously, and often of two storeys. Particularly in Aith, where there were a number of whalers at home during the summer, a number of houses were brightly painted, perhaps indicating a degree of affluence as compared to the whitewashing of the traditional croft dwelling. In this area also, the lairds of the Vementry estate, purchased from the Busta estate in 1900 by the Fraser family, adopted a policy different from that of most other lairds in Shetland in constructing a number of cottars' and replacement croft houses; for the latter they charged rents considerably higher than the croft rents previously obtained.

The first council housing in this area provided two Cruden houses at Tresta in the early 1950s followed by eight of the design known in Shetland as the Ackrigarth type at Aith in 1955. Two further houses were added to the Aith scheme in 1966; but in the 1970s with population increasing and considerable demand for housing, schemes at Bixter, Skeld and again at Aith provided sixteen, six and eight houses respectively. In addition seven sheltered houses were constructed at Skeld and eight at Aith, with a warden's house for each scheme. These sheltered houses are a particular success keeping the elderly (who might otherwise have to be accommodated in eventide homes in Lerwick) within the community; but it may be that for the moment the supply of general-purpose housing is equal to the demand.

In general, of approximately 300 inhabited houses in this area the total of 62 council houses is a much smaller proportion than would obviously exist in many other (especially urban) areas of Scotland. Aided in many cases by grant and loan schemes of the Department of Agriculture and Fisheries for Scotland, a considerable number of new croft houses were constructed, especially during the late 1960s and early 1970s; the result is the number of houses built or substantially rebuilt in the last 30 years is almost on par with the number of council houses. Steeply escalating costs have seen a considerable falling off in private house building in the past decade, but Local Authority and D.A.F.S. grants have ensured that most houses now have a reasonable standard of amenity, with few lacking the basic requirements such as inside toilets.

LEISURE ACTIVITIES

This parish is of course remote from established centres of entertainment, but there is strong community spirit as shown by the efforts made to support the village halls in Aith, Bixter and Skeld. The halls at Aith and Bixter were built between the wars while at Skeld the sail loft, which had proved to be a highly popular community centre as well as having a commercial function till the early years of the 20th century, was finally replaced by the building of a new hall at Skeld in 1950. Sadly the wartime hut used as a hall at Sand deteriorated badly, and at a time when lesser grants were available fell into disuse. Full use however has been made of the considerable grants available in recent years in Skeld and Aith, where improvements costing of the order of £100,000 and £90,000 respectively have been made.

All these halls are in frequent use for meetings of various organisations—S.W.R.I.'s in each area, youth clubs, Boys Brigade, badminton clubs, etc. Badminton in particular is popular as a winter sport, involving participants of a wide age range and in Aith the new school gymnasium is a popular venue, being used in addition to the hall. This gymnasium is also used by football and netball clubs for training.

Much the most popular provision in the new school however is the training pool fully used by clubs and family groups. Obviously in an area such as this where water based activities are for some a means of earning their livelihood, and for a great many more a popular pastime, the importance of being able to swim cannot be over-emphasised.

Whereas a hundred years ago most families would have had access to a boat of necessity, today boats are much more often pleasure craft, and regrettably (particularly over the last 10 years) the cheaper fibre glass is replacing the finer lines of the Shetland model and the ubiquitous outboard has replaced the sail. Regattas are held in Skeld, Aith and Tresta Voes each summer and are important social occasions in the calendar of the community, but there are now fewer local boats participating. In Skeld the attempt is being made to further this sport by having regular 'points' races during the summer months, and by providing tuition for youngsters.

Since the area was voted 'dry' in the early 1920s, closing the two licensed premises at Bridge-of-Walls and Tresta, no alcoholic liquor has been available for sale in this area. The abolition of the veto poll has made such premises again a possibility though their commercial viability is more in question; but a social club using former school premises is likely to open in Aith in 1983.

Television has made a considerable impact in the last 20 years with only a few isolated pockets still unable to get satisfactory reception. Undoubtedly it has had an effect upon community life though it may well be that people are now much more selective in their viewing. Certainly some community events have suffered, perhaps particularly the local variety concert, but the support given to the wide variety of social activities available indicates a lively community.

LIFEBOAT AND SHIPPING

At one time sea faring played a much larger part in the lives of the communities of the parish than it does today. With roads inadequate or non-existent, the sea routes were the main highways. Aith was for many years a port of call of vessels run by the North of Scotland Shipping Company, while especially during the boom times of last century Skeld and Reawick were involved in trade, with vessels sailing to Leith and other ports.

Inevitably, in communities such as these, closely linked with the sea, there have been over the years many instances of tragic loss of life. In the early years of this century on two occasions vessels on passage to Scalloway (one from Skeld and the other from Reawick) were lost; one went down with all three crew members, but in the other case a crew member saved himself by hanging on to two tea chests. In Aith Voe and off Vementry tragic accidents involving boats under sail also cost the lives of young men. There were of course many incidents prior to this century when fishermen were venturing to the 'far haaf' and beyond, though mercifully there were no disasters such as affected other areas of Shetland in 1832 and 1881.

The exposed coastline between Reawick and Culswick in particular has seen several shipwrecks; some of these were tragic as the case of the barque the *Avante Savoia*, which was lost with all hands near Culswick in 1915. On other occasions, as in 1930 when a vessel was wrecked at Silwick, the crew were more fortunate in being able to wade ashore.

It was, however the tragedy of the Aberdeen trawler, the *Ben Doran*, lost on the Ve Skerries off the west coast of Shetland in 1930 which remains most vividly in the public memory and which was to have the most significant effect. Men remained on board that stricken vessel for some time after she was wrecked, eventually lashing themselves to the rigging; but there were no rescue services available capable of mounting a successful rescue in these treacherous waters.

Subsequently, first at Lerwick, and then in 1933 at Aith the R.N.L.I. stationed lifeboats in Shetland. Aith now has her third lifeboat, the 1952 Barnet class *John and Frances McFarlane* which has been on station since 1961 and will perhaps soon be due for replacement.

The lifeboat moored at the head of Aith Voe is an extremely important feature in the life of the community, involving many people not just in ensuring that there is a ready supply of volunteers, but also in providing 'back-up' services, and in supporting an active Ladies Lifeboat Guild in their fund-raising activities.

Over the years many successful rescues have taken place, perhaps none so dangerous as the rescue of the crew from another trawler the *Juniper*, wrecked on Papa Stour in 1967, which won for coxswain John

Nicolson the silver medal and also vellums for the crew. But Aith does not have a monopoly of successful rescues. In 1979 survivors in a liferaft from a wrecked coaster, the *St Kentigern*, were snatched to safety near the dangerous Aa Skerry by the courageous actions of lobster fishermen Jim Scott and his Skeld crew in appalling weather conditions.

INDUSTRY AND EMPLOYMENT

The years preceding and following the Second World War were bleak indeed with agriculture offering a livelihood for some, but few employment opportunities available elsewhere. Little work was available in other areas of Shetland either, and the only real alternative was the sea. Many men joined the merchant service, while a number also found employment with Salvesens of Leith at the Antarctic whaling. In a depressed economy the whalers returning with a season's earnings almost intact appeared wealthy, though in fact their hourly rates were low for arduous and often unpleasant work.

Depression continued throughout the 1950s, but the local authority did make efforts to provide services to rural areas, and the various water schemes and council housing schemes provided some much needed (if temporary) employment. By the 1960s, however, some revival was taking place in the traditional industries in Shetland, and if work was not necessarily available for everyone in this area itself, it was possible to find employment elsewhere in the islands, as for example in the fish processing industry at Lerwick or Scalloway.

Regrettably, a substantial part of the workforce from this area still have to travel to other parts of Shetland, particularly to Lerwick or to the Sullom Voe area for employment. On the credit side, however, most of these commuters have strong roots in this area and are unlikely to leave.

During the construction phase at Sullom Voe few men from this area were directly involved, but a number of women were employed as cleaners, many of them now sadly unemployed. Sullom Voe has, however, provided a number of opportunities for men from this area, particularly those with a sea-going background. Some have obtained full-time work on tugs, as operatives on jetties, or in the process areas. These jobs are all the more important at a time when nationally the merchant service is in such severe recession.

A considerable number of both males and females commute to Lerwick to a wide variety of jobs, but firms such as the gas suppliers Rearo and Home Furnishing, which have strong links in this area, tend to employ a number from the Westside. Roadmen employed by Shetland Islands Council and employees of plant hire and construction firms also travel outwith this area to various destinations, depending where the work is at any particular time. Several plant hire firms (R. & D. Garrick; Johnston Tait; T. & S. Haulage; Robertson & Johnston; J. Ridland; Garrick &

Manson) providing diggers, bulldozers, lorries, etc., for the construction industry are based in or have their origins in this area, and most tend to employ their operatives from within this parish.

One of the plant hire firms, R. & D. Garrick till recently employed a few men in the production of breeze blocks widely used in the construction industry, though the scale of this operation is much smaller than that of the other two larger firms which produce these blocks in Shetland. Garricks did for a time also hold an agency for Daf cars but in recent years they have concentrated their garage operations on the maintenance of their own machinery. The Fiat agency is however still operated by a garage in Aith which has recently changed hands and is now trading as Aith Autos with two full-time and two part-time staff employed. Two individuals, both formerly employed as heavy vehicle mechanics, have separately started as one-man businesses in the Bixter and Tresta areas, the former providing garage services while the latter is providing black-smith facilities.

There are a number of firms of builders which operate from this area. Tulloch Construction is large enough to undertake complete contracts such as housing schemes, and they construct their own house kits at their workshop in Twatt and provide employment for tradesmen and appren-tices. Another of Shetland's larger building firms, Garriock Brothers, started in this area but has now moved the base for its operations to Lerwick. Two firms, Morrison and Garrick and J. and P. Johnson, carry out general building work; W. and J. Irvine and Morrison and Couper specialise in bricklaying and concrete work; while Nicolson and Hunter and L. and R. Anderson offer plumbing and electrical services. Each of these firms must however depend to a considerable degree on work outwith this area.

AGRICULTURE

A substantial number of people are involved in agriculture, but few on a full-time basis. Most of the crofts are too small to be viable economic units on their own, and even where several crofts are held the net income may be quite small. Soil is generally not of high quality and it is only by the application of considerable quantities of lime and fertilisers that good crops or even high quality grazing may be obtained.

In Sandsting and Aithsting according to D.A.F.S. figures there was in 1974 a total of 13,020 acres of which just over 2,000 acres were arable and the rest rough grazing. Of the arable acreage, however, only a small proportion is actually cultivated.

A century ago participation in the fishing was necessary in order to pay the rent while the croft was necessary in order to provide food for the family. Crops were grown not just for animal fodder, but more importantly for human consumption. Sheep certainly were numerous, though much less so than now, but cattle were much more highly regarded, their dairy products being vital to subsistence. Ponies too were kept, some of which were used in the transporting of peats, though Rev. John Bryden suggests that not as much use was made of them as one might have expected.

Now the whole pattern of agriculture has changed. Numbers of cattle have declined throughout this century, and since the Second World War at a much greater rate. In 1973 numbers were down to 589 and by 1981 had fallen to just 140. Such cattle as are kept tend to be in larger herds of perhaps 10 or 20, and the numbers of crofters who retain cattle are very few; indeed there may be hardly any in some entire districts.

Traditional methods involved most cattle being tied in a byre at night and milked perhaps three times a day. Calves were bucket fed, kept on tether, and required to be watered and flitted frequently. These practices were extremely labour intensive. Hay was cured and crops of oats and turnips cultivated also by methods which required a great deal of effort. Despite tractors becoming available to replace the ponies, of which (apart from a few children's pets) there are scarcely any now left in this area, it was as profitable and much less onerous to lay down crofts to sheep than to continue the amount of cultivation necessary in order to keep cattle. The majority of crofters now cultivate little more than a quarter of an acre of potatoes for home consumption.

Hay is still cured by many, but adverse weather can often mean a high labour input for a moderate quality crop. A number now prefer to import fodder from the south, but freight charges make this option extremely expensive. Only the few who have sufficient arable land and sufficient stock to justify the high capital outlay on pits and forage harvesters are able to make silage.

Sheep inevitably are increasing in numbers, from 26,260 in 1973 to 28,640 in 1981, but over the longer term the most significant changes may not be in numbers but in breed. Shetland sheep are still prominent, particularly on the large areas of scattald (hill grazing), but on in-bye and improved ground they are often crossed with the Cheviot to produce a popular first cross ewe. Suffolk tups are now widely used to breed with cross ewes and thereby produce good quality store lambs.

Many of the store lambs are shipped south on the hoof but an enterprise in Reawick, the Reawick Lamb Marketing Company, provides an important outlet, particularly for the slightly smaller carcases. This company, which has been operating since 1972, processes some 5,000 lambs per year, some for consumption within Shetland. It was particularly active when the construction camps at Sullom Voe were accommodating over 6,000 men, but with the rundown in that area other markets have been required. The Faroe Islands provided an outlet for a time, but in recent times consignments have been sent to mainland Britain and even to Gibraltar. Sheep and lamb skins are also processed by the same company and this provides valuable employment in the Skeld area. Sheepskins are also cured by T. Nicolson, Aith (a one-man business) while at Vementry a high reputation for quality lamb ensures the success of a small business providing fairly small carcases, mainly for the local market.

Some innovations have been attempted in recent years with varying degrees of success. The Gotland breed of sheep has been introduced and when crossed with the Shetland produces a sheepskin of high quality and value. The only mink farm in Shetland still operating is located in Aith. But fluctuating markets in the south have meant that both these enterprises have not been as profitable as might have been anticipated at the time of their introduction.

Though a considerable amount of land has gone out of cultivation, some substantial improvements have been made in agriculture in recent years. The Twatt area in particular has been in the forefront in a process of land regeneration which has converted much rough pasture to good quality grassland. Other areas are now following suit, particularly since the introduction in 1978 of a scheme by the Shetland Islands Council to assist with the cost of lime used. Many crofters have now applied for and been granted apportionments of their shares in common grazings, presumably with a view to improving this ground; and indeed in some areas, such as Clousta and the west side of Aith, there is now little of the former scattald left undivided.

The community as a whole is interested in agriculture as is shown by the support given to the show held at Walls but which also serves this area, and to the local sheepdog trials held at Skeld. There is no doubt that agriculture could be more efficient if units were larger and operated by full-time, active farmers. However crofting is for many, though inadequate in providing a livelihood, an important part of the way of life.

FISHING

The 19th century, as has been stated, saw the development of Skeld and Reawick as centres for the cod fishing, but its day was over by the end of the century, by which time steam was taking over from sail and the herring fishing had ousted that for cod for first place. The herring fishing tended to be concentrated in the larger stations elsewhere in Shetland though there was some activity at West Burrafirth in the early years of this century. In the years following the First World War with the fishing industry depressed generally there was no place for the crofter-fishermen and the small-scale operation. With little alternative employment available in the islands, large numbers joined the Merchant Navy while the process of emigration continued and the once-vibrant shore facilities became inactive and derelict.

The late 1950s, and more particularly the 1960s, saw an upsurge in a sector of the fishing industry previously little exploited in Shetland, the fishing for shellfish. From Skeld, Aith and West Burrafirth the lucrative lobster fishing was pursued by small vessels, usually in the 20 foot to 30 foot category, on a seasonal basis, the winter being used to make new creels and mend damaged ones.

The lobster was unable to withstand the over-fishing, particularly when larger vessels from other areas became involved in years of poor white fish landings. Diversification for the smaller boats was possible by fishing for crabs and (especially in recent years), for queen scallops. At present part-time fishermen and one full-time man operate from Aith, two full-time from Skeld and one from West Burrafirth, but shell fishing is very much seasonal and it is necessary for the full-time fishermen to move to other areas from time to time, depending on supply. One of the Skeld boats is at present also operating a ferry service from West Burrafirth to the island of Papa Stour.

Perhaps more important even than the success of the lobster fishing itself was the impetus it gave in encouraging young men, especially in the Skeld area, to involve themselves in the fishing industry. There are now three larger vessels which though not fishing from Skeld itself, are mostly crewed by men from that area. The *Hercules II* is a multipurpose vessel capable of fishing for sand eels, whitefish or shellfish; the *Aspire* is a 60 foot wooden seiner/trawler built in 1980 with joint owners in Burra Isle and Skeld; and the largest of the three and one of the most successful boats in Shetland is the 70 foot *Sunbeam*, which carries a crew of nine and is owned (and in the main crewed) in Sandsting.

Two recent developments in fishing are as yet only at the experimental stage, but one hopes for their success in the future. Skeld Voe and the Clousta/Vementry area are suitable locations for mussel rafts and indeed the first harvest of mussels was recently taken from rafts in Cribba Sound, these rafts having been at their location for almost two years. Mussel farming can probably never be other than a part-time activity but it may provide a useful supplement to the income of shell fishermen and perhaps of some crofters.

Perhaps more important in that full-time employment may result is the salmon rearing project presently taking place in Selivoe near Sand. Norwegian and Shetland interests operating jointly hope to develop this scheme and indeed other voes may well be suitable for future developments. But regrettably processing of salmon may have to take place in a place such as Lerwick or Scalloway in order to reduce the high costs that would be involved in a remote area.

KNITWEAR

The knitwear industry has of course traditionally been of great importance to this area, as to other parts of Shetland. Virtually every girl was taught to knit at an early age, and was expected to devote a very large part of her free time to the art. Indeed while carrying peats from the hill or even dung to the fields a woman of 100 years ago would most likely have had her knitting in her hands as well as her burden in a 'kishie' on her back.

Very coarse stockings were at one time the main articles produced but some items of the highest quality with Fair Isle patterns or of the finest lace have also been made over the years. Though every woman no longer spends a large proportion of her time knitting, there are still a number capable of producing truly excellent articles.

The hand knitting part of this industry is extremely difficult to quantify being very much cottage-based and in a number of cases the products being disposed of on a 'private order' basis. It is likely that during the past decade less attention was paid to knitting as more women found employment elsewhere, the returns from knitting even to the most efficient being very low in relation to the hours involved. But with recession looming one hopes for expansion again in knitwear.

One of the reasons for the growth of Aith this century has been the development of, and employment provided by, the knitwear industry. Introduced by Anderson and Smith, merchants, this trade was developed in the 1920s and 1930s by A. D. Clark who not only bought hosiery privately produced but also introduced machinery and employed a number of women to knit in a factory-style building at Gudataing. Wages were often low but much-needed employment was provided for a number of girls not only from Aith, but also from other parts of the Westside.

The knitwear side of A. D. Clark's business did not continue after his death but in the early 1960s the Lerwick firm of Peter Blance & Co. revived the industry using the Gudataing premises. Again a number of girls were employed, some engaged in finishing work while others operated hand-frame machines. With few employment opportunities available, a number of men became involved in the production side of the knitwear industry for the first time, introducing hand-frame machines into their own homes. A reasonable wage could be earned, but only if very long hours were worked.

Peter Blance and Co.'s activities in Aith were short-lived but by the end of the 1960s a young English couple, the Caldwells, had moved into the Gudataing factory and for a time operated a most successful business and eventually had a new purpose-built factory constructed in Aith. Trading as 'Shetland Fashions' they expanded rapidly, dressing and packaging being mainly carried out in the factory and the actual jumpers being produced and finished by cottage employees throughout the islands. At their peak employment was provided for 24 in the factory and a great number of full-timers and part-timers in their homes.

Oil developments and recession in the knitwear markets appeared to affect Shetland Fashions particularly badly and by the end of the 1970s their staff in the factory had been reduced to four. The Caldwells having moved back to England eventually sold the factory in 1982, and with considerable financial assistance from Shetland Islands Council the Lerwick firm of Judane took over the premises. Judane have introduced heavy production machinery and happily their operations appear to be expanding, providing employment for nine in the factory at present.

Judane concentrate on jumper production but in a smaller operation conducted from her home in Sand, Mrs Stuart has developed the firm

'Shetlands from Shetland' aimed very much at the top end of the market; it provides employment for a number of mainly hand-knitters and produces a variety of articles including scarves and berets.

TOURISM

Though an attractive area with excellent fishing there is little provision for tourism in this area. A substantial hotel at Clousta was unfortunately destroyed by fire in the early years of this century, while the Bridge of Walls hotel was converted into self-catering flats during the 1960s. Some bed and breakfast accommodation is available, and there are three chalets at Sand, and a number of cottages in various other areas, which are available for let. During the construction period at Sullom Voe much of the accommodation has been occupied on a long term basis, and few tourists have been noticeable.

WAY OF LIFE

The way of life of a community is perhaps the most difficult of all things to describe, and almost inevitably requires a more subjective assessment than the other sections. For many of the people living here however, there are considerable advantages in living in a community such as this, in spite of the undoubted remoteness.

Modern day amenities have been essential in retaining a viable population. If neglect has been felt at some times, for example when services were being concentrated in oil development areas in the mid-1970s, the local authority and other agencies must be complimented for the standard of provision overall. Much can still be done and road improvements come readily to mind, but most important must be the encouragement of developments which provide more jobs within this area for a greater proportion of the workforce.

Not all changes meet with unanimous approval. Particularly, many may regret the decline in the dialect and the fact that young people from this area share the same interests—motor cycles, discos and 'pop' music—as their counterparts in any other part of the country.

There is still, however, much more freedom here than one would find in a town. Apart from a few motoring offences, crime is minimal and no resident police presence is required.

The most isolated outposts of the community have become seriously depopulated but throughout the area there is a strong community spirit and now an optimism as to the future which was not so apparent in the bleak 1950s. One trusts that given adequate local and national support this optimism will prove to have been well founded.

April 1983

THE PARISH OF TINGWALL, WHITENESS AND WEISDALE

Original description by G. M. Nelson, 1951
New version by James R. Nicolson, M.A., B.Sc., 1983

PHYSICAL BASIS

The parish of Tingwall, Whiteness and Weisdale occupies a central position on the Mainland of Shetland. The three sections occupy broad and generally fertile valleys separated by parallel ranges of heather-covered hills. At the south end of Tingwall valley lies the village of Scalloway, the second largest settlement in the whole of Shetland.

The eastern boundary of the parish runs from the Atlantic coast three miles south of Scalloway in a generally north-easterly direction to the North Sea two miles north of Lerwick. The western boundary runs from the tip of Russaness almost due north behind the Hill of Weisdale before climbing the western slopes of Scalla Field and crossing the summit of Gruti Field. It then heads east to bisect Petta Water before turning south along the main road through the Kames as far as the Loch of Girlsta whence it turns due east to the North Sea at Catfirth.

About 14 miles long and 6 miles wide, the parish is deeply dissected by long sheltered voes including Weisdale Voe, Stromness Voe, Whiteness Voe and Scalloway harbour which is the major port on the Atlantic coast of Shetland. The voes on the east side of the parish, Dales Voe, Lax Firth and Wadbister Voe are little used although Cat Firth, most of which lies in Nesting parish, was an important base for seaplanes in the First World War.

To the south of Scalloway lies the large but thinly populated island of Trondra which is part of Tingwall although the neighbouring isles of Burra are part of Lerwick parish. Between Burra and Weisdale Voe is a string of small islands most of which are included in Tingwall parish. Some of them were formerly inhabited.

In this parish there is a close relationship between geology and topography. Parallel bands of schist, gneiss and limestone run roughly north-east and south-west giving a pronounced 'grain' to the landscape. The main valleys, ranges of hills and the voes all follow this direction. The most important of these rocks is limestone which normally forms the valley floors and outcrops in Tingwall, Whiteness, Weisdale and Girlsta to produce some of the best agricultural land in the whole of Shetland. The remains of small circular lime kilns can be seen at Utnabrake, Weisdale and Laxfirth, while the production of lime for building and agricultural purposes was for long a major industry at Girlsta and enjoyed a temporary revival after the Second World War. Stone for road metal and aggregate is quarried near Scalloway.

The parish contains a large number of freshwater lochs, the largest of which, Girlsta Loch, is the biggest in the Mainland of Shetland.

HISTORY OF THE LOCAL COMMUNITY

The area has been settled for thousands of years, as is clear from the large number of prehistoric remains. Gradually the best land was cleared and farms evolved on the valley slopes while even the hills were useful as grazing for sheep and ponies and as a source of peat for fuel. The population remained small until the 19th century when a rapid increase took place due in part to the effectiveness of inoculation as a means of combating smallpox.

As the population rose the farms were divided into less than viable units and the men had to look more and more to the sea for their livelihood. The expression, 'crofter-fisherman' aptly describes the situation of the average Shetlander during the 19th century. Unfortunately he had little say in the matter since it was usually stipulated in his agreement with his landlord that he had to serve as a hand on a fishing vessel during the summer deep water fishery and land his catches to his landlord, or to the latter's factor, at prices determined by the landlord.

In some important respects, however, this parish was not typical of Shetland as a whole. Having a central situation it was not suited to the deep water ling and cod fisheries upon which most other parishes depended, although some fishermen no doubt took part in this fishery operating from a remote station in vessels belonging to their landlord. It is known that in some parts of this parish fishing was not a condition of tenancy and many men chose instead to sail as hands on Arctic whalers. As early as the 1820s independent fish curers were in business at Scalloway and it seems likely that fishermen in this parish had a little more freedom than their counterparts in most parts of Shetland.

The parish had a unique asset in the shoals of cod that congregated in the 'North Haaf' and the Deeps west of Scalloway in the early part of the year. This gave rise to an important spring fishery in which men from Scalloway, Whiteness and Trondra took part, along with fishermen from Burra and the small isles. The discovery about 1819 of cod banks west of Foula gave a boost to this sector of the fishing industry. The firm of Hay and Ogilvy (who built the first deep water quay at Scalloway) and their rivals, Nicolson and Company, each had a fleet of decked sloops which brought prosperity to their owners until the cod banks failed in the 1840s.

Larger vessels were later acquired capable of fishing around Faroe and Iceland, while about 1860 prolific cod banks were found around Rockall.

Caught on handlines, the cod were gutted and beheaded and salted down in the vessels' holds where they remained for several weeks until discharged at numerous drying beaches along the West Side of Shetland. There were drying beaches at Whiteness (Nesbister and Hirpa) and Scalloway, and on the islands of Trondra, Burra, Oxna and Langa. About 1850 Hay and Company (successors to Hay and Ogilvy) set up a steam drying plant at their premises at Blacksness, Scalloway. But the process was expensive and was used mainly to finish off the drying of fish that had come in from the beaches. When drying was completed the fish were exported to merchants in Spain.

In the Second Statistical Account several ministers deplored the social conditions of the mid 19th century. In most places the people were entirely at the mercy of their landlords who owned their houses and crofts and even the boats in which they fished. The worst aspect of the system was the lack of security since the tenant could be evicted with only forty days notice. This right was exploited by several landowners in the latter half of the century when they discovered that sheep were more profitable than tenants on their estates. Many families were evicted, one of the areas most badly affected being Weisdale. Here the evictions were carried out by Mr D. D. Black who between 1846 and 1852 built up a large estate. The first evictions took place in 1849 and in the next 15 years he was responsible for the removal of almost 200 people from Upper Weisdale. The crofts were then amalgamated into large farms with names like Flemington (later known as Kergord), Milton and Stenswall, which were leased to farmers. Black died in 1875 and his estate was purchased for £6,500 by David Inglis who had been tenant at Flemington. Black is also remembered for his interest in tree planting which was taken up by others so that today the area around Kergord has several plantations of sycamore, larch and Sitka spruce.

Tingwall valley also suffered changes during the 19th century. There were some improvements with the establishment of large Scottish-style farms at Laxfirth, Veensgarth and Asta, but unfortunately in some cases eviction was an essential step in these developments.

It was only in 1886 that the Crofters (Scotland) Act brought security of tenure and ushered in a new era for Shetland. But an Act of Parliament could not tackle the economic problems, and emigration, which had begun years before, was seen by many as the only answer to their plight. The rise of the herring fishery, which replaced the cod fishery in the 1890s, halted the flow of emigrants for a time and some actually returned to Shetland to invest their savings in sailing drifters. The summer herring fishing fitted perfectly into the seasonal activities of the croft. Few crofter-fishermen, however, were in a position to invest in the more costly type of herring boat that came in the early 20th century —the steam drifter—and again the flow of emigrants became a spate.

The parish suffered badly during two world wars. The war memorial at Tingwall Churchyard bears the names of 38 men who perished in the first war and of 11 who lost their lives in the second. Whiteness and Weisdale have their own war memorial and there the figures are 21 and 14 respectively.

Farming in Tingwall received a boost between the wars following the introduction of legislation which gave the Board of Agriculture powers to establish smallholdings by agreement with the landlord or by compulsory purchase if necessary. In 1919 the farm of Asta was split up into three new holdings and one enlargement of an existing farm. In 1923 Veensgarth was divided into 19 new holdings and 10 enlargements.

Depopulation continued after the wars, being most marked in the island of Trondra—the smaller islands of Oxna, Papa, Linga, Hildasay and Langa had lost their residents many years before. The downward trend in the parish would have been more marked had it not been for the fact that Scalloway actually showed a small but steady rise in population during this period. As crofts became vacant they fell into the hands of remaining crofters some of whom were able to build up fairly extensive holdings. In most cases, however, crofting remained a part-time occupation, subsidiary to work in Lerwick.

Although little affected by onshore oil-related developments the parish experienced a considerable rise in population during the years of the oil construction boom in the 1970s. Vacant houses were refurbished and new houses were built both privately and by the islands council to meet the demand for more homes.

SCALLOWAY

The history of Scalloway is entirely different, owing much of its early importance to Earl Patrick Stewart who built his castle here in 1600 making it the seat of the islands' law court. The village appears to have declined during the 18th century but it included among its residents several of the islands' principal landowners. As mentioned already the village received another boost in the 1820s with the discovery of cod banks west of Shetland and during the second half of the century it was an important centre for the distant water cod fishing around Faroe, Iceland and Rockall.

The cod fishing declined towards the end of the century by which time Scalloway had become a major herring port. In 1881 the North of Scotland and Orkney and Shetland Steam Navigation Company introduced a weekly service that linked Scalloway with Stromness, Aberdeen and Leith. This enabled local fish merchants to find outlets for fresh haddock shipped to merchants and customers in the south. Haddock fishing became a major activity each winter, and with the herring fishing in summer brought year round activity to fishermen in the area. Increasing prosperity at the end of the century was shown in a rising population, more large houses, and shops and two hotels.

Although the Westside herring fishery declined steadily between the wars Scalloway maintained a reputation for the quality of its kippered herring smoked by three or four kippering firms, and for its 'matje' herring cured in the early part of the summer for immediate export to Germany. By the 1930s however, Scalloway was primarily a white fish port—a busy place in the wintertime. The Westside steamer service was withdrawn in 1939 by which time the growing importance of Lerwick had led to centralisation of trade and services there.

During the Second World War Scalloway became famous as the base from which a group of Norwegian patriots sailed their wooden fishing vessels across the North Sea to Norway then occupied by German forces. They landed ammunition and saboteurs and returned with refugees. Their barracks was the old sail loft belonging to Nicolson and Company and for overhauling their vessels they built the Prince Olav Slipway, visited by the present King of Norway in 1942. Late in 1943 the US navy loaned three submarine chasers for this important work. The mansion house of Flemington (Kergord) played a vital role in this operation, being used by Secret Intelligence Service and Special Operations Executive who co-ordinated the transport of Norwegian secret agents to and from Norway. The story of this daring operation was told by David Howarth in his book *The Shetland Bus*. Mr Howarth made his home in Scalloway for several years after the war turning his attention to the local fishing fleet and building several fine vessels before his yard had to close down for economic reasons.

Although herring fishing has been banned since 1977 following twelve years of overfishing, Scalloway is still an important fishing port with year round activity due to the presence of a fleet of twenty white fish seiners and trawlers owned by fishermen in Burra, Scalloway and Trondra. Catches increased during the Second World War when the seine net replaced the old-fashioned haddock line. Since then light trawls have been adopted with great success by the larger vessels in the fleet.

Until 1960 the bulk of the white fish catch was simply packed with ice in boxes and shipped via Lerwick to the Aberdeen market, or to merchants in Aberdeen and Glasgow. In that year however, a group of local businessmen set up Iceatlantic (Frozen Seafoods) Ltd and converted an old fish shed at Blacksness into a modern processing plant for filleting and freezing haddock and whiting. This sparked off a period of great development in Scalloway and indeed in Shetland as a whole. In 1964 a second processing plant, that of TTF (Fish Processing) Ltd opened its doors and the older firm of L. Williamson became one of the leading processors in Shetland. By 1970 these three factories were employing 150 people whereas only a few years earlier less than a score of people were employed in the fish sheds packing fish for shipment south.

As a result of these developments Scalloway, like the rest of Shetland, enjoyed nearly full employment in the early 1970s. To attract workers from other parts of the UK, the Islands' Council embarked on a building programme with sectional timber houses imported from Norway. Scalloway was allocated ten of these houses.

Transport costs and marketing problems in the UK remained a problem until TTF developed a market for Shetland fish in the USA and arranged a service with a Danish shipping company whereby the cartons of frozen fish were shipped from Scalloway to Boston, Mass. In 1971 4,500 tons of frozen fish were shipped from Scalloway to America, the produce of processing plants in several parts of Shetland.

Investment in new harbour works lagged far behind that in new vessels and processing plants. Around 1960 a new breakwater and a fish market were built at Blacksness at a combined cost of around £100,000 but the former provided little shelter and the latter was far too small for the catches of the growing fleet. These problems were not solved until 1981 when a new breakwater was built to the east of Blacksness Pier taking advantage of the natural shelter provided by the East Voe. This was part of a £4 million scheme completed in 1983 with the building of a large fish market.

Scalloway has played only a minor role in the extraction of North Sea oil. In 1972 a local firm, Nautical Services (Shetland) Ltd, was set up to offer a complete range of services to companies operating in Shetland waters. Within a month the firm was in operation supplying drilling mud, chemicals and water to a rig drilling west of Shetland. Since then there has been only sporadic activity west of Shetland and Scalloway's participation in the oil industry is limited to the occasional supply boat or standby trawler that calls for shelter or for repairs. This situation may change towards the end of the century when the oil companies turn their attention to the oil fields that are known to exist in deeper water west of Shetland.

HISTORICAL MONUMENTS

The parish is rich in ancient monuments and sites of archaeological interest. The remains of Stone Age cairns can be seen on Nesbister Hill, Hill of Olligarth, West Hamarsland and the Ness of Westshore, Scalloway, and at the Hamars near the north end of the Loch of Strom. Urns, apparently from the Bronze Age, have been found near Kergord while at Little Asta, near Scalloway, a two-storeyed cist burial was excavated in a roadside quarry. The relics from all these sites are preserved in the National Museum of Antiquities in Edinburgh. Standing stones can be seen near the south end of Tingwall Loch, at the top of Wormadale Hill and at Mailland in Whiteness.

Relics of Iron Age times are the brochs, all of which have been plundered as a supply of building stone. Traces of these stone fortresses survive at Hawks Ness, Wadbister Ness, Barra Holm, Holm of Burwick and at the Holm of Burland in Trondra. Burnt mounds can be seen at Heglibister, Vatster, Hoobie, Churchton, Swinister, Griesta and at the south end of the Loch of Asta where there are two. Another stands on the island of Trondra.

Early chapel sites are that of Our Lady Chapel at Sound (Weisdale), St Ola's Church (Whiteness), St Magnus Church near the present church of Tingwall and a reputed chapel site at Cutts, Trondra. Tingwall churchyard is of considerable interest because of its memorial and armorial stones.

A little to the south of Tingwall Church is the Law Ting Holm where the open-air Parliament for the islands was held in Norse times. Some time last century the level of the loch was lowered by improved drainage and the holm is now a promontory at the north end of Tingwall Loch.

Best preserved of all the ancient monuments in this parish is Scalloway Castle built in 1600 by Patrick Stewart, Earl of Orkney. A fragment of an earlier tower or castle stands on Castle Holm in the Loch of Strom.

Scalloway has two interesting old mansion houses both built by the Scott family, once the major landowners in the area, at the end of the 18th century. The older, the Old Haa', stands at the east end of Main Street while Gibblestone House stands a few hundred yards west facing the harbour and overlooking its stone pier, which is now swallowed up in the village's open-air swimming pool and paddling pool complex. Another old Scalloway family, the Mitchells of Westshore, had their mansion at the west end of the village. Now shorn of its upper storey and with its windows filled in with concrete blocks it serves as a private garage. The Mitchells' garden still survives, notable for its ancient trees which do not grow much higher than the surrounding wall. Salt-laden winds off the sea stunt their growth.

While actual relics of Norse times are comparatively few, the legacy of the Norsemen is still evident in the dialect which is spoken by the people and in the place-names. Almost every name on the map is derived from the old Norse tongue although in many cases the meaning is now obscure. Tingwall (originally *Ting vollr*) derives its name from the old Ting or Parliament; the name Whiteness incorporates the element *nes* or headland (originally *hvita nes*). Similarly the name Weisdale incorporates the element *dalr* or valley. Dr Jakob Jakobsen, the noted Faroese scholar pointed out that Visa is an old name for a river.

The old Norse word *stadir* (farm) is seen in the name Asta while *setr* (homestead) is particularly common in the Tingwall valley where we have Kirkasetter, and North, Mid and South Setter. The lonely croft of Vatster was originally *vatn setr*, the homestead beside the lake, and even today no name could be more appropriate. Girlsta is *Geirhilder Stadir*, named after Geirhildr, daughter of Flokki of the Ravens who was drowned in the nearby loch in the 9th century.

A reminder of the distant past is Scalloway's fire festival, traditionally held on Christmas night as if it were a relic of the pagan Norse festival of Yule. It took the form of a bonfire and torchlight procession. About the end of last century a model of a Viking longship appeared for the first time—clearly this festival was being influenced by the changes taking place in the festival of Up-Helly-Aa at Lerwick. Some time between the wars the date of Scalloway's festival was moved to Christmas Eve. It fell into abeyance in the late 1950s partly through the influence of ministers of the Gospel who believed that it was not right that a sacred occasion such as Christmas should be honoured in this way. There was a temporary revival in 1959 followed by another extended gap until 1979 when the festival was held on 28th December. It has continued for the past three years, always held on a convenient date between Christmas and the New Year.

Girlsta joins with Nesting in celebrating Up-Helly-Aa on the second Friday in February the festival being managed by an organising committee. It follows closely the pattern of Lerwick's great festival although on a much reduced scale.

POPULATION

The following table gives the Census population figures for the parish from 1801 to 1981:

1801	1,863	1901	2,273
1811	1,927	1911	2,110
1821	2,309	1921	1,766
1831	2,797	1931	1,531
1841	2,957	1941	no census
1851	2,874	1951	1,658
1861	2,697	1961	1,623
1871	2,491	1971	1,688
1881	2,385	1981	2,318
1891	2,329		

The census figures show clearly the tremendous rise in population that occurred between 1801 and 1841 when the peak of 2,957 was reached. Thereafter the decline was steady reaching a low point of 1,531 in 1931. In some parts of the parish the decline was especially pronounced. The population of Trondra, for example, dropped from a peak of 180 in 1841 to only 20 in 1961 although by 1981 it had risen again to 93. Since the building of a bridge linking Trondra with the Mainland in 1970, the island has become a desirable place to live. Old croft houses have been renovated and a new community of private bungalows has grown up around the long abandoned croft of Caldhame at the north end of the island.

In the smaller isles the decline in population began about one hundred years ago. Hildasay which had 19 inhabitants in 1861 had been abandoned by 1901. (This island once boasted a herring curing station and a granite quarry.) Langa with 8 people in 1861 had none in 1891. Linga which had 13 inhabitants in 1881 had only 4 in 1911 and none at all in 1921. Oxna had 36 inhabitants in 1901 and none at all in 1921.

Part of the reason for the modest growth between 1931 and 1951 was the growth of Scalloway as people moved from other parts of Shetland, enticed by the prospect of work at a time when unemployment was a serious problem in many parts of rural Shetland. The rise between 1971 and 1981 can only be attributed to the influx of construction workers etc., who made their homes in the parish. This was partly related to the building of a fairly large scheme of council houses at Weisdale.

While the bulk of the population at the present time was born in the parish (or more precisely in the maternity unit at Lerwick to parents whose homes are in the parish) the proportion of immigrants rose steadily in the 1970s. Information assembled by Mr John A. W. Fraser, headmaster of Scalloway Junior High School gives a clear indication of this trend. Pupils were asked to state whether one, both or neither of their parents had been born in Shetland and the results are as follows:

Born in Shetland	1978		1979		1980	
Both parents	164	60%	166	58%	154	54%
One parent	69	26%	75	26%	80	28%
Neither parent	39	14%	47	16%	52	18%

PUBLIC AND SOCIAL SERVICES

The traditional family home was the croft house—a simple two-roomed cottage with a roof of thatch. It was entirely independent, all the services being provided by the family themselves. Peat was cut for fuel; water for drinking, cooking and washing was carried from the well; and lighting came from simple oil lamps. Domestic rubbish was either thrown on to the midden or flung over the cliffs.

Whatever improvements were made in this simple lifestyle came through the efforts of the people themselves until the years after the Second World War when large sums were spent by the government and the local authority in improving living conditions for everyone. In the first place the North of Scotland Hydro Electric Board spent an enormous amount of money in providing electricity to virtually the whole of Shetland. Then came the public water schemes provided by Zetland County Council, the predecessor of the present Shetland Islands Council. The reservoir at Scalloway, fed from Njuggles Water Loch, was too small for the growing population and new storage tanks were installed; and a water supply was eventually piped to every house in the Tingwall valley and to those in the island of Trondra. Whiteness and Weisdale were supplied from a separate reservoir. The third main improvement of postwar years was in the road network as existing roads were improved and new ones built. It is no exaggeration to say that those areas that had a good road connecting people to Lerwick with its shops and jobs retained their population while those that had no road became depopulated. An example of the latter category is the hamlet of Burwick near Scalloway where in 1983 only one house is occupied.

In Scalloway the story is rather different. Unlike other parts of the parish it has long had roads and lanes which at the end of last century were lit by paraffin lamps. In the 1930s two firms of engineers acquired generators to provide electricity for their own premises. Gradually this service was extended to neighbouring houses, and in 1936 electric street lights replaced the oil burning lamps. By the outbreak of the Second World War William Moore and Sons were providing electricity to the whole western half of the village, while H. Williamson and Sons provided power to the eastern half. These private services were replaced by the North of Scotland Hydro Electric Board in 1949.

As early as 1906 Scalloway had a public water supply from springs at the top of the Scord. A drainage system was provided in 1910 but this did little to improve sanitation. By 1919 the local authority had power to force householders to instal water closets, but it was impracticable to do so in Scalloway until a satisfactory water supply was provided. In 1928, 111 out of 192 houses in the village had no toilets. Scalloway was designated a special scavenging district but the most convenient form of disposal was over the sea wall whence sewage was washed up on the beaches to create a nuisance every summer.

In 1932 a new water scheme was completed at a cost of £4,690 and with it began the slow transformation of the village as more householders installed toilets.

Scalloway's horse drawn refuse cart was replaced by a motor lorry about the end of the Second World War, refuse being tipped at a dump near the Scord quarry. Since then however the whole parish has been given a weekly collection service, refuse being taken to the rubbish tip at Lerwick.

Owing to the scattered nature of the population of the parish and the absence of a regular public transport service the number of private motor cars is high. Whiteness and Weisdale benefit from the transport service between Lerwick and the West Mainland (generally once a day in each direction), while Girlsta is on the route of the operators who serve the North Mainland. There has long been a regular coach service between Scalloway and Lerwick. The Scalloway firm, Georgeson and Moore, is now the largest operator in Shetland having taken over most of the rural services.

Haulage contractors used to play an important part in the life of the community. They were extremely busy during the herring season, while between January and August they were in demand to bring home peats.

Lately there has been a tendency for merchants to buy their own vans for transport, while crofters generally have a tractor and trailer. Many families now have a small trailer towed behind the family car which is used to bring home the peats.

The oil construction boom provided a boost to all haulage firms while Sutherland Transport of Scalloway inaugurated an important skip service for the removal of waste material.

HEALTH SERVICES

In the early part of this century Scalloway could boast of two or more doctors competing for their share of patients. By the 1930s however there was only one doctor and this arrangement continued after the introduction of the National Health Service. The practice was a large one including the whole of the parish, with the exception of a small part of Weisdale, and also including Burra Isle. As the population increased in the 1970s it became necessary to engage a second doctor to share the workload.

Nowadays very few babies are born at home, most mothers choosing to have their confinements in the maternity unit attached to the Gilbert Bain Hospital at Lerwick. Pre-natal care is of a very high standard and it is quite common for mothers to be flown to Aberdeen by air ambulance should complications arise. Loganair operate the air ambulance service from Tingwall airstrip which was opened in 1976.

Working under the supervision of the two Scalloway doctors are four nurses who take care of home nursing throughout the parish. Elderly people are especially well catered for, those living at home having the advantage of a home help service and 'meals on wheels'. Small flats for elderly people have been provided by Shetland Islands Council at Scalloway and Whiteness, while another scheme at Scalloway has a warden on call. One of Scalloway's two hotels has been converted into an eventide home run by the Church of Scotland through a locally appointed advisory committee.

EDUCATION

By the mid 19th century several schools had been established in this parish. The parochial school was situated at Sandersfield near Gott, schools founded by the S.S.P.C.K. had been established at Weisdale, Whiteness and Scalloway while schools provided by the General Assembly of the Church of Scotland had been established at Trondra and Laxfirth. The latter building still stands although it is now rapidly falling into disrepair.

Following the passing of the Education Act of 1872 which made education compulsory, substantial school buildings and school houses were built throughout the parish at Scalloway, Gott, Whiteness, Weisdale, Girlsta and Trondra. The children of Oxna and the other small isles were served by a single teacher who spent a month or so at each island in rotation.

The Education (Scotland) Act of 1946 introduced a new compulsory scheme of secondary education for pupils over the age of 11 or 12, and

Scalloway school became a junior secondary school, its catchment area containing all the primary schools in the parish and that of Nesting. As the population of the Girlsta area became reduced, that school was closed and the pupils transferred to Gott; and Weisdale school was closed its pupils being transferred to Whiteness school.

Following the construction of the bridges in 1971 Trondra Primary School was closed, its pupils being transferred to Scalloway; the secondary department at Hamnavoe, Burra Isle was also closed, its pupils being transferred to the secondary department at Scalloway.

As the population of the parish increased in the 1970s, and as educational standards generally became higher, some of the existing schools became inadequate. An entirely new school was built at Whiteness while work on a major extension to Scalloway school began in 1982.

For children of pre-school age there are playgroups at Scalloway, Whiteness and Weisdale, Tingwall and Girlsta.

The school rolls in January 1983 were as follows: Nesting, 28; Gott, 46; Whiteness, 81; Hamnavoe, 118; and Scalloway (primary), 133. At the same date there were 125 pupils in the secondary department at Scalloway Junior High School.

PUBLIC HALLS

Prior to the building of public halls functions such as dances and weddings were held in barns or croft houses, while in Scalloway the fish sheds, after the export of their contents to Spain, made a suitable venue for such functions in winter.

Scalloway Public Hall dates from 1902 while Tingwall Public Hall was opened in 1905, being followed by a more modest building at Whiteness. Tingwall Public Hall after standing empty for several years was sold about 1946 for conversion into a dwelling house, but it was replaced by a sectional timber building at Veensgarth which was used regularly for concerts, dances and weddings; it is also the home of the Althing Social Group whose debates attract enthusiastic audiences and many excellent speakers from all over Shetland.

Within the last few years fine new public halls have been built at Whiteness and Tingwall (Gott) while in 1983 work began on an extension to Scalloway Public Hall. The assembly halls of the various schools are often used for meetings, flower shows, etc., while the gymnasium of Scalloway Junior High School, built originally as a church, is still used for meetings of youth groups and for badminton matches.

SPORT

Football is a sport of summer in Shetland and the parish has two clubs, Scalloway and Whitedale (i.e. Whiteness and Weisdale). The former club enters teams for senior, junior and juvenile leagues while Whitedale has had a run of outstanding success in senior football. Badminton has long been popular as an indoor sport and there are three clubs in the parish at Scalloway, Tingwall, and Whiteness and Weisdale. Hockey is enjoying something of a revival at present in Scalloway. Another traditional sport is sailing which is organised through Scalloway Boating Club and Whiteness and Weisdale Boating Club. The sailing of model yachts is another traditional sport in winter time, and there are two active clubs at Whitedale and Asta. Within recent years several more clubs have sprung up indicating a widening interest in sport. These include Scalloway and Burra Athletic Club, Scalloway Swimming Club and Weisdale Equestrian Club.

Scalloway Fraser Park was opened in 1942 providing a football and hockey pitch, a tennis court, swings, see-saws, etc. The park is run by Fraser Park Trust who are responsible also for the swimming pool and paddling pool on the opposite side of Main Street. Whiteness has a football pitch and there are multi-courts at Scalloway (Fraser Park) and Whiteness Primary School. Play areas have been provided for children at Scalloway (Blydoit and Sycamore Avenue) and Tingwall.

OTHER ORGANISATIONS

The number of youth organisations has greatly increased within recent years. Scalloway has companies of the Boys' Brigade, Girl Guides and Brownies and a thriving Youth Club; while Weisdale Church Youth Club, Whiteness Methodist Church Youth Club and Whiteness and Weisdale Junior Club cater for young people in their respective areas. The Royal British Legion has an active branch at Scalloway its headquarters being a fine new clubhouse near the public hall. There are three branches of the S.W.R.I.—Scalloway, Weisdale and Tingwall and a similar number of senior citizens' clubs serve the same three areas. Scalloway Drama Group has an impressive record of success at the annual drama festival at Lerwick.

CHURCHES

The Church of Scotland has four churches in the parish. Tingwall church, built in 1790, stands near the site of the old Church of St Magnus which was built in the 11th century; the present church of Whiteness stands on a site where churches have stood since 1722; Weisdale Church of Scotland began its life as a United Free Church; and Scalloway Church of Scotland was built in 1841 to meet the needs of a rising population.

The Methodist Church has also been extremely active in the parish. From 1822 they held services in the old school at Scalloway before building their chapel there in 1861. Stromfirth Methodist Church was built in 1872, Girlsta chapel in 1896 and Whiteness chapel in 1905.

Before that the Whiteness congregation met for worship in the former Congregational Church at Wormadale.

Scalloway has a Congregational Church, which is the oldest church in the village; and for several years it had a United Free church which was closed when that congregation re-united with the Church of Scotland. The Christian Brethren have a meeting room at Scalloway. Their meeting rooms at Trondra and Haggister are now disused.

HOUSING

Considerable improvements in housing conditions were carried out in the late 19th century as croft houses were given felt or slate roofs in place of the roofs of thatch. Often the walls were raised at the same time to give two small bedrooms on the first floor reached by a steep stairway. Over-crowding was a problem, especially in Scalloway.

The first attempt to overcome this problem was made in 1938 when a scheme of 38 houses was built by Zetland County Council at Scalloway. The houses had not been completed when the Second World War broke out and several of them were requisitioned for a time to house service-men.

Many more houses were provided by the local authority in the immediate postwar period, especially at Scalloway, while four blocks of Cruden houses were built at Weisdale. Since then council houses have been built at Scalloway, Whiteness and Veensgarth (Tingwall) while a new village has virtually been created at Weisdale.

At the same time a considerable number of private houses have been built, especially at Scalloway, while everywhere croft houses have been modernised or rebuilt. In some cases smart new bungalows have replaced the older croft houses which now serve as garages or stores. Building societies in general are reluctant to grant mortgages on property outwith Lerwick, but many houseowners have taken advantage of building loans from Shetland Islands Council. Crofters are eligible for assistance in building new houses under the Crofters Holdings (Scotland) Acts.

The lack of land for building has become a problem in Scalloway, where the village has grown to the limits of its natural boundaries and is now encroaching on some of the best agricultural land in Shetland. This has been a hindrance to the development of the village as the second largest community in Shetland, especially during the era of the oil construction boom when both housing and commercial ventures were diverted away from Scalloway because of the lack of land for building.

In 1982 the croft of Blydoit was sold and the new owner in turn sold part of the land to Shetland Islands Council, who intend to use it as an industrial site and as a site for council houses. Blydoit is situated to the east of the East Voe of Scalloway and is seperated from the village by the East Voe and a narrow strip of agricultural land. More than twenty private houses and ten council houses have already been built along the eastern side of the East Voe, far outnumbering the original four or five croft houses.

In 1981 there were 764 occupied houses in the parish with 3,403 occupied rooms, which compares with 475 houses and 885 'rooms with one or more windows' in 1861. Of the 1981 total 269 were council houses, 179 of them being in Scalloway.

AGRICULTURE, INDUSTRIES AND COMMERCE

With some of the best land in the whole of Shetland the parish has long been noted for its agriculture. The past thirty years, however, have seen a great increase in the sheep population and a corresponding decrease in cattle stocks. Crofters no longer keep a cow to supply them with milk, preferring instead to buy milk in bottles or cartons at the nearest shop. Dairy farming is still important in the Tingwall valley although the last few years have seen a marked reduction, especially at the north end of the valley.

By 1950 the work horse had disappeared from the parish, being replaced by the tractor. The ploughing match at Tingwall in 1939 had nine pairs of horses and one tractor, while that of 1944 attracted nine tractors and one pair of horses. Before the war Tingwall hosted the islands' major agricultural show. Unfortunately its revival after the war was only temporary and today the nearest agricultural show is that of Cunningsburgh. The sheepdog trials at Tingwall are still a major annual event.

Hay is still cured for winter keep but silage making has been found far more dependable in this wet climate. Turnips and swedes are widely grown for fodder while of the potato crop a small quantity is sold to shops in Lerwick and Scalloway. As the numbers of cattle have declined the area under oats has also been considerably reduced.

The old method of burning limestone was abandoned in 1942, being replaced by a limestone grinding plant at Girlsta. This was operated privately until 1950 when it was taken over by a farmers' co-operative who ran it for several years. Today large quantities of agricultural lime are brought in from the North of Scotland.

The most important of postwar developments has been the improvement of hill land. Pioneer of land reclamation in this parish was Major R. D. Winton of Kergord who, shortly after the Second World War, acquired heavy caterpillar tractors and drainage machinery. Further improvements were carried out by crofters as they were given permission to apportion their shares of the common grazings. In 1955 the Crofters Commission introduced a scheme which provided grants for the reclamation of hill land and several crofters in this parish took advantage of this offer.

At the moment agriculture is in a state of transition. Of the old estates only Hayfield Estate is still in existence with extensive property in

Tingwall. Most of the other large landowners are themselves farmers, like the Smith family who run Berry Farm, the Leslie family of Laxfirth, and Mr Anderson of Stenswall. Several crofters have now purchased their crofts. A survey in December 1982 of 73 crofts in the parish showed that 18 were owner occupied while 55 were still tenanted, although many of these tenants were in the process of negotiating for a purchase. This process has gone on most rapidly in Whiteness where half the crofters now own their own crofts.

Many of the 'scattalds' (common grazings) are still run on a communal basis, the crofters of the area co-operating to gather the sheep for dipping, etc. Some, however, have been apportioned among the various crofters who hold grazing rights in them and who, after erecting fences, are going ahead with their plans for re-seeding or improvement. This process is most advanced in the Tingwall area.

It must be emphasised that in most cases crofting is only a part-time occupation—a useful addition to a full-time job elsewhere.

★   ★   ★

Fishing is by far the most important industry in the parish both in terms of employment and gross income. The industry is concentrated at Scalloway which is the base for a fleet of about twenty seiners and trawlers, most of them owned and crewed by fishermen from Burra. Whiteness is no longer a fishing community, the last two seiners to be owned by Whiteness men being sold in 1962 during a period of exceptionally poor catches.

The size of the local fleet has been reduced considerably since 1945 but the individual boats are generally larger and, by incorporating all the latest fish finding equipment and the most advanced types of fishing gear, can catch far more fish than their counterparts of forty years ago.

The most important species are haddock and whiting while an important sand eel fishery has sprung up within the last few years. Sand eels are caught from April to October and are converted into fish meal at a large factory on the island of Bressay, while smaller quantities are frozen by the Scalloway firm of Iceatlantic (Frozen Seafoods) Ltd and shipped to Finland as mink food. Herring fishing has been banned in the Shetland area since 1977 after the near destruction of the stocks due to over-fishing by purse seiners in the years following 1965. Supplies of herring are now imported from Canada and Iceland to enable Iceatlantic to keep their kippering line in operation. Scallop fishing is prosecuted by several small inshore vessels, but the catches of lobster have decreased considerably following an increase in effort in the 1960s.

In 1982 landings at Scalloway were as follows: white fish, 5,343 tonnes (with a quayside value of £1,688,465); sand eels 5,446 tonnes (£158,506); shellfish 32 tonnes (£13,086); this gave a combined value of £1,860,057—a record for the port.

Since 1981 Scalloway has been a regular port of call for ships of the Faroe Line which links Faroe with Denmark, calling at Grimsby on the way south and at ports in Sweden and Norway on the return journey. Using this service small quantities of fish products are exported to the Continent and larger quantities of general cargo, including cartons for the fish trade and wooden pallets, are unloaded at Scalloway. Refrigerated cargo vessels take consignments of frozen fish direct to America and consignments of frozen offal and sand eels to the Continent.

Scalloway is now heavily dependent on fishing and its ancillary industries. Over one hundred people are employed in the three main fish processing plants—Iceatlantic (Frozen Seafoods) Ltd, L. Williamson and TTF (Fish Processing) Ltd. At Westshore William Moore and Sons have three slipways for the repair of fishing vessels, the largest catering for vessels up to 90 feet long. H. Williamson and Sons specialise in the installation and maintenance of electronic equipment such as sonars, echo sounders and the Decca Navigator, and are agents for a large number of suppliers including Decca. Three firms of fishsalesmen handle the accounts of the local fleet—LHD Ltd, A. S. Fraser and Westside Fishermen Ltd; the last is a co-operative which also runs a ship chandlery store.

★   ★   ★

Knitting is still important to the women of the area. It is essentially a home industry, most women selling their produce to Shetland Woollen Company who finish the garments in new premises adjacent to Scalloway Castle. High quality silverware is produced by Shetland Silvercraft at Weisdale while Hjaltasteyn at Whiteness specialise in jewellery and ornaments incorporating polished stone of local origin. Shetland Litho, the Scalloway firm of printers, has expanded greatly in recent years and in 1982 applied for permission to build new, larger premises on the proposed industrial site at Blydoit.

There are several boarding houses in the parish, and hotels at Scalloway, Veensgarth and Whiteness. All of these benefited from the increased activity of the oil construction boom. Scalloway has two public houses and another opened in 1982 at Weisdale.

As a shopping centre Scalloway declined in the 1970s due partly to the proximity of Lerwick—seven miles away—where larger shops can sell goods more cheaply than their rural counterparts. Since then there has been a revival in the commercial life of the village which is at present well served. A rise in population of even a few hundred people might, however, stimulate a demand for a greater variety of shops. At present most people have to shop in Lerwick for clothing, footwear and a wide range of household goods. The benefits of a growth in population can be seen from the excellent service now provided by a thriving little general merchant's shop at Weisdale.

WAY OF LIFE

The 1970s have been years of change for this parish since, like most parts of Shetland, it was affected by oil related developments in other parts of the islands, especially Lerwick and Sullom Voe. High wages have led to higher standards of living for most—but not all—families. An inevitable outcome of the oil boom, however is an abnormally high cost of living and many people on low or average incomes are worse off now than they were before oil was discovered.

The landscape is changing. The area under cultivation is shrinking year by year, and land that used to produce good crops of oats or potatoes is now grazed permanently by sheep. As agriculture becomes less important many landowners are selling land as sites for houses thus interrupting the traditional pattern of distinct crofting communities. This process can be seen at Weisdale, Whiteness, Veensgarth and Trondra.

The people have changed in many ways. There has been a marked influx of people from outwith Shetland bringing different attitudes and different values. In many ways the mix of cultures has been productive but there have been problems. A minority of the incomers, especially the temporary residents, are trouble makers. Their loyalties are to homes and families hundreds of miles away. The crime rate has increased although serious crime, fortunately, is still rare. Local people are less trusting than they used to be, and are far more wary of strangers.

In some ways the oil boom has merely accelerated changes that were apparent long before the discovery of oil. Sunday in Shetland used to be a day of rest when the only forms of relaxation considered suitable were walking or a drive in the country. Now, as in other parts of the UK, it is quite normal to spend Sunday working in the garden or playing football or carrying on one's usual work. For many part-time crofters with a demanding job elsewhere, Sunday is often the only day available for penning the sheep for dipping, shearing, etc. Inevitably church attendance has suffered, although lately there have been signs that young people are becoming increasingly interested in spiritual matters.

Now the oil construction boom is over and Shetland is settling down to a quieter pace of living. Life has never been better and one of the most heartening results of the oil boom is in the opportunities for young people both in work and sport. There is a growing realisation, however, that the future of the islands depends on the traditional industries of fishing, crofting and knitting. These were the industries that sustained the islands in the past and there is no doubt that, with careful planning, they can do so in the future.

March 1983

THE ISLAND AND PARISH OF UNST

Original Description
by A. T. Cluness, M.M., M.A., F.E.I.S., 1951
Revised by Andrew J. Irvine and John Renwick, 1982

PHYSICAL BASIS

This parish, the most northerly in the British Isles, consists of the inhabited island of Unst (46 square miles) along with the uninhabited islands of Uyea, Balta, Huney, Haaf Gruney, Wedderholm, South Gruney, and the holms of Skaw, Burrafirth, Woodwick, Newgord and Heogaland.

The island of Unst is roughly rectangular; it is twelve miles from north to south and on average four miles from east to west. The north end of it is split by the long inlet of Burrafirth, the south indented by the bay of Uyeasound, while the east side broken by the long voe of Baltasound and the broader shallower inlet of Haroldswick. From south to north a valley divides the island; in it is a pleasant chain of lochs, those of Belmont, Snarravoe, Stourhill, Watlee and Cliff, this last being three miles long.

To the west of this central valley there extends along its greater part a steep ridge of hill called Vallafield which, after descending to the lonely beach of Woodwick, opposite the south end of Loch Cliff, continues under various names until it terminates in the lofty headland of Hermaness. Beyond this more than a mile out to sea is Britain's most northerly lighthouse on Muckle Flugga, and the Outstack (60° 51′ 40″ N), the most northerly part of the British Isles, a bare little rock on which Lady Franklin landed once during the anxious years of search for her explorer husband.

To the east of the valley for some distance the Vord Hill also runs north to south, but about the middle of the island the long inlet of Balta Sound, sheltered by Balta Isle, runs far into the land. Immediately north the hill ridge of Crussafield runs east and west and separates Baltasound from Haroldswick, beyond which the mass of hills again trends north to south culminating in Saxavord which rises to a height of 938 feet O.D., and looks down on the inhabited districts of Norwick to the south-east, Skaw to the east, and Burrafirth to the south-west.

The cliff scenery is striking, especially in the north-west. The best known cave is really a passage through the rocks at Hol Hellier on the east side of Burrafirth. On a calm day a rowing boat or motor launch can pass for a distance of perhaps a hundred yards through this narrow vaulted tunnel; and in summer the cliffs at either end are thronged with seabirds seated row on row.

The island has two good harbours. Baltasound, sheltered from the east by Balta Island, is one of the best natural harbours in Shetland, and afforded adequate space for several hundred boats in the palmy days of the herring fishery at the start of this century. Uyeasound, at the south end of the island, is protected by the island of Uyea from all directions but the south.

Modern developments have caused several alterations on the surface of the island. Most prominent here has been the building of a dam on the east side of the island between Colvadale and Watlee to provide a water reservoir for the whole island. This was done between 1954 and 1956 by Zetland County Council, and enlarged the two small lochs known as Heylaswater.

WILD LIFE

Wild life includes numerous rabbits. Rats were first recorded about 1903 and are now very numerous also. Mice were unknown in 1793 but have been plentiful for at least a century, although there are still none on the island of Uyea. There are no hares, hedgehogs, weasels, frogs, toads, snakes or adders. Seals are to be seen in fair numbers around the coast and the otter after being reduced to low numbers is now again very common.

Changes have taken place in the number, kind and even the habits of wild fowl. For seventy years there have been no eagles, merlins or goshawks. On the other hand, the fulmar petrel, exceedingly rare at the beginning of this century, now nests on every cliff; and for several decades it has also nested inland among rocks and ruins. 'Solan geese' (gannets) have a colony at Hermaness, which is now a bird sanctuary. The 'bonxie' (great skua), of which only three pairs were known in the world in 1904, has now spread from Hermaness to all of Shetland, Orkney and the north of the mainland of Scotland. Lapwings were once rare but have been common for many years. Wild swans since the 1940s have wintered at Easter Loch, Uyesound, but owls have disappeared. The 'chalder' (oyster catcher) has increased in numbers and now nests inland as well as at the coast. The Arctic skua is more numerous than ever before; and the redthroated diver nests here and there by lonely lochs: according to tradition there has always been a pair of the latter nesting on Heylaswater for the last two centuries. The stormy petrel is known to nest on Haaf Gruney. Gulls, terns, shags, puffins, guillemots and eider-duck continue to be very common. Land birds were formerly limited to larks, linnets and starlings, but now there are a few blackbirds and an occasional thrush.

The people of Unst have long since ceased to use as food any seabird except the wild duck. The only eggs occasionally taken for food in modern times have been those of gull and eider duck.

HISTORY

There are many indications that in the very remote past the island was relatively densely populated. There are Stone Age heel-shaped cairns at Crussafield and the Muckle Heog; there are standing stones at Clivocast and Lund; and there are several cairns on the Gallow Hill. There yet can be seen the ruins of several Iron Age brochs; at Hoganess, where the sea has taken away a portion of one leaving a central mass of ruins protected by two very deep trenches and semi-circular ramps; at Snabrough where the ruins project into a little loch; at Underhoull, Westing, there are traces of two brochs; there is a broch on the Brough Holm, Westing, which has probably been connected to the land by a causeway since washed away by the sea; some traces of one remain at the south end of Burrafirth; and at the Noup, north of Saxavord, is the most northerly of all the brochs; while the names Brough at Colvadale and Musselbrough at Uyeasound indicate the presence once of similar erections, though now no trace at all is left at the former place, and only a small skerry showing at low water at the latter.

Evidence of settlement from the Iron Age has now been revealed by archaeology at Underhoull, and here also have been found Viking long-houses. Portions of Viking houses had earlier been revealed by erosion of coastal sand at Millaskaera; here whorls and portions of steatite vessels, Viking combs and other artefacts have been found from time to time. In Muness there are ruins of a castle erected in 1598 by Laurence Bruce, Great Fowd (or governor) of Shetland. He was half brother of Robert Stewart (a natural brother of Mary Queen of Scots), who was at the time lord of the islands of Orkney and Shetland. It is the ordinary rectangular type of Scottish baronial castle with two round towers at opposite corners. It was inhabited only for a short time. According to tradition, it was built rapidly by forced taxation and labour, and it crumbles slowly and is unregretted.

CHURCH

The church from ancient times has left evidence of its presence, and succeeding stages can be traced in the very names. Papil in Haroldswick would seem to indicate a very old settlement of priests. Kjurkaby (Kirkaby) at the Westing must be as old as the tenth century. Kurkwall (Kirkhoull) at Uyeasound and the Kirknowe at the Westing have now no trace but the names. Clat Cna kirk at Uyeasound is now but a few stones and a legend of how it was never completed; the powers of darkness undid by night the work done by day. Ruins of medieval chapels with burial grounds still in use are found at Lundawick and at Sandwick. Tradition says that the latter place was first used as a burial ground in the twelfth century, and that the former burial ground was beyond Millaskaera and now half a mile out to sea. While the distance must be exaggerated, some proof of this has come to light in the storms of recent years. The sands have been largely swept away and skeletons are from time to time uncovered in the shallow stone graves opposite Millaskaera. Here too have been uncovered by sand erosion portions of houses of Viking times which have for long been covered with sand and earth to a depth of eighteen feet. Whorls and portions of steatite vessels, Viking combs, etc. are found from time to time. Colvadale has its chapel ruins and very ancient burial grounds. Cross Kirk near Clibberswick at Haroldswick was long held in veneration. Altogether there are said to be at least a dozen sites of ancient chapels and churches. The best preserved of them all is on the Isle of Uyea.

Near Watlee between Baltasound and Uyeasound the spring of Yela Brun (the 'healing spring') was long held in veneration.

The history of the church in Unst during the nineteenth century is largely the account of the labours of two men, the joint writers of the previous statistical account of this parish, the Rev. James Ingram D.D., and the Rev. John Ingram, M.A. The former, ordained in 1803 after twenty years in Fetlar, came to Unst and there in 1876 celebrated his hundredth birthday and the 73rd year of his ministry. He died in 1879. His son was associated with him in the charge from 1838, and in 1888 he too celebrated his jubilee as minister at Unst, dying at the age of 85 in 1892. Dr Ingram played a leading part in the Disruption of 1843, and most of his congregation accompanied him in leaving the Established Church. He was the father of the Free Church for many years and preached vigorously when well over ninety. John Ingram too was in time the last of the fathers of the Free Church in Shetland. In addition to his work in Unst he established the Free Church in Fetlar, and was there regarded by the congregation as their pastor for 23 years, until in 1866 they were able to call a minister of their own. In 1843 a church was built in Uyeasound too for the Free Church. In 1841 when the minister's stipend amounted to £249 annually, a day labourer's wage was one shilling per day, and a woman servant's wage was £2 per year. In those days the minister had no difficulty in maintaining his position and his great house with the aid of two or three or more servants. Great changes have since World War II taken place in churches and church buildings. There is now one Church of Scotland minister for the island and one manse situated at Baltasound, the Uyeasound manse having been sold some years ago; however the church at Uyeasound is used for one service weekly. The United Free Church at Baltasound has been demolished, and the Church of Scotland hall at Haroldswick is no longer used for services on Sundays. There is no longer a resident Wesleyan minister but one comes to Unst occasionally from the circuit on the Shetland Mainland.

Church attendance and membership have fallen considerably in recent years. The only evening service now is at Baltasound during the winter months. Sunday school attendance has also fallen, while Sunday work on crofts has increased, possibly due to the fact that so many crofters now have their main occupation and earnings elsewhere, and the croft is only secondary to these in importance, the work done on the crofts in some cases being mainly done on Sunday. Paradoxically the funds of the local churches have been better supported, and people give generously.

POPULATION

Despite clearances and emigration in the 19th century, the population rose to a peak of 3,060 in 1861. In 1841, there were estimated to be at least 1,200 people in the southern part of the island, but now the total is only about one-sixth of that. There is now no inhabited house between Muness in the south-east and Clugan, near Baltasound, although there are 29 ruined croft houses. From Belmont in the south-west to the north Westing, there are more than 40 abandoned homesteads and about 20 still inhabited.

Emigration from Unst was especially directed towards New Zealand; for example in May 1874, 104 people left in a group to join fellow islanders already settled there. The population continued to fall through emigration for a century, but has stabilised since 1951, and is now showing a slight tendency to rise. The total number of people in 1981 was 1,209.

For a considerable time, many of the population have lived some time beyond the allotted span. In the period since 1851, about 40 attained ages of 95 or more; and of these four died at over 100 years.

PUBLIC AND SOCIAL SERVICES

In the last 30 years there has been a considerable increase in public and social services, and the island has in several respects reached urban standards of provision.

In the 1950s the County Council laid a mains water scheme for the whole island; and in the same decade the North of Scotland Hydro-Electric Board provided it with mains electricity. Street lighting has been provided at all the sheltered homes, and at most of the council houses.

Since World War II there has been a great increase in the number of telephone subscribers; the total number in 1951 was 39, whereas in 1982 it was over 200.

SCHOOLS

For most of the period since World War II the school population has been around 150, although there was a considerable increase for a period in the 1960s. As education has become more centralised, four schools have been closed—at Pettister, Uyea Isle, Norwick and the Westing: the last named at the end of last century had over 60 pupils. Baltasound school was raised to the status of Junior Secondary in 1950, and has since become a Junior High; it now has 120 pupils and 17 teachers. There are also primary schools at Haroldswick (with 28 pupils and 2 teachers) and Uyeasound (with 12 pupils and 1 teacher).

The medical and social needs are provided by a doctor, a district nurse, a dentist, a health visitor, an ambulance, and a welfare officer.

There is a resident policeman, who we are proud to say is not overworked.

The safety provision has been strengthened by the setting up of a fire fighting unit. There is also a weekly refuse collection.

The number of shops has remained unchanged over the period since World War II; there are three in Baltasound, three in the Haroldswick area, and two in Uyeasound.

As late as 1876 the mails for Unst and the adjacent island of Yell were very small. Once a week the letter carrier set out from Haroldswick in the north of Unst and, collecting letters from Baltasound and Uyeasound, proceeded to Snarravoe. Crossing by boat the mile-wide tide stream of Bluemull Sound, he added the Cullivoe and Mid Yell letters before reaching Ulsta—a total distance of nearly forty miles, generally in one day. There he handed over the outgoing bag and received the incoming mail, and after a night's rest retraced his steps. In his later years he was sometimes met at Snarravoe by his daughter who came to assist him. His weekly bag contained the mail for 6,000 people.

Now there are 5 mails a week. There have been for decades three post-offices—at Haroldswick, Baltasound and Uyeasound, but since the 1950s the number of postmen has dropped from eight to four, and mail is now delivered by motor van.

TRANSPORT

In the 1950s and 1960s following much improvement of roads on the Shetland Mainland, the County Council continued the improvement programme into Unst. First this was by widening (where required) and then by tarring the island's main and side roads. Here a fact emerged which seems worth recording. The main road from Uyeasound to Baltasound did not require to be widened, although it was laid over a century ago. Roads to townships in crofting districts have been added to and upgraded, and now there are few inhabited houses more than 50 yards from a road. Admittedly the little village of Pettister on the north side of Cliff Loch has now been abandoned, mainly we would suggest (like Snarravoe and Colvadale in the south end of the isle) because of the lack of a road. For all these, roads would have been very expensive owing to the steep, wet, and difficult nature of any route. Names of districts and signposts, along with reflecting verge markers, and major and minor road signs, are useful modern additions.

Travel has accordingly become easier and more in keeping with modern methods. In 1950 very few private vehicles were owned, and road transport was handled by two buses and three car hirers. Almost every family now has a car, while vans, tractors, and lorries, are available as required.

In 1950 the main method of travel from the island was by steamer to Lerwick by the coastal vessel 'Earl of Zetland' which called at Unst three times weekly. There was also an overland service by bus through Yell and the Mainland, and launch over Bluemull and Yell Sounds five days weekly, leaving Unst and Lerwick at 9 a.m. and arriving at the respective terminals at approx. 2.30 p.m. Carriage of goods by such means was obviously impossible, and even luggage had to be limited; consequently anything larger than a pram or a motor cycle had to use the steamer service. This method of transport continued until 1973 when the Shetland County Council introduced the vehicle ferry services on Bluemull and Yell Sounds, making it possible for people to use their own cars for travel. Buses on the Mainland and Yell roads were also provided, and since then we have had the advantage of being able to visit the town or almost any part of Shetland and return the same day.

Also and perhaps most important, an airstrip, later to become an airfield, was sited at Baltasound and an air service provided by Loganair became available on scheduled services. This is available at all times for ambulance or hospital cases as required.

These new methods of travel meant the loss of the sea link, which was (although slow) the cheapest way of moving goods. Although fares and freights were kept as low as possible, it did contribute to a very considerable rise in living costs on the island. There is now talk of road-equivalent tariffs being introduced, but it is doubtful whether this would be an advantage. The present service really works well, and when we consider the strong tidal currents, and violent winter weather, the service has been proved to be almost as efficient and regular as any other form of travel service in the country.

HOUSING

From 1956 to 1966 the Shetland County Council carried out the building and letting of three groups of houses in Haroldswick, Baltasound, and Uyeasound, thus filling the long-felt need of accommodating at modern standards some of the non-crofting part of the community. At this time there had been little inflation, and at a weekly rent and rate total of 33/- these soundly built houses were considered very reasonably priced, meeting the needs of those who required them. In 1975 a further three groups were built in the same districts, and currently another group of twenty houses are in course of construction in Baltasound, erected by the Shetland Islands Council. At the completion of this scheme, the island of Unst will have approximately 70 council houses.

Since 1950 at least 20 houses have been built by private owners. In all there has been a much greater development of both private and council housing than for at least 60 years. Less than three per cent of the inhabited houses are without modern facilities.

As is frequent in crofting areas, the housing position has been complicated by the special position of the crofter in law. Rents for crofts, and the houses going with them, have changed very little since the end of the last century, while crofters have virtual security of tenure. In these circumstances landlords have no real incentive to maintain houses, although crofters themselves have fairly generally improved and modernised their own.

One of the less popular modern developments is that planning permission has now to be obtained for the erection of any buildings, however small.

There are two local firms involved in building and maintenance.

AGRICULTURE, INDUSTRIES AND COMMERCE

CROFTING

While the importance of the traditional crofting has fluctuated somewhat over the modern period, the general trend has been for it to become less and less; now it is largely a spare-time activity for men with full-time employment in other things. Cultivation has greatly decreased; and in livestock there has been a run-down in cattle and a rise in sheep.

In the inter-war period, some of the larger sheep farms were broken up and a considerable amount of land passed into the hands of crofters. With the serious recession in the fishing at this time, some crofters had acquired enough land to be worked full-time, but the inter-war Depression acutely affected the profitability of the sheep and cattle on which they mainly depended. This was followed, however, by the great stimulus to agriculture during World War II, with boom prices for livestock and wool, and increased mechanisation in the working of the land. With the subsequent return to normal peace-time conditions, production from the land continued to be the main economic basis of the island, and around 1950 it was popularly believed that three-quarters of the revenue of Unst came from sheep, thanks to high lamb and wool prices together with subsidies. As well as contributing to the domestic food supply, egg production gave a considerable part of croft incomes in the 1950s, but has now declined to minor importance.

Perhaps the greatest change in the island's life which has occurred during the last three decades is that the Unst man is no longer a fisherman operating from a crofting base, but generally speaking a wage earner deriving a subsidiary income from the croft on which he dwells. Gone is the cow and most of the cultivation. The number of cattle kept on crofts now would not reach double figures, and the cattle kept on the island now are in large beef producing units, while nearly all the milk used is imported. Sheep are now the main production of the crofts. The area of improved land has been considerably increased by reseeding and reclamation grants given by the Department of Agriculture and administered through the Crofters Commission, whereby crofters can not only be helped in the purchase of fertilisers and in the cost of hill ploughing, but also assisted in the purchase of fencing materials. The suitability of much of the hill land in Unst has made this development of hill scattald enclosure very much accepted by the crofters. A large proportion of the land so reclaimed is being used for sheep grazing and now carries about five times its former numbers.

In the 1950s a sudden rise came in market value of Shetland ponies, with year-old ponies and foals reaching hitherto unattainable values.

Animals with good blood lines often reached ten times their former value, and high-bred stallions with good stud potential were hired through the Department of Agriculture to be put in on the scattalds. This had a marked effect on the quality of the stock, but unfortunately for many crofters, market values have progressively deteriorated in recent years. This is regrettable from the point of view of good husbandry, because with the fall in the number of cattle kept, and a corresponding increase in sheep stock, any further reduction of ponies would tend toward unbalanced grazing, and deterioration of good grazing land through old rough grass remaining uneaten. The enclosure of apportioned scattalds has taken away some of the shelter provided by stone dykes which were the original hill boundaries of the crofts, the new boundaries being now of wire fencing. It is hoped that future governments will continue to provide help with these schemes, especially in fencing; otherwise the annual cost of upkeep might result in neglect and loss of what has been reclaimed. Years ago fence replacements were made in large part from driftwood, but as the high price of wood has led to fewer deck cargoes being carried, little can now be obtained from this source. Up to 1950, there were few mechanical aids on the croft, except on the bigger units. This has changed and now there is little hand work. Cultivation by spade, or by pony plough, except for small garden plots, is unknown. The scythe and the hay rake have been succeeded by the mowing machine and the hay baler, and in recent years, the communally owned corn binder and potato lifter have greatly improved harvesting methods. Hay is still the main crop for most crofts, with oats, potatoes, and turnips now considerably reduced. Silos are now fairly common, and barley has been tried recently with considerable success.

FISHING

Fishing has for centuries played a big part in the life of the people. As far back as 1793 it was recorded that there were 78 boats, each with a six-man crew, and that all men in health between the ages of 16 and 60 were employed in the fishery. Up to the late 19th century, the main fishery was for cod and ling, but in the 1880s there was the great Shetland herring boom, in which Unst (and especially Baltasound) played an outstanding part. This fishery developed largely in response to expanding markets in Europe, especially in Russia and Germany. Boats (more substantial than the traditional open sixareens) came thronging from Scotland, England, The Isle of Man, Holland, and France, and as many as 700 could be seen in harbour together at the weekend. In 1904 a quarter of a million barrels were cured in Baltasound alone. In summer over 8,000 people found employment at the herring stations. Work was to be had by all, by the men at the fishing and by the women at the gutting and packing of the herring. Some of the remoter crofts were abandoned for cottages or rooms nearer the fishing stations in Baltasound and Uyeasound; and this also brought people nearer shops and schools.

Subsequent developments have seen the fisheries dwindle to very minor proportions. While Unst concentrated on the herring fisheries in the decades before World War I, the decline in white fisheries was accentuated by the advent of trawling from mainland British ports. In the inter-war period there was the collapse of the European herring markets, which led to a great contraction in the fishing effort from Unst stations, and by 1950 it was only a matter of history. Small-scale fishing for lobster and crab was prosecuted through most of the period since World War II, but this has now been almost discontinued. Most fishing now is on a casual basis for domestic use, or for sport.

For a period after World War II, the whale fishery in the Antarctic gave employment to a number of men, but this ceased when Messrs Salvesens of Leith ended their operations in the 1960s. Numbers also went to the Merchant Marine, but these also have dwindled.

MINERALS

Since iron chromate was discovered here early in the nineteenth century it has from time to time been quarried. Exported in a crude state, it commanded a fair price until it became cheaper for Britain to import foreign ore. In times of war there is a revival. Even during the Crimean War the quarry at Hagdale was deep enough to drown three men on the 13th August, 1857. A revival to some extent of the industry occurred during both great wars. A commission which in the 1940s investigated the mineral resources of Scotland emphasised the great amount of workable serpentine in the island; this with suitable crushing and conveying machinery could be cheaply shipped. Talc is however the only mineral now worked and exported, and the same commission was of the opinion that about one third of Britain's annual needs (10,000 tons), could have been obtained here. There used to be limestone quarries at Ballista (the Bollarstadir of the Orkneyinga Saga) but these are no longer worked as such. Traces of gold have been found at Saxavord and the little stone hut used by the searchers still stands under the brow of cliffs. Diatomite is said to be present in small quantities in the south end of the island at the Sma Waters.

HOSIERY

For generations, Unst was famous for the beauty and quality of its woollen lace scarves and shawls, and women from the island for many years could be depended on to win prizes for these at the Royal Highland and other shows. However the very time-consuming nature of this work has rendered it obsolete.

For a considerable period after World War II, hand-knit garments, or machine-knit ones with hand-knit inserts played an important part in the island's economy, but the younger generation has entered very little into this occupation, and hosiery production has considerably fallen. A small knitting factory started on the island, but had to close mainly through lack of operatives. A few of the older generation still do fine hand work for shows and private sales.

SERVICE INSTALLATION

Since 1950, the Services installation of RAF Saxa Vord has provided employment for a number of civilian workers in catering, maintenance and ancillary works. It has also added a new social facet to the community life of the island, with mutual benefit to both Service personnel and local population.

TOURISM

The pattern of tourism has changed. Formerly visitors came for shooting and trout fishing, but both of these pursuits have now ceased to attract. Now hiking, camping and general nature study are more important. There are two good licensed hotels to cater for visitors; a youth hostel at Uyeasound which has proved popular; and at Baltasound a block of self-catering flats has been well patronised.

WAY OF LIFE

The impact of the great social changes of the last three decades does not appear to have markedly affected the characteristics of the islanders.

The people still retain their qualities of resource and practicality and often have multiplicity of skills, a thing which is not usually recognised or approved in the union-dominated work forces of mainland Britain with their principle of 'one man one job'. Perhaps the implication that trade unionism inhibits the islanders' freedom of choice explains why it has never been really strongly supported.

Peat was very much the traditional fuel, and there are still abundant supplies of peat at Vallafield and Saxa Vord, and in both cases the peat banks have been accessible by road for over 30 years. A motor lorry can now transport in one day the number of peats which at one time would have taken twelve peat ponies a fortnight.

There is an adequate supply of peat available at Ramnageo and Muness, but one of the reasons for the abandonment of the settlements of Sandwick and Colvadale was that local peat supplies had become exhausted. The west side settlement of Uyeasound and Snarravoe used to obtain this fuel supply from the neighbouring isles of Yell and Linga. As late as 1914 in summer a dozen boats could be seen crossing Bluemull Sound with their peat cargoes. It was hard but not unpleasant work, and the passage between the islands was made easier by the use of the strong tides in the sound; the tide running north helped to take boats to the peats, while the southbound tide brought them back. By the 1950s the use of peat had largely given way to coal, and this in turn has been partly displaced by fuel oil for heating.

Leisure pursuits have benefited from modern opportunities. We have for the greatest part of the last decade had the advantage of an excellent mobile library service, operating at monthly intervals, providing literature to suit all tastes, and bringing when requested specific books. This to a community with a high proportion of readers, and especially to the student and the housebound is a service of great value, especially when we remember that formerly the literature available to the average person consisted of newspapers, fairly limited school libraries, and the limited collections of books in individual households. In addition to this service, we now have magazines edited and published on the Shetland mainland. For nearly thirty years a magazine entitled the 'New Shetlander' has been issued quarterly, and is an excellent and informative periodical from all points of view. It contains local and national news items, folk lore, stories and verse. The latter are sometimes written in dialect by local authors of considerable ability, which does much to present and preserve our island way of life, both past and present, in a readable true-to-life presentation for our times. Recently another magazine, the monthly 'Shetland Life', has become available, and is doing excellent work in providing a contemporary account of island life, as well as recording much of our past. Although we cannot claim these as our island products, we find they contribute to our enjoyment, and we do not want to omit their mention; the fact is that few issues appear without some contribution to their pages from our island writers.

Literature and music have always had great prominence in our past, and it is a great pleasure to record that today they are by no means being neglected. Music, especially for violin and guitar is being taught in our schools, and some of the pupils are showing promise of great potential.

Island entertainment has altered out of all recognition. In the 1950s many people would gather in a house in the district, and spend much of the evening in playing bridge or other card games. Violin and accordion music also did much to help pass the evenings. There were never fixed visits; one simply called at a neighbour's house and could always be certain of a welcome.

Parties, except at Christmas were uncommon, and hospitality was always given without formality. While hospitality is still prevalent, the casual way of visiting neighbours without a previous invitation has changed. Organised parties and arranged visits have become more the social pattern.

Public entertainment has also changed. Except for the festival of Up-Helly-Aa and the annual regattas (which are still popular and in fact getting more sophisticated) there is now little or nothing of the old system of local concerts, which were mainly organised and carried through by local effort and talent. In the 1950s there would have been several such entertainments in the winter season, consisting of locally written and produced sketches, recitations, and musical items. Now there are few of any such gatherings. Vocal and instrumental parties from the Shetland Mainland, and 'pop' groups which tour the islands are more popular with present day audiences; and for the young element disco dancing provides the focal point for gathering.

For older folk who do not react to these later innovations, during the winter months occasional whist drives are held in each of the three district halls, which have all recently been enlarged and modernised. Recently a local history group has been formed, and it is endeavouring to find and encourage the recording and preservation of, stories and folk lore, which did so much to enrich our island heritage in the past.

One thing that has gained greater popularity recently is boat building, mainly to produce sailing craft for races in the harbours of Baltasound and Uyeasound. Quite a number of men have designed and built their own racing boats—no mean achievement. Some of these boats can hold their own against anything in their class. Races are held weekly during the summer season; there are also annual regattas in Unst and in the neighbouring isles, entry to which has increased from four or five boats to 26 locally owned and manned. Competition in sailing has increased more than in any other recreation. Soccer and hockey have progressed considerably, while easier travel has allowed inter-island and inter-county games; this has made for keener competition, and also has been socially advantageous. Schools have helped in this with training and organising, the junior high school at Baltasound having a P.E. instructor, with a games hall and other facilities. Also at the Baltasound School a wide ranging programme of evening classes is held. At Haroldswick and Baltasound there are very active and progressive S.W.R.I. groups which play a very active and prominent part in the life of the community. Their activities range from flower displays to sheep and pony shows, and to competitions for baking and agricultural produce.

DIALECT AND PLACE-NAMES

The language of the parish has greatly changed over the modern period. As late as 1895, Dr Jakob Jakobsen, the Faroese philologist found about 10,000 words of definite Norn origin still surviving in Shetland; and Unst was the parish in which these had survived best. But with the upheavals of two World Wars; the scattering of the young (and even not so young) of both sexes all over the world in various services; with the influence of four generations of compulsory education with English the basic language; with radio sets and television in almost every house; and with the passing away of old ways of life, much of the old language has passed too.

Shetland dialect is still the speech used in the average Unst home, although many of the words in use fifty years ago are now seldom heard. These are in the main the words used to describe implements, or methods of work which are no longer in use. The high proportion of non-local pupils from service families attending local schools, have oddly enough produced little or no diminution in the use of dialect amongst local children. The reverse in fact is the case, the non-native element has been inclined to adopt dialect, becoming reasonably proficient too in its use.

In this island and indeed all over Shetland, efforts are now being made to preserve the dialect words and phrases.

Several main usages of the dialect may be instanced. The parts of the boat from the *aers, ruth, kabes, humblibands, hinney spot, stammering, nile, rakki, stroods*, to the *rongs, fitlins, auskerri, tafts*, and *tilfers*, are all of Norse origin; the gear of peat ponies, the *flakkies, maeshies, rivvakishies*, the *klibbers* and even its *neebie* and *varnagel pin* are Norse enough; and Shetland weather is still best described in Shetland words. Everyone still speaks of *fanns* (drifts) of snow or *fivvles* (light powdering) and of *moorikavs* (dense blinding snowstorms). There may be a *stoorawind* (great wind) or *blash*, or *eestik*, or *njidder*, or *attri*, to give only a few instances. Sea birds still retain their Norse appellations. Except in presence of strangers here we speak of *maas* and *scories, tirriks, shalders, scarfs, tysties, haigris, shuis*, and *bonxies*, when we refer to gulls, young gulls, terns, oyster catchers, guillemots, shags, herons, arctic skuas, and great skuas. The second personal pronoun singular is still *du*, 'you' being reserved for strangers and elders. The verb to be is the auxillary with all verbs of motion, and generally with other verbs also. *Am been* for 'I have been', *He's geen*, for 'he has gone', *We'r dune it* for 'we have done it', etc. Many verbs still exist to describe exactly the sounds made by animals, many verbs to describe minutely the movements or methods of progression of men and animals, and many descriptive adjectives exist which have no exact equivalent in English.

Place names are still as a whole Norse though many are every year passing out of use. But names which to English ears sound strange (such as *Tonga, Millaskaera, Gamlagrind, Heogaland, Grunka Hellier, Do Keostins* and *Houllna Gruna*) still survive in great numbers, though the meanings of many are now forgotten.

SURNAMES

Surnames have not altered much since they became stabilised about 1820. Those ending in —son are much the commonest. There are several Andersons; a few Davidsons and Edwardsons; Edmonstons; several Hendersons and Hughsons; many Jamiesons and Johnstons; here and there a few Laurensons and Mansons; several Patersons; a few Robertsons and Sandisons; and some Thomsons and Williamsons. Smiths are common; there are no Browns, but some Grays. The surnames Stickle and Priest are common in Haroldswick but uncommon elsewhere. There are Inksters and Irvines and Hunters in fair numbers. And there are several surnames of obviously Scottish origin such as Bruce, Clark, Gifford, Mouat, Fraser, Fordyce, Scott and Sutherland. These have been supplemented in the latest phases by some surnames of new immigrants.

CONCLUSION

The impact of the great social changes of the past three decades, does not appear to have markedly affected the basic characteristics of the islanders.

The fact of this being a virtually classless society has done much to make the people very democratic in their outlook, and the religious, political and racial prejudices in other areas of the country are quite alien to their character even in this modern age. Time does not contain the same element of immediacy as it does in the timetable-dominated areas, and this is reflected in the initial reserve both in making social contacts and formulating opinions.

Having formulated opinions they adhere strongly to them, stubbornness being a salient characteristic. The islander may be led to the water, but drinking it would be quite another matter, unless it contained a potent additive. Essentially the islander is a survivor, because he is the end product of a people who have contended over the centuries with the elements, invasion, tyranny and oppression, extreme poverty and hardship. He yet still retains his individuality, and can still deal with the problems of today.

December 1982

THE PARISH OF WALLS AND SANDNESS

by Alexander Pearson, M.A.

PHYSICAL BASIS

The parish of Walls and Sandness consists of the butt of the peninsula of the West Mainland of Shetland, together with a number of offshore islands of which only three—Papa Stour, Foula and Vaila—are inhabited. The name 'Walls'* represents an anglicisation of the 'Waas' of Shetland speech; and the latter itself is an altered form of the original Old Norse Vagr ('bay'). Sandness is in fact an accurate topographic description of the north part of the parish—promontory with sandy soils.

At its landward end Walls and Sandness is bounded by the parish of Sandsting and Aithsting. The bedrock for the main part are the sedimentary rocks of the Old Red Sandstone, but Papa Stour is composed mainly of volcanic rocks. Much of the land consists of low hills, smooth in outline, although in Sandness Hill to the north-west it reaches a height of 817 feet O.D., and The Sneug in Foula reaches 1,373 feet O.D. The surface is also broken by a considerable number of small lochs. The great part of the coast consists of spectacular cliffs, and in the case of The Kame on Foula, rise almost sheer to a height of 1,200 feet.

HISTORY

There is evidence that this parish, like many other parts of Shetland, was settled in the Neolithic period, by a date around c. 3000 B.C. Neolithic period homesteads have recently been uncovered at Scord of Brouster by a team from Southampton University. Burial cairns and cists, and various early boundary walls, are often more in evidence than house-sites. Part of the reason for this is that not a few settlement sites were covered by the

---

* The name 'Walls' is not pleasant to the ear of local people, who call it 'Waas'. The origin of the name is Old Norse 'vagr', meaning voe or inlet. Våg is the word in Norway today, and is pronounced 'voe'. The English plural 'voes' may have come in because there is more than one inlet. In time the Scandinavian 'v' apparently gave place to 'w'; and there appears to have been confusion over the letter 'å' in Scandinavian, which is alternatively written as 'aa', although it is pronounced 'o'. Hence the name became 'Waas', but map-makers, taking it for a Scottish dialect form, changed it to 'Walls'.

growth of peat following a climatic change to cooler and wetter conditions c. 2000 B.C. It is now thought that the type of house associated originally with Neolithic farmers showed little change for 3,000 years. Little definite evidence of the Bronze Age has yet come to light, but there are three stone circles in Walls that are not listed in any published inventory: they are all c. 100 yards in circumference, but none is above a metre in height because of past generations taking the stones for other buildings. The period of the broch builders, now thought to be between 600 B.C. and 200 A.D. and associated with the Iron Age, saw the building of a series of these fortifications, at Watsness, Setter, Broch, Footabrough, Burland, Burrastow, Loch of Kirkigarth, Pinhoulland, Bousta, Ness of Garth, Holm of Melby and Huxter. These also have been robbed of building stones by later generations. However, relatively little has been done by archaeologists to investigate the many ancient monuments.

The Christianisation of the area by missionaries of the Celtic Church in the Dark Age period is in effect commemorated in the name of Papa Stour ('big priest isle'), and it is thought that this was a base for mission. The Pre-Norse population of Shetland may well have had at least a Celtic component in it, but evidence for this in place-names is controversial.

From c. 800 the area was settled by the Norse, and the big majority of the place-names are indubitably of Norse origin. Examples include Lera Voe ('muddy bay'), Foratwatt ('sheep grazing land'), Stennistwatt ('land with the stone house'), Brunatwatt ('land by the bridge') and Brouster ('farm by the bridge'). Recently Dr Barbara Crawford of St Andrews University has excavated on Papa Stour what may be the remains of the residence of Duke Haakon of Norway. The earliest Shetland document from 1299 states that the King of Norway had a farm on the island, and that the Duke's house had a wood-panelled room called a 'stofa': the building conforms with the known 'stofa' style, although excavation is still incomplete.

In the later 15th century Shetland along with Orkney came under the Scottish crown, and there was an influx of Scots towards the end of the 16th century, consisting mainly of landowners and clerics. This information can be gathered from the Shetland Court Book 1602-1604, which Professor Gordon Donaldson states 'can properly be regarded as the earliest volume of Shetland record which has survived'. From these records we learn that 'Robert Swinton, who was minister of Walls, but who had many secular interests, had three (boats); and Nicol Gutteromson in Cullivoe and Nicol Thomasson at Brek in Walls each had two'. When this Mr Swinton died in 1612 the inventory of his goods included 'four old herring nets'.

A variety of cases came before the court in Walls. For example, 'in Walls in 1604, Marion Cromarty was accused of the theft of ling from Andrew Nicolson's skeo'. Again 'in the court of Walls in 1604 a German called Edward Mair was accused of assault, and a Walls man who died in

1612 owed money to three Germans, Bernard Lening, Claud Mathowsone and John Gausborg!'. These and other items make interesting reading in the book by Professor Donaldson entitled 'Shetland Life under Earl Patrick'.

Gradually the old Norse laws were dispensed with in preference to Scots Laws, and in place of the Norse Udal system there came into force the Scots Feudal system. The land in the parish came largely into the hands of the Cheynes of Vaila and the Scotts of Melby. In 1576, when the Scottish king confirmed the grant of the island of Vaila to Robert Cheyne in that year he gave the right 'to big ane hous and fortice upoun the saidis landis of Valay for sauftie thairof fra the hiland men, perattis, and otheris invasionis'. However, in 1792 there were twelve proprietors in this small area, possibly a survival of the great number of proprietors in Norse times. These large estates were superimposed on a settlement pattern of small nucleated townships and isolated farms along the north (Sandness) and south (Walls) shores of the peninsula, with the main scattald in between.

In Earl Patrick Stewart's time, in the early 16th century, there were trading centres at convenient points throughout these islands. Walls and Papa Stour both had trading 'booths'. The traders were from the ports of Hamburg and Bremen and they came for the summer months. Commodities such as brandy, wheat meal, linen, muslin, soap, and candles were traded for fish and fish oil. They also paid in money, and this gave a strong incentive to fishing rather than farming. This was a period of relative prosperity.

However, after the union of 1707 strict measures in the form of customs duties and a salt tax in 1712 ended the summer visits of these German merchants. Scots 'landmasters' took their place. They did not at first have markets so well organised as the foreign merchants had had; but they did make use of an iniquitous truck system, which varied from place to place and time to time. In general it resulted in keeping the majority of tenant fishermen-crofters bound to fish for these lairds at rates of remuneration below what could be obtained elsewhere. As markets expanded greater pressures were put on the fishermen to catch more fish. From using four-oared boats (four'eens) they progressed to using six-oared boats (sixareens) and fished further from land. The landmaster rented the boats and the gear to the men. Because of rent for holdings and amounts credited for meal and other essential goods the amount the fisherman earned was minimal; more often than not he was in debt. And, as indicated in the First Statistical Account, stiff penalties of fines or eviction were imposed on fishermen who were tempted to transgress by selling their fish to merchants offering more than the laird. This was the era of the 'haaf' (deep sea) fishing.

In 1742 landmaster John Scott of Melby petitioned the Presbytery for a 'fixed school' in Sandness. In his letter he stated there are 'no Gentlemen, no Merchant, no tenant of any tolerable stock or substance residing in that parioch, nay few, very few that are capable to pay half of their just debts, but the far greater part are (to my experience) so plunged in Debt, that I question much if there be any Parioch in the country so deeply and universally depauperate'.

The First Statistical Account stresses the iniquity of the practice of subdivision of holdings and alludes to the clandestine selling of fish to merchants who would give a better price. Some landmasters built look-out towers from which to keep an eye on boats coming to land, and it may well be that the tower on Vaila at the entrance to Wester Sound was built for such a purpose.

In the early 19th century a merchant class superseded the class of landlords, and the 1872 Truck Commission Report 'crushed the power of the landmaster'.

In 1838 on the island of Vaila the noted philanthropist Arthur Anderson of P. and O. Company fame started the Shetland Fishery Company. He did this, partly we can assume, with a view to improving the lot of the fishermen by paying them adequately for their labour. This enterprise for a few years brought a degree of prosperity to the fishing community of Walls and district. Spanish vessels anchored in Vaila Sound to load the fish from the nearby drying beaches. Unfortunately this enterprise flourished only briefly and the company was wound up in the 1840s.

By the middle of the 19th century larger decked boats were in use, and the writer has it on good authority that two of these were built at Seafield, Walls. The builder was a Mr Moodie, grandfather of the late Daniel Fraser of Skarpigarth.

Population figures in the parish had risen from 1,967 in 1801 to 2,315 in 1841, and to 2,579 in 1871. This was mainly due to the 'impolite rage for prosecuting the fishing' mentioned in the First Statistical Account. To encourage early marriage, and thereby increase the man-power, land holdings were carved up into smaller units. Needless to say the rents were not reduced accordingly. These small crofts were cropped more intensively than ever before, but even so enough food to last the year through could not be produced. Vaccination against smallpox is also given as a reason for the rise in population.

With disasters in the 19th century among 'haaf' fishing boats and the introduction of decked vessels the 'haaf' fishing declined and herring took its place from around 1880. There were four herring stations in Walls and one in Papa Stour. In summer people came to these new stations in large numbers; they included curers from mainland Scotland with their coopers, and women gutters recruited from the Moray Firth, the Western Isles, and even Ireland. Local people found summer employment, some in fishing, some in working ashore. No one became rich—certainly not the fishermen or the shore workers. Goods and services had to be provided and at one time there were nine shops operating in Walls and Mid Walls. There were two blacksmiths, there was a bakery at Burnside, and a shoemaker at the Closs of Voe.

It must be said here that not all the parish manpower was engaged in this herring boom. Since 1886, when the first Crofters Act had given security of tenure to crofters and fixed fair rents, many young men had joined the Merchant Navy, and many (even with families) had emigrated. Between 1871 and 1901 the population fell from 2,579 to 1,995, and it was to continue falling.

The herring fishery in this parish was not as enduring as the 'haaf' fishery, lasting only half as long. An auction system for herring was started in Lerwick which meant an improvement in conditions for the fishermen who had previously worked on an engagement basis. A more important change was the advent of steam drifters which began operating around 1900. These needed bunkers which Lerwick and Scalloway could best supply. Also many sailing boats were converted to motor fishing boats, and these too had fuel needs which could best be met at the larger centres. The steamers' pier, built in Walls around 1910, largely through the enterprise and financial help of the landlord, Herbert Foster Anderton, had come too late. Commercial fishing in Walls ended with the First World War. The North of Scotland Shipping Company steamer continued its West Side service (including calls at Walls) until 1939 and then discontinued it owing to the opening up of road transport.

Between the wars, and during the Second World War, many men from the parish served in the Merchant Navy. After this a few small boats found fishing for lobsters remunerative as a part-time enterprise. At the time of writing there is one boat from Walls engaged in fishing for lobsters and queen scallops during the summer months. One man in Sandness is likewise engaged. Two men belonging to the parish, engaged in fishing, have taken up residence in Scalloway. One Burra Isle fisherman has come to Sandness but carries on fishing from Scalloway. Two other fishermen resident in Walls do likewise.

The report of the Crofters Commission, which led to the first Crofters Act already mentioned, contains interesting information on crofting conditions in the report of a hearing at Walls held in July 1883. A parishioner of no mean stature locally, James David Robertson, presented the case for the crofter-fishermen. Their complaints were (1) excessively high rents for land generally of inferior quality in this region. (2) No security of tenure, giving no encouragement to improve holdings. (3) No compensation on leaving a holding for improvements carried out. They also complained of the crushing burden of rates. Poor rates and school rates alone came to 7s 9d per pound, half of that amount being paid by the tenant. Although road money was paid, scarcely any of it was being expended in country districts. The people of Sandness, which was half the parish, had 8 miles to walk over tracks through the heather to reach the highway.

The proposal was put to the Commission that where rates exceeded 5s per pound the Government should provide relief. It was argued that as the Government gave help towards maintaining lunatics and paid the doctor to care for the poor, it should also pay something towards maintaining the poor.

Robertson in his evidence to the Commission stated that the Road Trustees had started building a road but had not completed it. The proprietor and tenants had never done anything towards making a road, and that tenants would not unless compelled make a private road at the instigation of the proprietor. When asked if the tenants would do something on their own part without payment if the proprietor paid half the expense, the reply was that the tenants would now do nothing without payment.

There was no complaint against the lairds or factors, simply against the law as it stood. There had been no evictions similar to the clearances in other parts of Shetland. The great fear was that the landlord might enclose the scattald (common grazing). There had been advantages in Walls not found anywhere else in Shetland. Under a number of lairds the people of Walls had had relatively more liberty than elsewhere. A great advantage in keeping down rents was emigration to New Zealand, and the fact that owing to 'the natural formation of the parish', it could not easily be let for farms.

LOCAL PERSONALITIES

Though not of local stock, Herbert Foster Anderton without doubt has a claim to local fame. He was of a Yorkshire family of mill owners and came to Shetland for fishing and shooting holidays, in conjunction with purchasing Shetland wool for his mills. He was so struck with the summer beauty of the island of Vaila that he decided to buy it; and with it he bought the remainder of estate of which it was a part and which comprised much of Walls and Sandness but excluded Foula. He reconstructed Vaila Hall to what it is today, developed a farm on the island, and ultimately came not only for summer holidays but to spend his retirement there. He is chiefly remembered for his philanthropic works in the parish. He helped the community by forming the Vaila Harbour Trust, by constructing the Vaila Sound pier at Walls, and in various other ways. Sadly, other schemes he had in mind, such as the building of a chapel on the island to seat at least 100 persons did not materialise; the First World War intervened. Typical of him was the fact that he kept on his mill workers during the inter-war depression while other mill-owners laid off their work force; and in doing so he sacrificed his fortune. He died in 1937 and was buried on Vaila in the garden he had created.

The Walls' poet, T. A. Robertson, probably better known by his pen name 'Vagaland', who died recently was known to the writer as the most quiet, friendly and unassuming person one could possibly meet.

He was among the first country schoolboys to qualify for and take advantage of secondary education obtainable at the Anderson Educational Institute in Lerwick. From there he went on to graduate M.A. at Edinburgh University. He trained as a teacher and spent his working life teaching in the English Department of the Lerwick Central School, which is now part of Islesburgh House Community Centre.

Only in later life did he publish poems, written mostly in the dialect, and including many masterpieces of rhythm and linguistic beauty. These appeared in the *New Shetlander* magazine and always won the hearts of his readers. He was ever the champion of the old well-tried ways, and though everyone would not agree that the old ways were in every respect the good ways, yet nostalgia is catching, and Vagaland knew how to present it in poetry of character. His works are published as *Laeves fae Vagaland* and *Mair Laeves fae Vagaland*. There is also *The Collected Poems of Vagaland* published after his death.

The following is a tribute to a noted skipper of the Foula mail-boat, Magnus Manson, who died in 1913. It is taken from the book *The Isle of Foula* by Professor Ian B. Stoughton Holburn who was laird of Foula for the thirty-five years from 1900 to 1935.

'One of the most perfect gentlemen it has been the writer's lot to meet was not one of the old British aristocracy, although they are very hard to beat, but the skipper of the Foula mail-boat, who died in 1931.

'He was a man of eighty-four, a superb seaman still handling with splendid skill the open sailing boat, only some 25 feet over all, that carried the mails through twenty miles of the stormiest seas in the northern hemisphere. He was a man of strong personality, to whom others instinctively looked for leadership, and he took his responsibilities very seriously. He never allowed the chance of making a passage to slip by, and many a morning before the first streak of dawn, he would send his crew wading up the burn in their sea-boots, feeling for stone to serve as ballast for the little vessel. He suffered from a disease which kept him in constant pain, yet he was never anything but cheerful.

'Magnus Manson was a small man with a noble head and a singularly beautiful face through which his fine character shone. His dark locks curled about his neck, and his clear eyes wore the expression of a mariner whose gaze was habitually fixed upon the far horizon. His manners were absolutely natural, as he had never been anywhere to learn them, but to see him take off his hat to greet a lady, or hand her into a boat, was a lesson in perfect deportment from which any young aristocrat might profit.

'He was a deacon at the little chapel and a spiritual inspiration to the whole isle. The language of his theology may have been old-fashioned and narrow but his heart was broader than his theology. Like Enoch, he was a man who walked with God, and when, as occasionally happened, the minister asked him to lead the congregation in prayer, it was a revelation. A grand old man if ever there was one!'

POPULATION

The population at selected Census dates since 1801 is given below:

Year		Year	
1801	1,967	1911	1,745
—	—	1921	1,346
1851	2,442	1931	1,102
1861	2,570	1941	no census
1971	2,579	1951	830
1881	2,262	1961	670
1891	2,057	1971	539
1901	1,995	1981	652

There was a considerable rise in population in the earlier part of the 19th century, when the landlords promoted fisheries and emigration was limited. Limited employment in the parish led to the subsequent decline in the era of smaller families and considerable emigration; but the tide has at last turned in the last decade with the opportunities caused by the 'oil boom'. 20 male and 21 female births were registered in the parish in the 1971 to 1981 decade.

The age structure for the different parts of the parish is given below:

	0-15		15-65		65 +		Totals		Overall totals
	m	f	m	f	m	f	m	f	
Walls	39	39	124	119	41	54	204	212	416
Sandness	12	14	34	36	18	24	64	74	138
Papa Stour	6	4	9	9	1	1	16	14	30
Foula	8	6	14	13	2	3	24	22	46
	65	63	181	177	62	82	308	322	630

At the present time immigrants from outwith Shetland into Walls proper account for 16 per cent of the population. During the years from 1960 to 1975 there was a total of 197 (90 males and 107 females) who passed through primary school; and of these 42 males and 60 females subsequently settled outside the parish. Against this 21 members of the 1960-75 group subsequently brought spouses into the parish.

About 65 houses in Walls that were occupied within living memory are now empty. Another 20 are in a ruinous condition. The farther from the centre one goes, the more derelict houses one finds. Crofters however are slow to decroft these houses despite the grants available to modernise them for let.

Papa Stour lost between 20 and 30 of its population around 1962-63. Someone is said thereafter to have put an advertisement in a mainland newspaper for people to populate the island. As a result a number of people came, and these included several children. There was a constant coming and going for a time and eight houses were occupied with as many as fifty people at the peak of the influx. Only three houses are now occupied by these immigrants.

The number of children in the parish for 1983 is given below by households:

Number with 1 child	27
Number with 2 children	23
Number with 3 children	13
Number with 4 children	3
Total households with children	66
Households with no children	162

A hundred years ago parents depended upon their children to help work the crofts. Those were the days of subsistence crofting. Large families were of necessity part of the system. It was a fragile system, and when it became possible to move out into the world beyond the confines of the croft, it began to break down. Young people sought opportunity elsewhere. Parents have sought in recent years to plan their families.

The composition of the households of the parish for 1983 is given below:

	Persons per household							Total households
	1	2	3	4	5	6	7	
Walls	37	43	23	25	16	5	2	151
Sandness	13	16	10	3	4	4	1	51
Papa Stour	3	3	2	1	1	1	—	11
Foula	3	3	3	3	2	1	—	15
	56	65	38	32	23	11	3	228

It will be noted from the above table that more than half of the households contain one or two people; in most cases these are elderly people.

PUBLIC AND SOCIAL SERVICES

Public order in the 18th century was, at parish level, dealt with largely by the Kirk Session. There were also officials named 'Ranselmen', the last of whom were sworn in on Fair Isle in 1869. These had authority to search in cases of suspected theft or appropriation of the contents of wrecked vessels belonging by law to the crown. Justices of the Peace were also sworn in to help settle disputes.

Kirk Session records of this parish (from 1735 onwards) give accounts of investigations into various types of misconduct and the penalties imposed. Particularly, the Session was hard on those who broke the Sabbath by grinding corn or by saving wreckage. It appears that, at the time the First Statistical Account was written in 1798, the minister was himself settling the quarrels that arose among the people. 'The task is unpleasant,' he says, 'yet, should these differences be entirely overlooked, though of a civil nature, unchristian conversation would more generally prevail.'

The Kirk Session also became the leaders in establishing education in the parish. In 1724 the assembled heritors of the islands and the Sheriff Depute established parish schools under the direction of the heritors, the ministers, and the Kirk Session.

Roads, as such, were unknown until the 19th century. In the 1840s there were crop failures, particularly bad in the case of potatoes, and food was in short supply. A 'free' distribution of meal, provided by the government, was made. However 'free' the government intended this distribution to be, the parish recipients had to work for it by making a road. The remains of this road can be seen leading from the vicinity of the Stove cattle grid towards the east. It was called 'da Mel Rod'. In the second half of the 19th century there was a series of developments. A Zetland Roads Act was passed in 1864; Parish Councils, School Boards, and District Councils were set up, and in 1918 the Education Authority was established.

Among the changes in local government that have taken place more recently, perhaps one of the most significant has been the formation of Community Councils. These are formed from locally elected persons with the Shetland Islands Council member an ex officio member. With air strips on Foula and Papa Stour, and with funds from the Shetland Islands Council made available for charter flights, the members from these remoter parts of the parish are enabled to attend meetings and to have their requirements considered on a par with the remainder. A direct link with the Islands Council is thus maintained. The Walls and Sandness Community Council concerns itself with a variety of objectives and has funds which can be spent in helping to provide gravel roads to houses, for example. It recommends works and services to the various departments of the Islands Council. Lately it has taken an interest in promoting a bakery in Walls and has recommended to the Islands Council the purchase of The Aurora Knitwear building which was formerly the Walls Congregational Church. It is at present organising the removal of the wrecks of old cars which so much encumber the area.

EDUCATION

The greatest credit for the establishment of permanent schools in the parish must go to the minister, the Rev. James Buchan, who took up duties in 1735, and to Mr John Scott of Melby who became laird about the same time. These men spared no effort in persuading the Presbytery, the Society for the Propagation of Christian Knowledge, and the other heritors and heads of families to set up schools. They met with resistance. Finally Mr Buchan offered, as a gift, four acres of his land in Walls to be an encouragement to the setting up of a legal or parochial school. This land was secured in perpetuity by title deed to the first and all succeeding head teachers of the school. Mr Buchan also offered £30 out of his own pocket towards the cost of building the school and schoolhouse. The reaction of the populace to this generous gesture was co-operation. There were 42 young men in Walls 'who were willing to contribute liquor and tobacco to the workmen'! The building took 33 days instead of the 25 originally estimated. The name 'Happyhansel' was given to the building, 'hansel' meaning a gift to bring good luck. Not so long ago the walls of this schoolhouse were still standing. Recently they were knocked down and a house was built on the site. The school, a much smaller building, is still intact and occupied. Four teachers in succession served the community of Walls in this school and it was held in high repute.

After the passing of the 1872 Education Act three schools were built in Walls, and one each in Sandness, Papa Stour, and Foula; and all had schoolhouses attached. It is an eloquent commentary on the changes of the present century that Sandness school, which in living memory had over 100 pupils on its roll, now has 17. Also Mid Walls and Dale of Walls schools, which had at one time 60 and 36 pupils respectively, are both now closed. Happyhansel School in the village of Walls, or 'Doon Waas' as it is called, can now muster only 49 pupils though it collects pupils from Dale of Walls, Mid Walls, and West Burrafirth as well as its immediate area.

There was a period from 1949 to 1970 that Happyhansel was a Junior Secondary School, providing both primary and secondary education up to the age of fifteen. Selection at the age 11 plus was the practice during those years, with the result that pupils more forward in English and Arithmetic passed on to the Anderson Educational Institute as it then was, and the others remained in their rural school. With a small secondary roll of between 20 and 30, and dwindling in later years to nearer 10, it was not possible to have adequate specialist staff or accommodation to allow for the spread of classes when visiting teachers were present. Prefabricated huts, as were common all over Scotland, were erected to accommodate the secondary pupils. Provision of mid-day meals in canteens with large coal-burning cookers was also a feature of this period.

By 1970 many of these small secondary departments were being closed. Secondary pupils from Happyhansel School were thereafter transported to the Aith School, which was raised to the status of a junior high school.

In 1982 a new Happyhansel School opened; it is situated to the rear of the old school which was built in 1878. This new school, costing in the

region of £300,000, has every modern amenity. The changes are staggering to contemplate. Radio and television programmes to schools broadcast
by the B.B.C. have been available for several years. During the 1950s,
1960s and 1970s schools had to raise half the cost of any piece of capital
equipment such as a projector or a television set. Now these items are
supplied. Playgrounds are obsolete. We now have multi-courts and indoor
gymnasia. There is no walk out in the fresh air to toilet or canteen, these
facilities all being under the same roof as the school. There is hardly
anyone walking to school any more. Either a school bus or car will pick
the children up, or parents living within walking distance will drive their
children to school.

HEALTH SERVICES

The first record of organised health provision involved the Kirk
Session, and in 1748 ' "Dr" Dunbar, "Dr" Fraser and "Dr" Innes were
paid to cure diseases which would formerly have been isolated and left to
destroy their victims'. Whatever the significance of the 'Dr' title at this
time, this was obviously an early form of medical provision.

It is however, difficult to determine what level of medical provision
there was up to the middle nineteenth century. The Poor Law (Scotland)
Amendment Act of 1845 laid on parishes the duty of seeing that 'there shall
be proper and sufficient arrangements made for dispensing and supplying
medicines to the sick poor' and of securing 'proper medical attendance for
the inmates of every Poorhouse'.

In 1912 the Highlands and Islands Medical Service Committee was
given the task of advising 'as to the best method of securing a satisfactory
medical service there-in'. The situation in this parish was examined by
this committee. Dr James Duncan Cochrane answered questions providing
information. Probably his chief complaint was that he had no secure
tenure of a suitable house, and this contrasted with the ministers of
religion who lived in amply built and comfortable manses. He lived at the
Bridge of Walls. Previously doctors had been housed in Melby House,
Greenland, and Lochside House.

After the First World War progress was made. A doctor's house was
built in Walls in 1924, though it was not until the 1970s that a surgery and
waiting room were added. In the 1930s a nurse's house was built at the
Bridge of Walls. Previous to that the district nurse was lodged in Sandness.
Papa Stour and Foula generally had nurses, in many cases the wives of
teacher-missionaries.

At present there is a resident nurse on Foula but there is none on
Papa Stour. The provision of landing strips on these two islands has
overcome the difficulty of reaching patients who might need medical
attention in weather that would prevent boats landing.

If the conditions in Dr Cochrane's time are compared with those
obtaining now under the National Health Service, one would conclude

that now there is little left to complain about. Roads lead to almost every house. The motor car has taken over from the pony and the motor cycle. Holidays for doctors are arranged simply by the doctor in the adjacent parish looking after his colleague's practice during his absence. Trained nurses take care of patients from day to day, and no longer is the neighbour woman left to deal with confinements. Medicines are dispensed at the doctor's surgery. There are prescription charges varying from time to time, with certain categories such as old age pensioners, children, and those with certain chronic diseases having treatment free of charge. There is no charge for doctor's or nurse's visits. Specialist staff such as chiropodists, occupational therapists and (for schools), speech therapists, are all available. School children are particularly well taken care of, each child being examined periodically by the Chief Administrative Medical Officer (CAMO) or his staff.

Out-patient clinics are held regularly in Lerwick by the two resident consultant surgeons, and visiting consultants from Aberdeen supply all other specialist medical needs. An efficient air-ambulance system is available for transfer of patients requiring medical care outside Shetland.

HOUSEHOLD AMENITIES

The Local Authority provided mains water in 1963 to all of Walls and Sandness, with the exception of the Dale of Walls and Watsness areas at the west end of the parish. Both Papa Stour and Foula subsequently had public water supplies provided.

Walls and Sandness have had mains electricity since 1954, when it was installed by the North of Scotland Hydro-Electric Board. On Papa Stour and Foula the people still depend for electricity on their own generators, but the possibility of laying a submarine cable to Papa Stour is at present being explored.

Gas comes in cylinders, the distributer making weekly deliveries.

Oil-burning cookers and heating systems are to be found in many homes, especially in those where the occupants are too old or infirm to cut and cure peat for themselves. The oil is brought in tanker lorries from depots in Lerwick. These depots have their supplies brought in tankers from the south; such is the ironic position while the main part of the national oil supply is piped ashore in Shetland.

Peat for fuel has been cut for many centuries. The Shetlander uses a long handled cutting tool with a right angled blade called a 'tushker', (cf. Icelandic torfskeri). After the top turf has been removed the tool is pushed downwards, and then with a levering out and lifting action, the cut peat is laid alongside the peat bank to dry.

As centuries passed the peat moor was cut back until the distance the cured peat had to be transported became a problem. There was a time when people living round the Voe of Walls chose to cut and cure their peat out round the heads at Ola's Voe and transport it home over the water. Four boat loads were a year's fuel. This practice was discontinued when lorries, and later tractors and trailers, came on the scene.

Papa Stour in time ran short of peat moor. Peat was also used for animal bedding and for supplementing the animal manure. Crops in former days were all important. By removing too much peat, harm was done to the common pasture. In time the people of Papa Stour also had to transport peat across the sea. They too discontinued this arduous and time consuming practice, and have been importing coal for many years.

Sewage is piped to septic tanks wherever there are Local Authority houses. An increasing number of private houses have their own septic tanks, but there are still a few who do not have this amenity.

There is a weekly collection of household refuse.

TRANSPORT

Since the last war all roads on the mainland part of the parish have been surfaced with tarmac. Previously they were water bound gravel roads with gates at various points within the townships. Cattle grids have taken the place of these gates. All roads in the parish, including the main one, are single track with passing places. A welcome feature of the recent period has been the making with grant aid of gravel roads to croft houses and to areas of the common grazing which have been improved.

With improved roads and more money in circulation, the number of motor vehicles in the parish since mid-century has risen strikingly. Then they could have been counted on the fingers of one hand.

The following table shows a recent count:

Cars per household	1	2	3	4	5	
Households	62	15	9	2	1	
Total cars	62	30	27	8	5	132 grand total

In addition there are 33 tractors, 3 buses, and 3 excavators. Vans deliver goods to the one remaining shop in Walls and the one shop in Sandness. The Walls shop delivers by van to outlying crofts. The three buses are owned by the Isbister family who from the 1920s ran the Walls Daily Service to Lerwick. A year or two ago they gave up the service and have since been engaged in private hiring. The firm Georgeson and Moore now run the service on the same days as formerly, i.e., every week day except Wednesday. Passengers from Sandness and Papa Stour have to connect with this service.

The Papa Stour service crosses the sound from West Burrafirth. The boat is the *Ivy Leaf* and it crosses thrice weekly, weather permitting. There is also the bigger *Spes Clara* which brings in heavier goods and takes out livestock. The Local Authority subsidises the cost of these services.

The Foula mail boat, a converted lifeboat, calls at Walls once a week, again weather permitting. Often in the winter time no crossing can be made for five or six weeks at a stretch. There is a slipway in Ham Voe on Foula, which was built in 1948-49. The wind has to be in a favourable direction, however, before the boat can be launched.

COMMUNICATIONS

Since the early decades of this century Post Office telephones have done much to improve communications. A little later telephone kiosks and private telephones arrived. The day exchange in Walls Post Office was rehoused in Rocklea and became a day and night service. Radio telephones connected Papa Stour and Foula with the mainland and a telephone cable was laid to the isle of Vaila.

In 1975 the system became S.T.D. (Subscriber Trunk Dialling) and was fully automatic. A new exchange building was erected east of the Public Hall. There are now 107 private telephones in Walls alone.

The postal service is now daily. Before 8 a.m. each day (Sundays excepted), a Post Office van from Lerwick arrives. The mails are sorted and two postmen with vans begin delivering, one through Walls and the other through Sandness with some deliveries in Walls en route. People of middle age remember the mail being delivered by postmen on foot or on bicycles; there were three postmen in the Walls area alone.

P. and O. Ferries send out a large van to the parish twice weekly carrying heavy goods.

SOCIAL ACTIVITIES

Sandness and Walls each have public halls. Walls Hall, built in 1925, was modernised in the 1970s, giving it a better stage, a committee room, and a larger floor area to accommodate badminton. This cost at the time over £30,000 of which the local community found one eighth, the rest being made good by grants from the Scottish Education Department, the Shetland Islands Council, and the Highlands and Islands Development Board.

Foula is at present raising funds for a community hall. Papa Stour has to make do with use of the school.

Evening classes have been popular for a very long time. Navigation was taught in Walls more than a hundred years ago. With the opening of a secondary school in Walls in 1949, classes in needlework, woodwork, cookery, engineering, and Norwegian were regularly organised. Lately pottery and computing have been offered.

There is a Youth Club in Walls and it is equipped with 'disco', table tennis, pool table, darts, and other facilities. A rota of parents and immigrant young people supervise the activities.

A small hall, known as the parish hall, adjacent to the parish church manse in Walls provides a locus for meetings of Cubs and Brownies and a Play Group. The minister of the united parishes of Walls, Sandness, Sandsting and Aithsting runs a company of the Boys Brigade.

Walls has a branch of the British Legion with 30 members, and both Walls and Sandness have groups of the Women's Rural Institute, each having about 20 members. The Walls branch celebrated its fiftieth anniversary last year. Badminton teams from the parish take part in tournaments organised to include most districts in Shetland.

Walls Regatta Club was started before the First World War by the landlord, Mr Anderton. Yachts actually competed in the club's earlier days. Later only Shetland model boats took part, with the addition of a dinghy section after the Second World War. For a time Sandness also held a regatta but now Sandness crews join forces with the Walls Club.

Points races provide excellent sport and entertainment during the summer months and Regatta Day is a very popular event.

Much thinking has gone into the hull design of the racing boats. Care is taken to preserve its traditional shape. The ballasted boat is becoming obsolete and instead a three man crew uses body weight to hold the boat upright. Sails, masts, rigging, and running gear are professionally manufactured on the mainland.

Recently Walls Regatta Club has had a new club house built. This, with improvement to the Bayhall pier, shows that the club intends to keep up with the times.

To end every Regatta Day there are two houses of a concert and a lively dance.

Vying in popularity with the Regatta held in July is the Walls and District Agricultural Show held in August. This show formerly had its venue at Greenland. It shifted from there to Brouster, but now has its permanent site on a piece of ground behind the Methodist Chapel and Manse.

It is greatly to the credit of the organisers of this show that, whereas the other Shetland shows at Voe and Tingwall were discontinued, this show was maintained along with that held at Cunningsburgh in the South Mainland. It must be noted that although held in Walls, its catchment area extends to the whole of the West Mainland.

At this show there is keen competition and something of interest for everybody. All kinds of livestock are brought to be judged in competition. Despite the fall in numbers of crofters keeping cattle, there are still ample numbers brought to compete. Knitters and wool producers have hundreds of exhibits. Flowers in a variety of classes make a beautiful show. Home baking and farm produce, art and craft exhibits, garden and field produce, all find a place. Sheep penning and pony riding provide afternoon entertainment and the day finishes with two houses of a concert followed by a dance.

There is little in earlier accounts on the social and recreational aspects of life. From handed down information we know that music and dancing were enjoyed as much then as now. Fiddle playing has a long tradition in every parish in Shetland. The house of Finnigarth was noted for its fiddlers. There is a dance still performed known as 'Da Muckle Reel O' Finnigirt' with a tune having the same name. Papa Stour was noted for 'Da Papa Stour Sword Dance' which has its own tune and brings in the seven saints of Christendom. It bears resemblance to the Long Sword Dance of the North of England, and could well have come in with immigrants. Foula has its Foula Reel, somewhat similar to 'Strip the Willow'. The traditional tune is 'Da Shaalds (shallows) O' Foula.'

The country dance known as 'The Shetland Reel' was universally popular, and was danced to tunes such as 'Da Merry Boys O' Greenland', 'If I get a boany Lass', 'Kale an' knocked Coarn', 'Laurie Tarrell', 'Ahint da Daekes O'Voe', 'De'il stick de Minister', 'Da De'il among da Tailors', 'Jeck brook da Prison', and many others.

Weddings, before the days of public halls, lasted for two or three days, and the dancing and feasting took place in houses or barns cleared for the purpose.

Today, while radio and television provide entertainment in music and drama, there are in the parish quite a few traditional fiddle players, accordionists, guitarists, and mandolin players. Drama, when performed by local artistes, is very popular and, with the help of producers from the south in the early stages, local players have competed commendably at drama festivals in Lerwick.

Bar facilities are now available in Walls in both the Public Hall and the Regatta Club House. Buffet suppers are often held with dancing to visiting bands, and even cabaret type functions are not uncommon.

CHURCH

The original parish church of St Paul's in Walls is thought to have been situated by the loch on the croft of Kirkigarth. The next was in the present graveyard near the voe. The third was on the present site, and the rebuilt church of today is the fourth to bear the name.

The churches of St Paul's at Walls and St Margaret's at Sandness, along with those of Papa Stour and Foula first became included in one united Ecclesiastical Parish under the Roman church. Some centuries later, at the Disruption in 1843, the parish minister with two of his elders left the established church and Mid Walls church and manse were built. The Mid Walls church was reunited with the parish church in 1929 on the reunion of the national church.

For a trial period (1730-94), the church of Foula was taken from this charge and made part of the charge of Fair Isle, Foula, and Skerries(i.e., a joint charge of the remoter islands). The scheme was a failure.

The earliest Church of Scotland manse is thought to have been at the Closs of Voe. A story concerning this manse goes as follows: There was a path, long before council houses ever came on the scene, which led straight down to the church. Large slabs of stone had been laid down in a boggy part to allow the minister to pass dry shod. A crofter, after the manse had fallen into disuse, needed the stones for lintels and removed them. In spring he planted his crops on his croft but he did not survive to reap the harvest.

Other manses were built. What is now the 'Haa' at Watsness was a manse and for a time the minister rode a pony over the hills to his charge in Sandness. The present St Paul's manse is a 19th century building of good solid structure and may in the near future have money spent on modernising it to make it the manse for the united parishes of Walls and Sandness, Sandsting and Aithsting. The two parishes were linked under one minister last year.

The Methodists have churches in Walls and in Sandness. Their minister resides in his manse in Walls. His charge covers Gonfirth, Wester Skeld and Gruting, as well as Walls and Sandness.

Declining membership caused the Congregational Church to close in the 1960s. Its manse, near the pier, is now a private residence. There is a small nondenominational chapel at Dale of Walls, served by both Church of Scotland and Methodist ministers. Mid Walls manse, once the home of the United Free Church minister and later Church of Scotland missionaries, is now also a private residence.

There is one lay reader residing at Sandness who assists the parish minister.

With the decline in population there has been a corresponding decline in the number of communicants belonging to the churches, Walls and Sandness had 201 communicants in 1965, falling to 149 in 1975, 129 in 1979 and then increasing slightly to 136 in 1983 but this number includes 11 on a supplementary roll. The Methodist membership numbers are 42 in Walls and 31 in Sandness.

Church of Scotland services in Papa Stour are taken twelve times in the year. The minister visits Foula once a year, and there is a resident teacher/missionary on the island.

HOUSING

There have been vast changes in housing in the last century. 18th and 19th century crofter tenants were given a measured house site on their holdings and some help towards the cost of buildings. As late as the 1880s there was no compensation for improvements and no security of tenure.

The house was built of stone gathered or quarried from near-by. Walls were thick and filled in with gravel to keep out draughts. The roof was clad with thin slabs of turf (called 'pones'), then with heather torn up by the roots (called 'flaas') and finally with straw secured by net and ropes. The ropes were made of twisted heather or straw and called 'simmints'. 'Link stanes' held the roofing material securely in place.

There was no chimney as such. The smoke (or some of it) from the open peat fire escaped through a hole in the roof. However, before the end of the 19th century chimneys were built in to the gable ends in most houses.

After the First World War, when some earnings had been saved and tenure and compensation for improvements had been secured, the pace of house improvement quickened. Wooden roofs covered with felt took the place of thatch, wooden floors or cement floors took the place of earth floors. Very many croft houses were heightened as can be seen today when one looks at the walls. These improvements were aided when the Board of Agriculture began providing building materials at subsidised rates.

These improved houses are still the main types seen in the parish today. Other improvements have been added—asbestos or tiled roofs, indoor toilets, sewage to septic tanks, and kitchen facilities. Some have added more bedrooms, and all engaged in crofting have byres and barns built away from the house. The minister visiting now would not be met by calves, sheep and young pigs, as he was in 1841.

The largest house is, of course, the laird's house, Vaila Hall. As already mentioned the King of Scotland ordered the tenant of Vaila, Robert Cheyne, to build 'ane hous and fortice' in 1576. It is uncertain what was built at that time. The older part of the present house is thought to have been built by the Mitchell family of Girlsta whose coat of arms and the date 1696 is to be found above the original door. A booklet, complete and written by the present landlord of Vaila estate, Mr Henry Anderton, bearing the name 'Vaila Hall' and printed by the 'Shetland News' gives the story of the estate and Vaila Hall.

In brief, the elegant building overlooking Wester Sound owes its stately lines to Mr Henry Anderton's grand-uncle, Mr Herbert Foster Anderton. During the years 1895-1900 approximately he planned and had constructed the north wing which formerly comprised out-buildings and a courtyard, but is now the hall. The freestone as well as the masons were imported from the south. The hall, built in Scottish Baronial style, is the feature which strikes the visitor most forcibly. An arched fireplace, stained glass windows, and an intricately carved ceiling all combine to give the impression of elegance.

Across the narrow sound entrance stands Burrastow House, also the residence of lairds of bygone times. In the 18th and 19th centuries it belonged to the Henry family. To judge by its appearance, it could have been renovated last century. In the early years of this century it was extended. It was then the summer residence of Col. Foster who was married to Mr Anderton's sister. The estate came to be called the Vaila and Burrastow Estate.

The house called 'Bayhaa' was also a laird's seat. It too was occupied by a branch of the Henry family. It is one of the oldest houses in the village and for many years was in a dilapidated condition. Lately it has been restored and made into council flats.

Unlike some other parishes, Walls had a number of lesser lairds who represented a measure of continuity from pre-Scots days in Shetland. 'The Haa' and Grutquoy on the road to Stennistwatt, Bardister House and Lochside House are examples of their houses. Spurries House was once a factor's house.

Vaila Hall, Burrastow House, Melby House and Bayhaa are now listed buildings.

In Sandness, Melby House, once the residence of the Scott family of landlords, has been greatly modernised. The 'Haa' on Foula, built as an occasional residence by the Scotts, is at the present time being re-conditioned.

The 1981 Census Scotland gives the following details:

		Permanent buildings						
		Tenure			Number of rooms			
Resident population	Households	Owner occupied	Council etc	Other	1-3	4-6	7-	Total
647	232	82	52	98	52	171	11	1,001

	Amenities			
Bath and WC				
Exclusive use of bath	One or both shared	Lacking bath and or WC	Exclusive use of WC	Over 1.5 persons per room
182	3	49	188	5
Without car	Not in self-contained accommodation	In non-permanent buildings	Occupier absent	Vacant
103	3	3	7	29

These last few years have seen more restoration of older houses and building of new houses than anyone can remember. Those on croft land have had grants and low interest loans to build new houses to laid-down specifications, or to improve existing houses. In the latter case, to leave only a small portion of the old dwelling untouched was enough to qualify for aid. Others have taken advantage of Local Council grants towards the building of bathrooms and kitchens. In all cases planning permission has had to be obtained to satisfy the authorities that regulations are being observed.

Gardening in the parish is pursued by quite a number of enthusiasts. When the lairds built their residences they added high walled gardens, knowing what wind could do to flowers, fruit bushes and trees in this area. And yet, when one visits the flower and vegetable display at the annual Agricultural Show one is surprised to find that so much can be achieved under conditions that are so often adverse. Winter frosts are generally no great menace if care is taken to protect tender plants. Gales are very much more destructive, and in the vicinity of houses, where gardens are usually situated, protective fencing can often be of little effect. However, the advantages of the long daylight in May, June and July, and the more often than not moist atmosphere, give rich rewards in gorgeous flowers and thriving vegetables. Strawberries, given a summer with some sunshine, do exceptionally well as do bush fruits where they have protection from the wind.

The visitor to the parish would find that the best tended gardens are probably those of council house tenants and cottars. These compare favourably with what may be seen in comparable situations in other parishes. The croft houses are widely scattered, and rarely are found having gardens except of the most rudimentary form. However, there will be found, often in a corner of the kale yard, a little garden that is giving inestimable pleasure to its owner.

AGRICULTURE, INDUSTRIES AND COMMERCE

The main production in Walls and Sandness is from crofting agriculture; there is a certain amount of other employment although this is mainly from service occupations.

Trends in crofting in the parish over the last century have seen the type of changes familiar in the West Highlands and Islands with the great contraction in the cultivated area and a marked decline in cattle numbers, while sheep stocks have greatly increased.

The great part of the parish consists of rough grazing, the area of which has been put at c. 27,000 acres. In 1841 it was estimated that there were 1,000 'farmed acres'; and by 1870 this had expanded to c. 1,500 cultivated acres, but the total area actually cultivated in 1980 had shrunk to only 146 acres, while the area in sown grass, negligible till the end of the 19th century, had expanded to c. 1,000 acres. Underlying these changes is the decline in domestic food production and the growth of a grassland type of stock husbandry. Cultivation now is largely restricted to domestic supplies of potatoes and a restricted amount of oats and barley.

With the decline in tillage the need for agricultural contractors scarcely exists, but there are still one or two who attend to the ploughing and haulage needs of the parish. The 33 tractors counted in Walls do a multiplicity of useful tasks. Sandness has three balers and Walls about the same number. The reaper and binder in use in Walls in the recent past is now having less to do. On Papa Stour there are two land-rovers, five tractors and one baler. On Foula there are seven tractors, four motor cars, and one excavator.

With these changes, the number of effective agricultural units has greatly declined. Although there are still 318 crofts on the Crofters Commission register, the number of holdings according to the Department of Agriculture and Fisheries (i.e., those requiring at least 26 man-days per year) was 130 in 1970. An independent count at this time shows the extent of holdings amalgamation in the mainland part of the parish:

Number of crofts held	1	2	3	4	5	6	7	8	9	10	11
Number of holders	47	22	7	9	4	1	—	—	—	—	1

Foula has 38 original holdings with some amalgamation.

Papa Stour has had systematic amalgamation bringing their number of holdings to nine of 30 acres each, together with a manse glebe.

The Isle of Vaila of approximately 800 acres, owned and occupied by the largest proprietor in the parish, Mr Henry Anderton, is at this present time up for sale. The property includes Vaila Hall, farm and farm house, caretaker's house, grazing land, piers and moorings.

In livestock, cattle numbers in 1870 were over 2,000, in circumstances when virtually every household kept at least a milk cow. Since then breeds have changed and numbers have greatly decreased, the total in 1980 being 173. About 1900, the main cattle stock was of Shetland breed—duns, reds, whites, and black and whites being common. After the First World War Friesian and Ayrshire bulls were brought in to give heavier animals, and later black poll (Aberdeen Angus) bulls as well. It is an ironic fact that the one surviving Shetland bull in Britain is owned by Mr Rosenberg, an American. There are however in the parish three black and white Shetland breeding females, with one bull calf and one heifer calf. Efforts are now being made to restore the Shetland breed. On the other hand, black poll-Hereford crosses and Shorthorn-Charollais crosses are also to be found. It is now common practice for cows to suckle their calves—a practice which would have scandalised crofter wives of half a century ago.

Sheep numbers have increased from 5,000 in 1870 to 19,700 in 1980.

The Shetland breed of sheep, small, hardy, and fine woolled, are kept on the open 'scattald' (common grazing). In winter they often resort to the seashore to vary their meagre diet with sea ware. The fleeces weigh from $1\frac{1}{2}$ to 2 pounds. In summer the fleece begins to fall off of its own accord from many of these sheep, and at a sheep 'crø' at shearing time 'rooin' (or plucking), the wool off is common practice.

Cross-bred sheep are kept on in-bye pastures and fed in the spring time. These are Cheviot, Suffolk, and now some Gotland crosses.

Shetland pony numbers have been falling. In the early years of the century small, broad, heavy ponies were still wanted for the mines. The 1950s to 1970s were boom years when ponies of 36 inches were wanted. Buyers came from abroad and these ponies were exported. Fillies would sell at from £60 to £300, while colts would fetch only £10. Now in the 1980s only half the former number of stallions is provided on the scattalds and the pony looked for has to be 40 to 42 inches for riding. A year-old colt can be bought for £9.

One household in Sandness, immigrants to the area, keeps pigs. No one seems able to make a profit out of keeping poultry. This was tried in the 1950s apparently without success. Now most people who have the facilities and the interest keep poultry only for their own use.

Sheep sales are held at convenient places throughout the parish, including Papa Stour. Animals are also sometimes disposed of to buyers who come round; and the Reawick (Shetland) Lamb Marketing Co. Ltd. has in recent years provided a convenient outlet.

For many years cattle sales were held at the Bridge of Walls but have now been discontinued.

Appended is an account written by a practising crofter.

AGRICULTURE OVER THE PAST 50 YEARS

Prior to 1947 cultivation was largely done by hand and carters were on hand to plough, seed, transport peat, and do various haulage tasks by horse and cart. They were P. Law, J. Wishart, A. Robertson, P. Nicolson, and M. Fraser.

In 1946 the Ferguson tractor was introduced to this area by the late M. Fraser. This tractor with its associated 'modern' implements led to an upsurge in cultivation to the point where in the 1950s three tractors were working 18 hours a day from mid-March to November. The contractors were A. Robertson and C. G. and M. Fraser.

With no mains electricity we were still in the days of 'reested' mutton, salted fish, and vegetables grown on the croft. Cash products were mainly wool, eggs, and mutton. All crofters sold eggs to the local shop, and lambs and cattle at local sales. Milk was sold from door to door in the village, by P. Law, P. Jamieson, and the late J. Jamieson. Such food sales are now of course illegal.

Self sufficiency was in fact still the main aim of crofting up to this time.

The 1955 Crofters Act encouraged larger holdings by amalgamation and gave the right to apportion one's hill shares while giving realistic grants for housing, land, and fencing. Improvements injected real money into the croft system for the first time in history, with the result that many young couples on crofts and with the aid of the knitting machine were able to raise families without outside employment.

In the late 1950s and early 1960s Shetland ponies and foals fetched staggering prices which could reach £250, and at the same time a good second hand tractor could be purchased for £75! Now ponies fetch from £5 to £40, but second hand tractors cost £1,500!

By the 1970s however the cost of oil, fertiliser, and machinery was slowly stifling extensive cultivation, while the need for money was becoming more evident. However at this time the price of all produce fell, or failed to keep up with inflation; and the rates of improvement grants also lagged behind. The short-sighted official answer to this was to increase dramatically the sheep subsidy payments only; this led to most crofters 'ranching' their crofts with sheep and taking up other employment, not from choice but from necessity.

By the 1970s the employment opportunities available during the oil boom led to a further decline in interest in crofting, as the yield from crofts could not hope to match the wages now available. Self sufficiency was now a 'hippy' dream. The proceeds from a few gallons of milk and dozens of eggs could not now compete with the wages packet offered by B.P.

The following table gives some idea of how the working population of the parish is employed:

15-65 Age Group

	Crofting only		Crofting with other employment		Other employment only	
	m	f	m	f	m	f
Walls	19	17	11	7	80	41
Sandness	12	16	12	5	15	12
Papa Stour	6	3	1	3	3	2
Foula	9	8	—	—	—	—
	46	44	24	15	98	55

Out of over 160 households in Walls over 100 persons have paid employment. Fifty of these households are cottar households. The numbers employed are as follows:

General services—shops, roads, P.O., janitor, home helps, guest house management	27
Contracting and the trades	20
Professions	20
Hirers and drivers	17
Clerical	8
Labouring	9
Domestic	10
Seamen, including officers	7
Fishermen and fishworkers	6

Most of these jobs are located outside the parish, chiefly at Sullom Voe. The local shop has had a staff of four for a number of years. Students at weekends and holiday times augment the present-day staff as and when required. The school employs three permanent teachers, two canteen staff, and a part-time janitor. One postman serves the whole of

Walls, and similarly one serves all Sandness. Three local men have permanent employment on the roads. There are three building contractors who work far and wide beyond the boundaries of the parish and two excavating contractors who also move about to where there is work. There are two hirers. There is one industry that appears to thrive, namely knitting, though it is impossible to put a value on its products to the parish as a whole. The 1950s saw the coming of the domestic knitting machine. With high demand for knitwear products, hand and machine knitting were taught in schools. The Sandness shop bought wool and knitwear whereas the shop in Walls had given up this branch of business. In the 1960s a redundant church building in Walls was converted into a knitwear factory and for a time employed ten or a dozen in-workers and a varying number of out-workers. The trade fluctuated. In 1970 the factory was bought over by Messrs Tulloch of Shetland. However, when women workers were wanted at the construction camps connected with the oil industry the factory was closed.

Handknitting continues to be taught, and with efforts being made throughout Shetland to design and market there is hope that useful earnings will continue to be made.

A very significant milestone in the history of the textile industry of the parish is the establishment at Sandness by the Jamieson family of merchants of a spinning mill, the first in Shetland. The work done at the moment on rather out-dated machinery is a pilot scheme, but plans are well advanced for the installation of new machinery. The future of the knitwear industry for the whole of Shetland looks promising.

WAY OF LIFE

Compared with past centuries conditions of life have greatly improved. The pressures of over-population, scarcity of resources and repressive measures imposed by some landlords had in earlier times led to a certain amount of petty crime and unrest. There were also however, reforms associated with religious revivals, and over the past century old problems and tensions have substantially disappeared; the parish is now a very agreeable place in which to live. Some relaxing of former strict Sabbath observance has taken place, but there is little evidence of the people of the parish giving up their traditional quiet Sunday. Church attendance, however, is somewhat thinner than formerly, due doubtless in part to the alternatives now available in the form of television, radio and sport. The removal of the privation and suffering of the past can lead people to become more secularly minded. When churches can provide a measure of entertainment in their services attendance is noticeably better; this is especially so with children's performances.

Television has opened up windows on the world for this generation, and this has accelerated the natural process of change. The local dialect has slowly been eroded over the centuries. English we must have, but the English also preserve the traditions of their 'rude forefathers'. Similarly, a knowledge of one's roots at parish and county level would be a desirable addition to what is provided in the school and in the home. A very commendable innovation has been the appointment in Shetland of a county archivist. An upsurge of interest in local history is very evident in this parish.

The middle of the 18th century has been noted as a time when civic consciousness blossomed in the establishment of places of learning. The late 19th century saw crofting discontent brought to a head, and local crofters sent their representatives to give evidence before the Crofters Commission. This present century has to its credit halls and club rooms for social gatherings, a variety of such gatherings for both men and women, youths and children of all ages. Especially noteworthy is the role of the Community Council which draws members from the outlying islands of Foula and Papa Stour as well as from mainland parts of the parish. For this purpose too a new electoral boundary has been made by which East Selivoe, Staneydale, Gruting, and West Burrafirth (all in the parish of Sandsting and Aithsting) are included with Walls and Sandness.

Disturbance in family life in the parish through divorce or separation of parents is minimal; and there is no real problem of school truancy or child delinquency. With more work in the islands now fewer youths have to leave home and seek employment elsewhere, and fathers see more of their families than formerly.

THE FUTURE

In Shetland, fishing is a prosperous industry despite its modern problems. Although the direct involvement in it of the people of the parish is now marginal, it could still be one of the best prospects for the future; at present however, there are to be resolved problems of co-ordination between fishermen and processors as well as the difficult task of effective conservation of the stocks.

It is difficult to envisage the shape of agriculture in the future. The Shetland Islands Council is offering grants to encourage a return to more cattle rearing, partly to provide more locally produced meat and milk; and this would involve more cropping. Probably some few crofters with suitable land will take up this offer.

Training schemes for youths are on foot to equip them to service the oil installations and man the oil rigs, quays and boats at Sullom Voe. One would hope that oil will flow for a long time, but the flow will one day stop, and employment prospects thereafter are an unresolved issue for the future.

Knitwear could have a continuing contribution to make to the gross earnings of the islands, and of the parish in particular, especially with a wool mill producing fine Shetland yarns within the parish.

Little is done in the parish to cater for tourists. There was a Youth Hostel on the Island of Vaila, but with the island up for sale its future is uncertain. One family have erected chalets but these seem to have been taken up by semi-permanent residents. Burrastow House caters for visitors in the holiday season. Many campers and caravan holiday-makers visit the parish where they have ample unimpeded choice of sites.

Something holds the typical Shetlander back from making money from catering for tourists. Some have been known to have started and to have charged so little as to fail to break even. Probably courses in simple business management and catering would prepare the way for more effective participation in the tourist industry.

April 1983

THE ISLAND AND PARISH OF YELL

Original description by Rev. Frederick W. D. Houston, 1954
New version by Robert L. Johnson, 1983

PHYSICAL BASIS

The island of Yell is the second largest in the Shetland group. In length it is seventeen miles, with a breadth of around five miles. On its south and west it is separated from the Shetland Mainland by Yell Sound, while on the east Colgrave Sound separates it from the island of Fetlar, and Bluemull Sound from the island of Unst. It has an area of 83 square miles.

Included in the parish are the islands of Linga, Hascosay and Uynarey; and the island of Bigga is partly in the parish of Delting and partly in that of Yell. Both Hascosay and Bigga were settled at one time, but have been deserted for many years.

Yell consists of Precambrian rocks of the Dalradian series. The greater part of the island consists of garnetiferous mica plagioclose gneiss, the foliation of which has a general north to south trend, and the overall inclination of which is steep and to the west. The north-eastern coastal strip and the south-east corner of Yell, together with the island of Hascosay, are underlain by striped granulitic oligoclase gneiss, some bands of calc-silicate rock and a band of gneiss with augen of microline; these outcrops appear to be separated from the main part of the island by a major dislocation, which could be a continuation of the Nesting Fault.

West of the east coast strip the geology is varied in detail and a sequence of six lithological units have been recognised although they are poorly defined. The highest land in the middle of the island is on thick lenticular quartzite which forms the Hill of Arisdale and the Ward of Reafirth. The western coastal cliffs of Yell consist mainly of evenly foliated muscovite biotite gneiss together with some silvery mica schists.

The relief of Yell is dominated by ridges trending in a general north–south direction in sympathy with the geology; at their highest, in the Ward of Reafirth and the Hill of Arisdale they are over 600 feet in height. The great part of the island is covered with blanket peat. The exposed parts of the coast regularly consist of cliffs, and in the north-west many of these are over 200 feet in height. The Ness of Sound, the Holm of Copister and the Ness of Galtagarth are all examples of off-shore islets linked to the main island by tombolos built by wave action.

HISTORY

The early phases of human occupation in Yell are shown by a series of archaeological remains, although these have been little investigated to date.

At Windhouse are the ruins of a building which was excavated by the proprietor during the First World War; it shows chambers which could be related to the Stone Age remains of Jarlshof in Shetland or of Skara Brae in Orkney.

Ruins of Iron Age brochs can be discerned at Burravoe, Gossabrough, West Sandwick, Copister and Cullivoe. However the best preserved of the brochs is at Ness of Burraness, where the external wall at one point is still about 14 feet high, and the foundations of other buildings on the site can still be traced. At the Burgi Geos on the north-west coast is a promontory structure which has been described as an Iron Age fort.

At Windhouse there are foundations of Norse buildings. Also at the Sands of Breckin at the north end of the islands, artefacts have periodically been observed in the past as the sand has moved, and this site is at present under archaeological scrutiny.

Like all of Shetland, Yell was settled and dominated by the Norse from the 9th century, as is still shown by the place names; and it also came under Scots rule from the 15th century. However there was not the building up of big estates in Yell; and in modern times there has still been a big number of different proprietors: in 1868 for example there were 68 listed on the valuation roll. Although in that year Mr Cameron Mouat owned a good proportion of North Yell, Joseph Leask had West Yell and J. R. MacQueen the Burravoe district, there was a considerable number of owner-occupiers, as there still is today.

The land and the sea were inter-twined in the traditional life of the people, the land being rented from the landlord under a system of fishing tenures. The tenants could hold directly from the proprietor, or from a merchant to whom the property was given in tack.

The croft land was the provider of most of the food supply and was worked mainly by the women. The men were away at the fishing stations for the 'haaf' fishing for ling and cod during the months from May until August.

The cow was the mainstay of this subsistence existence; it provided milk for direct family use and also other products, the first of which was butter. The buttermilk was used both as a drink and for the baking of bread; and it could also with the addition of boiling water be made into 'kirn milk', the whey of which (known as 'bland') was an important thirst quencher. Milk was thus used in a series of ways in the home, and in addition, surplus milk was always sold. From the 1850s until the start of the First World War in 1914, the price of a cow did not change much in value. In 1866 the prices given were as follows: a cow in calf £5; a fat cow £4; a 2 year old bullock £2 6s.; a cow in milk £2 10s.

If a crofter had the misfortune to lose a cow it was something of a major disaster, for it usually left a lot of very hungry mouths.

Sheep did not play such an important part in the croft economy in the 19th century although the wool was hand spun and knitted into garments, the surplus of which were sold. In 1864 wool was sold for 3¾d. per pound but the very fine wool reached 11d.

Eggs were also a source of income, the people receiving from the merchant 3½d. to 4½d. per dozen if they wanted cash, but if they took goods from the merchant he allowed an additional penny per dozen. This was part of the Truck System which was subject to a Commission of Enquiry in 1871, and subsequently such practices were generally ended.

Sheep were less important to the people than cattle, and this was not lost sight of when some of the landowners anticipated that they would get a bigger yield from sheep on their land than from crofters with fishing tenures. About 1835 Windhouse, Vollister, Lumbister, Setter and Graveland had their tenants evicted to make sheep farms; but this did not prove the anticipated success, and in 1849 and 1850 houses were rebuilt and tenants (11 families in all) put back into Setter, Vollister and Lumbister. However in 1865 the lands of the Garth estate were taken over by its factor, John Walker. He introduced a policy of separating the scattald (hill grazing) from the crofts while at the same time increasing the rents. In this way he could force people to leave their homes. In 1868 about 28 tenants left the townships of West-a-Firth and Burraness in North Yell; and eight tenants from Lumbister and Vollister also had to find new homes. Later, in 1875, the six tenants of Setter all left, and the land was put under sheep.

The 'haaf' fishing for ling and cod was carried out in open 'sixareens' from outlying stations nearer to the main fishing grounds. The places of operation of the men from different districts reflected the stations controlled by their landlords, or by the merchants holding tacks from the landlords. In the north half of Yell (i.e. north of Whalfirth and Mid Yell Voe), men fished from the two beaches at Gloup Voe. Those from Mid and East Yell operated mainly from Funzie in Fetlar; from South Yell a considerable number of men were based at Out Skerries; while those from West Yell, West Sandwick and the Herra fished from Fethaland in Northmavine parish.

In July 1881 a sudden storm caught the boats from the Gloup stations at sea, and they were forced to reach land on a weather shore, with the result that six boats with 36 men from the area were lost. Due to this disaster and to the beginning of trawling off shore, from this time a decline set in in the 'haaf' fishing and by the end of the century this type of fishing had become but a memory.

About the start of the 1880s there was a boom in herring fishing with drift nets from decked boats, and boats from as far afield as the Isle of Man came to take part in the bonanza. Curers erected stations at all convenient voes, and Cullivoe, Gutcher, Basta Voe, Mid Yell, Burravoe, Ulsta, West Sandwick and Whalfirth all had stations for the curing of salt herring. During the next twenty years this herring fishing was the most important activity in the island's life, as bigger and better sail boats were procured, and a large number of women were employed in gutting the catches. However with the advent of the steam drifter from 1900 onwards the sail boats were outdated and unable to compete, and the fishery became more and more centred on Lerwick. The last herring curing station operating in Yell was at Cullivoe just after the Second World War.

POPULATION

The peak of the population was in the census year of 1871 which recorded 2,728 residents on the island; from that time there was a steady decline for a full century, as the following census figures show:

Year		Year	
1871	2,728	1931	1,883
1881	2,529	1941	no census
1891	2,501	1951	1,483
1901	2,483	1961	1,152
1911	2,318	1971	1,143
1921	2,129	1981	1,213

While a variety of factors are behind this population trend, basic has been the move away from a situation in which much of the food supply was produced on the crofts, while fishing was the main source of cash income. Instead the people looked more and more to income earned outside the islands. A considerable number of men went to the merchant marine, and subsequently some settled with their families in ports such as Leith and Liverpool. Others emigrated to Canada, the United States, Australia and New Zealand. Two World Wars also took a high toll of young men from the island. Just after the Second World War a number of Yell families left the island for new homes in Lerwick, and the district around Basta Voe was affected particularly by this.

There has, however, been an upward trend in numbers more recently, largely due to the employment available at the Sullom Voe oil terminal; and an increase of 70 people was recorded in the 1981 Census.

PUBLIC AND SOCIAL SERVICES

The whole island is supplied with mains water. North Yell, including the district from Gloup to Sellafirth, is supplied from the Loch of Brough.

The central area, including places from Basta to Gossabrough on the east, and also the Herra and West Sandwick on the west, is supplied from the Burn of Laxa. The remaining districts in the south and south-west between Burravoe and West Yell are supplied from the Loch of Kettlester.

Yell was relatively late in getting mains electricity, but the North of Scotland Hydro-Electric Board installed this for the whole island in 1968 after putting a submarine cable across Yell Sound, which connected with the grid supplied by the Lerwick power station.

Medical services are supplied by a doctor whose surgery is at Hillend, Mid Yell; he is assisted by two district nurses, both resident at Mid Yell. There are home helps in all districts who assist the elderly to keep their houses tidy and clean, while a 'meals on wheels' service provides substantial meals for those unable to cook for themselves. At the time of writing a care centre is being built at Linkshouse, Mid Yell, thereby supplying a need which was mooted by the late Dr Taylor as long ago as 1902. This will provide for those patients whose condition is not such as to require hospital treatment, but who cannot be properly cared for at home. It will also be used for patients convalescing after hospital treatment. There is an ambulance stationed on the island, and for emergency hospital cases the vehicle ferries will make a special crossing, including at any hour of the night if required.

EDUCATION

There are now two primary schools on the island—at Burravoe and Cullivoe, and a junior high school at Mid Yell. Prior to the Second World War there were also schools at Gutcher, Colvister, the Herra, West Sandwick, West Yell, Ulsta and East Yell. There were also side schools at Vatster and Gossabrough for young children unable to walk the three statutory miles to a main school.

The 1982 school rolls show 114 pupils at Mid Yell, with 34 at Burravoe and 26 at Cullivoe. The Mid Yell school educates pupils up to the O-grade certificate; and those taking a full secondary course leave for Lerwick at the age of 14.

CHURCH

Most of the people belong to the Church of Scotland, and the minister now responsible for the whole island lives at Mid Yell; the island of Fetlar is also part of his charge. At one time there were also ministers at Cullivoe and Burravoe, with missionaries at Sellafirth and West Sandwick.

There is a Methodist chapel at East Yell and an Episcopal Church at Burravoe, and both of these are now served from Lerwick.

An Apostolic Church was established at Mid Yell 25 years ago, and has a continuing small congregation.

COMMUNICATIONS

For most of the modern period the main outside contact of Yell was by boat with Lerwick. This service between Lerwick and the North Isles was first operated by sailing smacks, and subsequently by the more reliable steam ships. Prominent here was the first *Earl of Zetland* which operated the service for 68 years beginning in 1877. The *Earl of Zetland II* was intended to succeed her in 1939, but this was postponed till after World War II, and the second *Earl* in her turn was succeeded by drive-on ferries in 1973. At one time the steamer called at Burravoe, Ulsta, West Sandwick, Gossabrough, Mid Yell, Basta Voe, Gutcher and Cullivoe; and as there were no piers, flit-boats had to transport passengers and goods to the landing stages. With the development of motor transport within the island the number of calls was reduced; and after years of delay a steamer pier was built at Mid Yell in 1952, and this became the only port of call.

Government subsidies became necessary for the operation of the service, and with the issue of replacing the second *Earl* arising, it was decided to change the transport system completely by providing drive-on ferries to link up the North Isles of Shetland. Two vessels now operate between Ulsta and Toft in Delting parish, while another plies between Gutcher and the islands of Unst and Fetlar. These ferries have greatly reduced the effect of isolation, as services operate on them at most times of day. This compares with the four round trips a week operated by the *Earl* even in its later days when the schedules had been accelerated by the elimination of many ports of call.

A bus service operates from Lerwick daily, and carries passengers and mail to and from the North Isles.

HOUSING

For a considerable period up to the Second World War very few houses were built. The first council houses to be built in Yell were at Burravoe where ten houses were erected in 1948; Cullivoe had ten built in 1951; and at Mid Yell ten were erected in 1953. With the advent of a public water supply and mains electricity in the 1960s came the impetus for improving existing houses and building new ones. Substantial grants coupled with low-interest loans made it possible for crofters to replace their homes or completely renovate them to modern standards. At the present time there are 405 inhabited houses in Yell; of these 165 have been built since 1950, the majority within the past ten years.

AGRICULTURE

The pattern of agriculture has changed during the past thirty years from crofting with cultivation and cattle to a sheep-orientated system. To a great extent what was the arable land on the croft has been laid down to grass, the cattle being disposed of and replaced with cross Cheviot ewes put to a Suffolk tup for the production of store lambs. There are now only about twenty holdings which are full-time units; the now dominant sheep husbandry allows the crofters to have full-time outside employment, and this has enabled them to have a better standard of living. Hay is the main crop now grown for winter keep, the growing of oats having gone out of favour. Small quantities of potatoes are grown for home use. Several of the larger producers make silage for winter keep for the livestock.

The open hills are stocked with Shetland sheep, the main product of which is the wool. Unfortunately, this has not maintained its price in relation to the inflation of recent years; in actual fact the producer receives less in real terms than he did 25 years ago.

With the grant aid available a considerable number of new fences have been erected, thus allowing a better control of stock. The better areas of the scattald have often been reseeded and this will lead to the raising of a more marketable product.

FISHING

The fishing fleet is small but relatively modern. There are two boats based at Cullivoe, one of which was built in Norway three years ago. Also built in Norway was the one boat based at Mid Yell and her sister craft at Burravoe; these two boats are at present engaged in pair-trawling. There have been efforts in recent years to build up a larger fishing fleet, but these have not been sustained, the men involved having opted for a more comfortable and secure livelihood ashore.

A white fish factory was established at Mid Yell at the end of the 1960s but closed four years ago; however at the time of writing, moves are being made to reopen it. If this succeeds it would give employment to about twenty people and would be a great asset to the island.

Mid Yell also has a Norwegian processing company's factory which processes crab into paté, and several other products are also made, e.g., salmon and tuna paté, all being sold under the John West label. There are about twenty people fully employed at this plant which came into production in 1969. This year the rearing of salmon for commercial purposes has been started using cages anchored in Mid Yell Voe. It will be another eighteen months before the product is ready for market. If this proves a viable proposition it will be another asset for the factory, which has to import all its salmon at present.

OTHER EMPLOYMENT

There is a range of employment in Yell with no single thing outstanding.

The hosiery industry is still substantially a cottage industry. During the 1960s there were two factories operating, both of which employed knitters while women operatives washed and finished the garments. Only the factory in East Yell survived the oil boom, and it today has no knitter on the premises although all the dressing is still done there.

The Shetland Islands Council is now the largest single employer on the island, and its main work is the improvement of roads; a two-way road between Ulsta and Gutcher is at present nearing completion, and is an essential link between the drive-on ferries in the North Isles.

The Sullom Voe oil terminal is accessible via the vehicle ferry, and at present about thirty are fully employed there, on the site and on tugs and pilot boats.

In 1983 a trial was made with peat production on a commercial basis. If successful this could provide work during the summer months for several people.

Since the coming of the oil industry to Shetland, Basta Voe has been consistently suggested as a site for a base for the supply of off-shore rigs and platforms. While attempts to have a supply base built have not yet met with success, there are still hopes that this may become a reality.

SOCIAL LIFE

Each district has its own public hall, most of which were erected prior to the First World War. There are halls at Cullivoe, Sellafirth, North-a-Voe, Mid Yell, the Herra, West Sandwick, Ulsta, Burravoe and East Yell. During the past few years substantial grants have been available to modernise these premises, and have been utilised. At East Yell a completely new building has been erected, while the halls at Mid Yell and Burravoe have been extensively renovated and brought up to modern standards; and at Cullivoe a new building is soon to be erected.

There are three public houses on the island—at East Yell, Mid Yell and at the Motel at Cunnister. The Mid Yell Boating Club converted the old Mid Yell School Canteen in 1982 into club rooms with a licence to supply drinks to its members.

Each district has a very active Women's Rural Institute, and these meet regularly during the winter. It would be very difficult not to find some social activity each night during most of the year.

There are ladies' guilds in each district, and they meet monthly in the Church Halls.

Badminton is a popular game, and the island has several teams which have done well in competition within Shetland. Football is played in summer, although Yell teams have not been as successful in competition as they have at badminton.

CONCLUSION

At present the situation in Yell is more favourable than it has been for some considerable time. What is needed now is that advantage should be taken of the grants and loans available from such public bodies as the Highlands and Islands Development Board and Shetland Islands Council to promote continued development.

August 1983

BIBLIOGRAPHY

Compiled by Roy Grønneberg

Anderson, Basil R.: *Broken Lights*, Edinburgh 1888
Anderson, Iain F.: *To Introduce the Orkneys and Shetlands*, London 1939
Anderson, Peter D.: *Robert Stewart, Earl of Orkney and Lord of Shetland*, Edinburgh 1982
Angus, James Stout: *An Etymological Glossary of Some Place-names in Shetland*, Lerwick 1910
    A Glossary of the Shetland Dialect, Paisley 1914

Baldwin, John R.: *Scandinavian Shetland—an ongoing tradition*, Edinburgh 1978
Balfour, David: *Oppressions of the 16th Century in the Islands of Orkney and Zetland*, Edinburgh 1859
Balneaves, Elizabeth: *The Windswept Isles*, London 1977
Banks, Mrs M. M.: *British Calendar Customs: Orkney and Shetland*, London 1946
Barclay, Robert S.: *The Court Books of Orkney and Shetland 1614-15*, Edinburgh 1967
Barnard, Frank: *Picturesque Life in Shetland*, Edinburgh 1890
Beenhakker, A. J.: *Hollanders in Shetland*, Lerwick 1973
Berry, R. J. and Johnston, J. L.: *Natural History of Shetland*, London 1980
Black, C. F.: *Examples of Printed Folk-lore Concerning the Orkney and Shetland Islands*, London 1903
Brand, J. A.: *A Brief Description of Orkney, Zetland, Pightland Firth and Caithness*, Edinburgh 1701-03
Brøgger, A. W.: *Ancient Emigrants*, Oxford 1929
Bulter, Rhoda: *Link-stanes*, Lerwick 1980
    A Nev Foo a Coarn, Sandwick 1977
    Shaela, Sandwick 1976
Burgess, J. J. Haldane: *Rasmie's Büddie*, Lerwick 1891
    Rasmie's Smaa Murr, Lerwick 1916
    The Treasure of Don Andres, Lerwick 1903
    The Viking Path, Edinburgh 1894
    Young Rasmie's Kit, Lerwick 1928
Button, John (ed.): *The Shetland Way of Oil*, Sandwick 1976

Campbell, Dr: *Account of the Dutch Herring Fishery &c., in Zetland, by a Gentleman who Resided Five Years There*, London 1750
Cant, Ronald G.: *The Medieval Churches and Chapels of Shetland*, Lerwick 1975
Catton, Rev. James: *The History and Description of the Shetland Islands*, Wainfleet 1838
Clausen, E., and Jamieson, H.: *Up Helly Aa 1881-1981*, Lerwick 1981
Cluness, Andrew T.: *The Shetland Isles*, London 1951
    Told Round the Peat Fire, London 1955
Coleman, Vicki and Wheeler, Ruth: *Living on an Island*, Findhorn 1980

Cowie, R.: *Shetland and Its Inhabitants*, Edinburgh 1871
Cox, Maurice: *The Shetland Pony*, London 1965
Crawford, Barbara E.: 'The Earldom of Orkney and Lordship of Shetland: A Reinterpretation of their Pledging to Scotland in 1468-70', *Saga-Book*, vol. xvii, parts 2-3, 156-76
Crawford, Rev. J. M.: *The Parish of Lerwick 1701-1901*, Lerwick 1901

Deyell, Annie: *My Shetland*, Sandwick 1975
Don, Sarah: *The Art of Shetland Lace*, London 1980
    Fair Isle Knitting, London 1979
Donaldson, Gordon: *The Court Book of Shetland 1602-04*, Edinburgh 1954
    Northwards by Sea, Edinburgh 1978
    Shetland Life Under Earl Patrick, Edinburgh 1958
Dunn, Robert: *The Ornithologist's Guide to the Islands of Orkney and Shetland*, London 1837

Edmondston, Arthur: *A View of the Ancient and Present State of the Zetland Islands*, Edinburgh 1809
Edmondston, Eliza: *Sketches and Tales of the Shetland Islands*, Edinburgh 1856
Edmonston, Thomas: *An Etymological Glossary of the Shetland and Orkney Dialect*, Edinburgh 1866
Eunson, J.: *Words, Phrases and Recollections from Fair Isle*, Lerwick 1976
Evans, Arthur and Buckley, T. E.: *A Vertebrate Fauna of the Shetland Islands*, Edinburgh 1899

Fenton, Alexander: *The Northern Isles: Orkney and Shetland*, Edinburgh 1978
    The Various Names of Shetland, Edinburgh 1973
Fojut, Noel: *Prehistoric Shetland*, Lerwick 1981

Gifford, Thomas: *Historical Description of the Zetland Islands 1733*. London 1786
Goodlad, C. A.: *Shetland Fishing Saga*, Lerwick 1971
Goudie, Gilbert: *The Celtic and Scandinavian Antiquities of Shetland*, Edinburgh 1904
    The Diary of the Reverend John Mill 1740-1803, Edinburgh 1889
Graham, John J.: *The Shetland Dictionary*, Stornoway 1979
Graham, John J. and Robertson, T. A.: *Nordern Lichts*, Lerwick 1965
Grant, Francis J.: *Zetland County Families*, Lerwick 1893
    Zetland Family Histories, Lerwick 1907
Grant, Roderick: *The Lone Voyage of Betty Mouat*, Aberdeen 1973
Gray, Joseph: *Lowrie*, Lerwick 1933
Greig, P. W.: *Annals of the Parish of Delting*, Lerwick 1892
Grønneberg, Roy: *Island Futures*, Sandwick 1978
    Island Governments, Sandwick 1976
    Jakobsen and Shetland, Lerwick 1981

Halcrow, Adam: *The Sail Fishermen of Shetland*, Lerwick 1950
Hamilton, J. R. C.: *Excavations at Clickhimin, Shetland*, Edinburgh 1968
    Excavations at Jarlshof, Shetland, Edinburgh 1956
Heineberg, Dr Heinz: *Changes in the Economic-Geographical Structure of the Shetland Islands*, Inverness 1972
Henderson, Thomas: *Shetland From Old Photographs*, Lerwick 1979
Hibbert, S.: *A Description of the Shetland Islands*, Edinburgh 1822
Holbourn, Prof. I. B. S.: *The Isle of Foula*, Lerwick 1938
Howarth, David: *The Shetland Bus*, London 1951

Irvine, Fred: *Pictures from Shetland's Past*, Lerwick 1955
Irvine, James W.: *Footprints*, Lerwick 1981
    Up Helly Aa, Lerwick 1982

Jakobsen, Jakob: *Dialect and Place-Names of Shetland*, Lerwick 1897
    Det Nørrøne Sprog på Shetland, Copenhagen 1897
    Etymological Dictionary of the Norn Language in Shetland, London 1928-32
    The Place-Names of Shetland, Lerwick 1936
Jamieson, Peter: *Letters on Shetland*, Edinburgh 1949
    The Viking Isles, London 1933
Johnson, L. G.: *Laurence Williamson of Mid Yell*, Lerwick 1971
Johnson, Robert L.: *Shetland Country Merchant*, Lerwick 1979
Johnston, A. W. and Amy: *Orkney and Shetland Records*, vols. i-ii, London 1907-23

Kemp, Rev. Dr J.: *Observations on the Islands of Shetland*, Edinburgh 1801
Kidd, Tom: *Life in Shetland*, Edinburgh 1979

Laing, Lloyd: *Orkney and Shetland: an Archaeological Guide*, Newton Abbott, 1974
Laurenson, Arthur: *The Shetland Dialect*, Lerwick n.d.
Linklater, Eric: *Orkney and Shetland*, London 1965
Livingstone, W. P.: *Shetland and the Shetlanders*, London 1947
Low, George: *Tour Through the Islands of Orkney and Schetland 1774*, Kirkwall 1879

McGregor, Shiela: *Traditional Fair Isle Knitting*, London 1980
McNicoll, Iain H.: *The Shetland Economy*, Glasgow 1976
Manson, T.: *Lerwick During the Last Half Century*, Lerwick 1923
Martin, Simon: *The Other Titanic*, Newton Abbot 1980
Marwick, Ernest: *The Folklore of Orkney and Shetland*, London 1975
Milne, E. O'H.: *Wi Lowing Fin*, Lerwick 1962
Mitchell, C. E.: *Up Helly Aa*, Lerwick 1948
Monteith, R.: *Description of the Islands of Orkney and Zetland*, 1845
Møller, Asger: *Shetland*, Aarhus 1969
Morrison, Ian: *The North Sea Earls*, London 1973
Mykura, W.: *Regional Geological Guide: Orkney and Shetland*, Edinburgh 1976

Neill, P.: *A Tour Through the Islands of Orkney and Shetland 1806*
Nelson, George M.: *The Story of Tingwall Kirk*, Lerwick 1965
Nevis Institute, The: *The Shetland Report*, Edinburgh 1978
New Statistical Account of Scotland: The Shetland Isles, Edinburgh 1841
Nicolson, James R.: *Lerwick Harbour*, Lerwick 1977
    Shetland, Newton Abbot, 1972
    Shetland and Oil, London 1975
    Shetland Folklore, London 1981
    Shetland's Fishing Vessels, Lerwick 1981
    Traditional Life in Shetland, London 1978
    Hay & Company—Merchants in Shetland, Lerwick 1981
Nicolson, John: *Arthur Anderson*, Lerwick 1932
    Folktales and Legends of Shetland, Edinburgh 1920
    Shetland Incidents and Tales, Edinburgh 1931

O'Dell, A. C.: *Historical Geography of the Shetland Islands*, Lerwick 1939

Perry, R.: *Shetland Sanctuary*, London 1948
Peterkin, A.: *Notes on Orkney and Zetland*, Edinburgh 1822

Peterson, John: *A Photographers Notebook*, London 1948
Pløyen, Christian: *Reminiscences of a Voyage to Orkney, Shetland and Scotland in the Summer of 1839*, Lerwick 1894

Rampini, Charles: *Shetland and the Shetlanders*, Kirkwall 1884
Renwick, Jack: *Rainbow Bridge*, Lerwick 1963
Robertson, T. A.: *Collected Poems of Vagaland*, Lerwick 1975
    Da Sangs A'll Sing ta Dee, Lerwick 1973
Robertson, T. A. and Graham, J. J.: *Grammar and Usage of the Shetland Dialect*, Lerwick 1952
Robson, Adam: *The Saga of a Ship*, Lerwick 1982
Royal Commission on the Ancient and Historical Monuments of Scotland: *Inventory Ancient Monuments Orkney and Shetland*, 1946
Russell, J.: *Three Years in Shetland*, Paisley 1887

Saelen, Frithjof: *Shetlands-Larsen*, Bergen 1947
Sandison, A.: *Tracing Ancestors in Shetland*, Lerwick 1972
Sandison, C.: *The Sixareen and her Racing Descendants*, Lerwick 1954
    Unst, Lerwick 1965
Saxby, C. F. Argyll (Ed.): *Edmondston's Flora of Shetland*, Edinburgh 1903
Saxby, H. L.: *The Birds of Shetland*, Edinburgh 1874
Saxby, Jessie: *Shetland Traditional Lore*, Edinburgh 1932
Saxby, Jessie and Edmondston, Biot: *Home of a Naturalist*, London 1888
Scott, Sir Walter: *Northern Lights*, Hawick 1982
Second Report of the Commission Appointed to Inquire Into the Truck System (Shetland): Edinburgh 1872
Senior, W. H. and Swan, W. B.: *Survey of Agriculture in Caithness, Orkney and Shetland*, Inverness 1972
Shaw, Frances: *The Northern and Western Islands of Scotland: Their Economy and Society in the 17th Century*, Edinburgh 1980
Shennan, Hay: *A Judicial Maid-of-all-work*, Edinburgh 1933
Shepherd, Stella: *Like a Mantle the Sea*, London 1971
Shetland Islands Council: *Shetland in Statistics no. 11*, Lerwick 1982
    Shetland Oil Era, Lerwick, 3rd edn. 1981
Sinclair, Catherine: *Shetland and the Shetlanders*, Edinburgh 1840
Shirreff, J.: *General View of the Agriculture of Shetland*, 1814
Simpson, W. Douglas (Ed.): *Viking Congress, Lerwick 1950*, Edinburgh 1954
Simmons, Jenni: *Shetland Cook Book*, Lerwick 1983
Small, A.: *Excavations in Unst*, Lerwick 1961
Small, A., Thomas, C. and Wilson, D. M.: *St Ninian's Isle and its Treasure*, London 1973
Smith, Hance D.: *The Making of Modern Shetland*, Lerwick 1977
Smith and Twatt: *Shetland Pattern Book*, Lerwick n.d.
Spence, Catherine Stafford S.: *Memoirs of Arthur Laurenson*, London 1901
Spence, David: *Shetland's Living Landscape*, Sandwick 1979
Spence, J.: *Shetland Folk-lore*, Lerwick 1899
Stewart, George: *Shetland Fireside Tales*, Edinburgh 1877
Sutherland, Stella: *Aa My Selves*, Lerwick 1980

Tait, E. S. Reid: *Hjaltland Miscellany* (5 vols.) Lerwick 1934-1957
　　Lerwick Miscellany, Lerwick 1955
　　Some Notes on the Shetland Hanseatic Trade, Lerwick 1955
　　(Ed.): *The Statistical Account of Shetland 1791-9*, Lerwick 1925
Tait, William J.: *A Day Between Weathers*, Edinburgh 1980
Thompson, W. P. L.: 'Funzie, Fetlar: A Shetland Run-Rig Township in the Nineteenth Century', in the *Scottish Geographical Magazine*, 1970, vol. 86, pt. 3, 170-85
Tudor, J. R.: *The Orkneys and Shetland*, London 1883
Tulloch, Bobby: *Shetland Birds*, Lerwick 1970
　　Shetland Mammals, Lerwick 1978

Venables, L. S. and U.: *Birds and Mammals of Shetland*, Lerwick 1955
Venables, Ursula: *Life in Shetland*, Edinburgh 1956
Viking Society for Northern Research: *Orkney and Shetland Miscellany*, Vols. 1-10, London 1907-1946

Wainwright, F. T.: *The Northern Isles*, Edinburgh 1962
Willcock, Rev. John: *A Shetland Minister of the Eighteenth Century*, Kirkwall 1897
Williamson, Kenneth: *Fair Isle and its Birds*, Edinburgh 1965
Wills, Jonathan: *Linda and the Lighthouse*, Edinburgh n.d.
　　The Travels of Magnus Pole, Edinburgh 1975
Withrington, Donald J. and Grant, Ian R. (Eds): *The Statistical Account of Scotland*, vol. xix: Orkney and Shetland, Wakefield 1978

Zetland Education Committee: *The Shetland Book*, Lerwick 1967

March 1983

INDEX